WORLD WAR II AND THE WEST IT WROUGHT

WORLD WAR II
AND THE WEST IT WROUGHT

Edited by

Mark Brilliant and

David M. Kennedy

STANFORD UNIVERSITY PRESS ▮ STANFORD, CALIFORNIA

Stanford University Press
Stanford, California

This book has been published with the assistance of the Bill Lane Center for the American West.

Printed in the United States of America on acid-free, archival-quality paper

Library of Congress Cataloging-in-Publication Data is available upon request.

ISBN 978-1-5036-1157-3 (cloth)
ISBN 978-1-5036-1287-7 (paperback)
ISBN 978-1-5036-1288-4 (electronic)

Cover design: Jordan Wannemacher

Cover photo: Ercoupe, assisted by six jets under the wings, leaves the Piper Cub still taxiing. Courtesy NASA/JPL-Caltech.

Typeset by BookMatters in 10/14 Minion Pro

CONTENTS

ACKNOWLEDGMENTS

In addition to the contributors to this volume, we thank Tim Egan and Alex Nemerov, who delivered keynote addresses at the 2017 conference that launched this project, as well as the several commentators whose remarks on that occasion informed the revisions of the chapters collected here. In alphabetical order they are: Cathryn Carson, Sandra Eder, Rebecca Herman, Ana Raquael Minian, Christian Paiz, Daniel Sargent, and Louis Warren.

We give special thanks to Stanford University's Bill Lane Center for the American West for organizing the conference, graciously hosting all participants, and supporting the publication of this book.

WORLD WAR II AND THE WEST IT WROUGHT

INTRODUCTION

MARK BRILLIANT and DAVID M. KENNEDY

Few episodes in American history were more transformative than World War II, and in no region did the war bring greater change than in the West. Having lifted the United States out of the Great Depression, World War II propelled a massive westward population movement, ignited a quarter-century economic boom—underwritten by unprecedented public investment in manufacturing, education, scientific research, and infrastructure—and helped redefine the West as the nation's most dynamic region. Amid robust economic growth and widely shared prosperity in the postwar decades—a rising tide that lifted all boats—westerners also made significant strides toward greater racial and gender equality, even as they struggled to manage the environmental consequences of their region's surging vitality. Richard White once evocatively encapsulated the catalyzing effect of World War II on the West: "Never in western history did changes come so quickly or have such far-reaching consequences as between 1941 and 1945. It was as if someone had tilted the country: people, money, and soldiers all spilled west."[1]

Abundant evidence in these pages affirms this perspective of World War II as watershed—and for good reasons: First and most obvious, since the broad Pacific region was one of the war's principal theaters, the West Coast was the natural staging area for America's Pacific war. Second, then as now, the West had the nation's lowest population density and greatest expanses of federally owned land. Those unique assets provided the space and the secrecy to test jet aircraft, practice bombing, and develop weapons, conspicuously including the plutonium manufactured in Hanford, Washington, for the bomb that incinerated Nagasaki on August 9, 1945.

Third, World War II proved so transformative for the West because the West was fortuitously primed for transformation. Industry in the region remained comparatively underdeveloped down to the eve of the war and was thus spared the cumbersome process and costly expense of retooling existing, older factories for war production. Instead, new factories were built afresh, incorporating the latest technologies.[2] Western industries were also able to tap the enormous supply of hydroelectric power made possible by dam building in the West in the immediate prewar years, especially the immense systems that rose on the Colorado and Columbia Rivers. Hydroelectric power proved to be especially important for the energy-intense manufacture of aluminum and plutonium. Some 50 percent of the energy required for the wartime manufacture of those critical materials flowed from the turbines of just two dams on the Columbia River in the Pacific Northwest—Grand Coulee (completed in 1942) and Bonneville (completed in 1937).

Among the westerners best positioned to appreciate the dramatic impact of World War II was the California-based industrialist Henry Kaiser, who became famous for the hundreds of Liberty and Victory transport ships that splashed down the ways from the shipyards that bore his name along the West Coast, especially in the San Francisco Bay Area. "The day of the West is at hand," crowed Kaiser at the December 1942 inauguration of his Fontana, California, steel mill—the first ever to fire up its blast furnaces west of the Rockies.[3] That pronouncement proved to be more prophetic than even Kaiser could have imagined. The United States had been the world's leading industrial power since 1890, but the pace of industrialization had varied greatly by region, with the West markedly lagging. On the eve of World War II, for example, only 5 percent of the Los Angeles County labor force was employed in manufacturing—two-thirds the average level in some thirty other comparable US cities.[4] But massive federal spending during World War II compressed into half a decade a veritable industrial revolution in the West that might otherwise have taken decades to accomplish.

Whereas Andrew Carnegie had raised a little more than $1 million in private capital to build his first steel mill in Pennsylvania in 1872, Kaiser Steel's initial capitalization at Fontana half a century later—all $100 million dollars' worth—came from a single source: the United States government, in the form of loans from the Reconstruction Finance Corporation.[5] To be sure, public financing of private ventures was certainly not without precedent in American history, in the West in particular (the transcontinental railroads, for example). But the scale of government engagement with the private sector during World War II dwarfed anything that had gone before. New Deal programs expended some $7.5 billion in the American West between 1933 and 1939. Yet during just four years of World War II, the federal government poured some $70 billion into the region.[6] A good chunk of this spending went toward expanding western energy infrastructure and manufacturing—from dams that generated hydroelectric power for making ships and airplanes and plutonium in the Pacific Northwest, to more ships along San Francisco Bay and still more airplanes in Southern California, which became the nation's airplane manufacturing hub, employing some three hundred thousand wartime workers (almost half of them women).

Western steel production had long been artificially stifled by the "Pittsburgh-plus" formula, a transportation premium levied on steel shipped from Pittsburgh. Not for nothing did famed writer Bernard DeVoto describe the prewar West as a "plundered province."[7] The war dramatically changed all that, unburdening the West of its historically crippling, quasi-colonial terms of trade with the rest of the nation. "For the first time in American history the Pacific states and much of the West were independent," wrote historian Bruce Cumings, "in oil, steel, factories, and investment capital," as San Francisco's Bank of America surpassed Chase Manhattan as the nation's biggest bank.[8]

"The most important things in this war are machines," Josef Stalin quipped to Franklin Roosevelt and Winston Churchill at the Tehran Conference in 1943. The United States, he said, "is a country of machines."[9] He could have added that within the United States it was the West where a disproportionate share of those machines—especially airplanes, ships, and nuclear weapons—were built. Among the biggest corporate beneficiaries of this river of federal dollars flowing westward in wartime were the several aerospace companies in the Los Angeles area—Douglas, Lockheed, Hughes, and Northrop; the steel, aluminum, cement, and shipbuilding companies of Henry Kaiser; and the San Francisco–based building company Bechtel, the largest construction and civil engineering company in the United States today.

The essays in this book grew out of a conference convened at Stanford University's Bill Lane Center for the American West to mark the seventy-fifth anniversary of America's entry into World War II. While some of the authors are known for their work on the western United States, others are better noted for scholarship that reaches beyond the region. As much as the contributions to this volume reconfirm the narrative of World War II as western watershed, they also offer reason to revise it. By expanding their analytical lens to survey both prewar and postwar periods, the chapters suggest that World War II did not so much represent a break with the past but rather an extension of it. From this perspective, the war proved to be less transformative than catalytic—less watershed than water project, to borrow from Richard White's fetching metaphor in the book's afterword—with the war serving to channel, redirect, and amplify prewar flows.

For example, as Jared Farmer details in chapter 1, "Executive Domain: Military Reservations in the Wartime West," large swaths of the American West had long been managed by federal agencies, including the National Park Service, the United States Forest Service, and the Bureau of Land Management. World War II introduced a new federal landlord into the mix: the Department of Defense, which quite literally conscripted Department of Interior lands into Department of Defense military service, where they largely remain today. These isolated and extensive military land withdrawals concentrated in the intermountain West also included some Native American, state, and private property. For Farmer, executive action for the sake of conservation undertaken a half century earlier by President Theodore Roosevelt set the stage for executive action in pursuit of military superiority undertaken by President Franklin Roosevelt. FDR's initiatives, in short, were "novel in magnitude rather than kind."

The long, intertwined histories of expansion, conservation, and militarization that Farmer braids together serve to foreshadow the story Mary L. Dudziak tells in chapter 7, "How the Pacific World Became West." Just as pre–World War II precedents prepared the ground for military land withdrawals in the interior West, so did they pave the way for the postwar projection of military power into the Pacific, where Dudziak focuses on Guam and Bikini Atoll.

While Farmer and Dudziak consider the Department of Defense's wartime conscription of territory, Daniel J. Kevles explores the conscription of knowledge. In chapter 2, "Enlisting the Laboratories: Science, Defense, and the Transformation of the High-Tech West," he examines the role of federal funding for aerospace engineering at California Institute of Technology (Caltech) and nuclear science at the University of California at Berkeley, both of which predated World War II, although the war dramatically shifted their priorities from basic research to national defense. Professor Ernest Lawrence's cyclotrons at Berkeley switched from neutron and radioactive isotope production for medical research to splitting atoms for atomic bombs. Similarly, aerospace engineering at Caltech converted from supporting the development of commercial airplanes to designing jet engines that enabled bomber take-offs from short airstrips and fighter take-offs from aircraft carriers.

In chapter 3, "World War II, the Cold War, and the Knowledge Economies of the Pacific Coast," Gavin Wright considers the "knowledge economy" clusters that dotted the West Coast from San Diego to Seattle. Like Kevles, Wright acknowledges the pre–World War II primacy of place of Southern California as the nation's leading aircraft center (and Caltech as the nation's foremost aerospace research hub), with Seattle not far behind, thanks to Boeing's production of seaplanes in World War I. In shipbuilding, too, the West Coast possessed a comparative regional advantage prior to the war, which in turn facilitated the production of just over half the vessels launched in wartime. These pre–World War II developments certainly contributed to the flourishing post–World War II "knowledge economy" clusters. Yet in Wright's account it is Cold War–era military spending (for both R&D and its commercialized products) that gets the major credit for transforming the once isolated American West into the nation's most economically dynamic region, with Silicon Valley (as it was christened in 1971) and Seattle emerging as the world's high-tech innovation capitals.

After postwar demobilization, cuts in defense spending, and recession accompanied by fears of slipping back into the prewar depression, it was Kim Il Sung's fateful decision to dispatch military forces across the 38th parallel in Korea in June 1950 that led Congress to quadruple defense expenditures. Dollars now flowed even more disproportionately westward than they had during World War II.[10] As Wright noted, "whereas the Pacific states received just 12.3% of military prime contract awards during [World War II], that share jumped to 23.9 percent in 1961," with California receiving the lion's share. Meanwhile, some 85 percent of R&D funding for electronics flowed from federal agencies. The military in turn dominated the developing markets for transistors and integrated circuits. In this way, Wright—like Farmer, Dudziak, and Kevles—also complicates the narrative of World War II as western watershed, albeit from a post-1945 perspective.

Economic dynamism's partner was demographic transmutation. Nearly eight million people lifted their heels for states west of the Mississippi between 1940 and 1950. Almost half of them settled in California.[11] The western population grew three times faster than that in the rest of the country. African

Americans poured in at a commensurate clip, increasing their numbers during this period in California from 124,306 to 462,172, in Washington from 7,424 to 30,691, and in Oregon from 2,565 to 11,529.[12]

In 1962, California surpassed New York as the nation's most populous state. The Pacific Northwest and the Southwest also exploded. Throughout the region white westerners flocked to mass-produced ranch-style single-family homes in ever-expanding suburbs, where a majority of all Americans dwelled by century's end. Meanwhile, nonwhite (especially black) westerners fought pervasive housing discrimination in the West's ballooning metropolises. Los Angeles became the epicenter of the legal campaign against racially restrictive housing covenants, which covered large tracts of developing suburbia until the United States Supreme Court invalidated their court enforcement in 1948.[13] Battles over housing discrimination and segregation continued to rage for decades thereafter, with fair housing legislation serving as one of the defining issues in the emerging "red-blue divide," as Matthew Dallek documents in chapter 4, "The Politics Wrought by War: Phoenix, Seattle, and the Emergence of the Red-Blue Divide in the West." Like other authors in this volume, with respect to Phoenix and Seattle, Dallek locates in the prewar period the headwaters of the transformations that swept over the region in the wartime and postwar years.

Demographic upheaval on the scale unleashed by World War II disrupted inherited political habits nearly everywhere in the West. Los Angeles went so far as to experiment with government-funded child care well into the postwar period, as Rebecca Jo Plant reveals in chapter 6, "'No Private School Could Ever Be As Satisfactory': The Fight for Government-Funded Child Care in Los Angeles." Meanwhile, wartime battles over issues like civil rights, labor rights, and anticommunism foreshadowed the political polarities that came increasingly to define the landscape of the West and the nation. Interestingly, the "red" side of this divide included a small but influential minority of Mexican Americans for whom, as Geraldo L. Cadava highlights in chapter 5, "The Roots of Hispanic Conservatism in the Wartime West," the war provided a seedbed for a strand of Latinx political conservatism that flourished in the postwar decades and continued to bolster Republican ranks well into the twenty-first century.

World War II also redefined—even revolutionized—relations between the United States and the rest of the world. As Cumings wrote, World War II "created for the first time in world history a continental nation with a combined integral industrial economy from the Atlantic to the Pacific, an 'organic whole' that emerged from the war unscathed...constituting 50 percent of global industrial production."[14] The United States no longer stretched merely from sea to shining sea. Now both an Atlantic and a Pacific power, it reached across the world's two widest oceans. The war and its aftermath hugely amplified the West's and therefore the nation's engagement throughout the Pacific basin, as evidenced by the Korean and Vietnam Wars and swelling trade with Asia. The resulting legacy of commercial, environmental, and military ties has shaped the global economic and geopolitical landscape ever since, as Dudziak makes clear with respect to the military basing and weapons testing that unfolded in the Pacific in the immediate postwar decades.

■

The acclaimed novelist Phillip Roth got something profoundly right when he described the immediate postwar era as the "greatest moment of collective inebriation in American history."[15] That giddy moment endured for the next few decades in the United States, and nowhere more giddily than in the West. *New York Times* columnist Nicholas Kristof has described the period as the "golden decades after World War II when growth was strong and inequality actually diminished."[16] As with any drunken bender, however, intoxicating glee eventually gave way to a painful hangover. Though the Cold War postponed this morning-after reckoning, ultimately the consequences of World War II began to have their own consequences, "countering some of the changes that the war brought" and creating their "own weather that would disrupt further progress," as Richard White writes in the afterword.

For White, the defining attributes of this new weather pattern include the growth of a "new conservatism in the West" and the expansion of economic inequality as the "great problem of our time," along with climate change and related effects of the post-1945 "Great Acceleration." These developments, White adds, were not yet discernible to the scholars in the 1980s and 1990s who "first forged the consensus on the impact of World War II on the West." But they are of central concern for the historians whose essays are assembled in this volume. Their studies at once affirm, qualify, and challenge the paradigm of World War II as western watershed. Put another way, just as the "consequences of consequences" of World War II have become more apparent, so have their antecedents.

It is therefore altogether fitting that Dallek pays heed to the pre–World War II roots of political conservatism in Phoenix; that, relatedly, Cadava focuses on a latent strand of Latinx conservatism that became more pervasive as the political center of gravity in the West shifted from New Deal liberalism to Reaganite conservatism; that Plant highlights a liberal policy road abandoned shortly after the war; that Dudziak draws attention to the projection—and, implicitly in the shadow of America's two-decade-long War on Terror in the Middle East, overextension—of US military power into the Pacific; and that Wright connects the West Coast's war-spawned knowledge economies to the demise of well-paying blue-collar jobs and the concomitant rise of high-tech-driven income polarization. As with so much of the story of World War II and the West it wrought, the West, ironically enough, has arguably led the way into a New Gilded Age.[17]

Attention to these dimensions of the history of World War II and the West it wrought attests to the ways in which "each age writes the history of the past anew with reference to the conditions uppermost in its own time," as America's first—and perhaps most famous—western historian, Frederick Jackson Turner, put it in 1891.[18] Taken together, the essays assembled in this volume compel a reckoning with the discomfiting question of whether the salutary changes that World War II helped set in motion were nothing more or less than an exceptional interlude between stubbornly recurring eras of inequality.

1

EXECUTIVE DOMAIN

Military Reservations in the Wartime West

JARED FARMER

The Second World War didn't end in 1945. That truism is especially true in the US West, the forefront of America's home front, the proving ground for the Atomic Age. It remains apt. Regardless of what happens to the post-1945 and post-1989 international order—an open question after 2016—the United States seems committed to maintaining an action-ready military with nuclear and aerial supremacy. For as long as the nation keeps that commitment, millions of acres of federal land in the US West will remain militarized. These properties—Air Force bombing ranges, Navy gunnery ranges, Army training grounds—have existed in perpetual wartime since the presidency of Franklin Delano Roosevelt.

Some preliminary real estate numbers are in order. By recent count, the US government owns approximately 640 million acres, more than one-quarter the nation's landmass. This acreage is overwhelmingly located in the far western states, including Alaska. Four agencies explicitly manage federal lands: the US Forest Service, the US Fish and Wildlife Service, the National Park Service, and the Bureau of Land Management (BLM). But there is a fifth major landlord, one that doesn't have a land management mission—the Department of Defense (DoD). Of the DoD's twenty-five million total acres of "base structure," roughly sixteen million are federal lands in the US West. This aggregate area, larger than West Virginia, is spread across the Great Basin Desert, the Mojave Desert, the Sonoran Desert, and the Chihuahuan Desert. The top four military states, in terms of acreage, are, in order, New Mexico, Nevada, California, and Utah. Each of the three largest base complexes—White Sands Missile Range, the Nevada Test and Training Range, and the Utah Test and Training Range—meets the obligatory "larger than Rhode Island" standard. In Utah the DoD's total acreage exceeds the combined acreage of the "Mighty 5" national parks (Arches, Bryce, Canyonlands, Capitol Reef, and Zion) for which the Beehive State is renowned around the world.[1]

Since the 1970s, antiwar activists have deployed a charged phrase to describe military reservations in the western deserts: "national sacrifice areas." That classification is too simple. Militarized landscapes like White Sands are wasted *and* wild, contaminated *and* conserved, emptied *and* populated, remote *and* developed. Desert bases constitute tax bases for local and state governments, employing large numbers of workers in private and governmental sectors. Adding to the complexity, most of the restricted land in the arid US West "owned" by the DoD is technically on loan from the Department of the Interior. As historian Brandon Davis has argued, "Nearly all aspects of America's condition of permanent war are predicated on the military's ongoing occupation of public land." In the language of federal law, such land is *withdrawn*. Although Congress during the Cold War placed constraints on future nonemergency land withdrawals, it condoned and effectively permanentized the withdrawals executed during World War II.[2]

Across the arid West, then, the legal year remains 1941. Or maybe the time is 1940—or 1939? As historian Mary Dudziak has shown, it's impossible to say when exactly peacetime became wartime during the administration of FDR.[3] Surely it was well before the attack on Pearl Harbor, December 7, 1941, and the congressional declaration of war the next day. One can point to Army appropriation bills, or the Selective Training and Service Act of 1940, or the Lend-Lease Act, signed on March 11, 1941, or various executive actions that nudged the United States away from neutrality—a process constitutional scholar Edward Corwin called the "war before the war."[4] For example, days after Germany invaded Poland in September 1939, FDR proclaimed a "limited" national emergency without clarifying any limitations.[5] For good measure, on May 27, 1941, six months *before* Pearl Harbor, FDR issued a sweeping new proclamation: "An unlimited national emergency confronts this country, which requires that its military, naval, air and civilian defenses be put on the basis of readiness to repel any and all acts or threats of aggression directed toward any part of the Western Hemisphere."[6] The White House understood the utility of emergencies: they permit deliberate preparation as well as hurried action.[7]

As a historian of the Great Basin, I want to call attention to another temporal marker on the continuum of peacetime to wartime, a moment that never appears in timelines of World War II, a day that does not live in infamy: October 29, 1940. On that date, FDR signed a pair of executive orders withdrawing 3.6 million acres of public land in southern Nevada and 1.6 million more in western Utah. The acreage was reserved for an unspecified period for the War Department's use as aerial bombing and gunnery ranges.[8] For his authority Roosevelt somewhat dubiously cited the Army Appropriations Act of 1918, which had granted the president the power to reserve land for "aviation stations, balloon schools, [and] fields for testing and experimental work."[9] Coming just after the onset of the London Blitz, FDR's pair of executive orders were, on the one hand, extraordinary proto-wartime acts. On the other hand, they were ordinary and un-newsworthy because they superficially resembled any number of previous western land withdrawals for nature reserves. Indeed, part of the Nevada bombing range had previously been reserved by FDR as the Desert Game Range (now the Desert National Wildlife Refuge).[10]

The sudden strategic importance of the Great Basin was a stunning role reversal. The playas of Nevada and Utah had long served as the US settler state's definition of "wasted": unused, unusable, uninhabited.[11] Thanks to World War II, the Great Basin's inarable void was finally "reclaimed"—not by the Bureau of Reclamation but the Department of War, not by plowshares but swords. In the language of military planners, the "natural endowments" of the desert had utility in war.

"War is in fact the true nurse of executive aggrandizement," warned James Madison during the first term of the first president. "In war the public treasures are to be unlocked, and it is the executive hand which is to dispense them."[12] Applied to the Great Basin during World War II, Madison's maxim holds true, albeit with an inversion. The executive could unilaterally *lock up* public lands in the western deserts precisely because they had been untreasurable. But the premise that the Great Basin was vacant, and therefore public, and thereby available to militarization, was a historical and legal fiction made possible by violence. When FDR withdrew the lands that would become the test-and-training ranges in Nevada and Utah, he encroached upon Numic territory whose title had never been extinguished. Treaties of "peace and friendship" signed during the Civil War, later ratified by the US Senate, recognized Western Shoshone and Goshute claims to tens of million acres. The signatories authorized the executive to establish military posts on Numic land and to create reservations for tribal use. Presidents would go on to exercise the former power maximally, the latter power minimally. Thus the "empty land" available for World War II militarization was *emptied* land—the spoils of attacks on indigenous sovereignty.

The histories of US expansionism, conservation, and militarism need to be connected. Over the long nineteenth century, the management of war and the administration of western lands each made the executive more powerful, and during World War II these related realms of power amplified each other exponentially. Expressed in biographical terms, conservation president Theodore Roosevelt bequeathed to war president Franklin Delano Roosevelt the precedent of using executive power to remake the western map with strokes of a pen. As tallied in total reserved acreage, T. R. ranks as the greatest conservationist in US history, while FDR ranks as the greatest militarist. But, of course, Theodore was himself a military expansionist—apologetic historian of the Indian wars, volunteer soldier in Cuba, de facto president of the Philippines. Contemporary Americans who celebrate the creation of nature reservations (national forests, national monuments, national wildlife refuges) by Rooseveltian presidents would do well to consider how the presidential sword cuts both ways. In terms of property law, the sacralization *and* the militarization of the western deserts was foremost the result of executive action. T. R.'s peacetime prerogative offered a template for FDR's wartime power. The latter's expedient role was novel in magnitude rather than kind.

Military historians are unaccustomed to discussing nature reserves in conjunction with military bases. More surprisingly, legal and diplomatic historians have not analyzed military land withdrawals alongside two related terrains of sovereignty: American Indian reservations and US overseas territories.[13] Through a joint reckoning of these extraordinary legal spaces, US Americans can better understand how land and power operate together in national history. In this short history of wartime property in the arid West, I trace two lines—one going temporally backward and spatially westward, another going temporally forward and spatially oceanward. In other words, my regional case study from the Second World War gestures to the founding foreign policy of the United States—relations with American Indians—and its current ambivalent role as warden of global empire.

I. Wartime Preparation

Military land withdrawals during World War II did not come out of nowhere. The original US Congress, through the Articles of Confederation, asserted federal primacy over unorganized western land, a legal precedent that proved enduring despite political contestation from states. The Constitution reinforced federal ownership through Article IV, Section 3, which states unambiguously: "Congress shall have power to dispose of and make all needful Rules and Regulations respecting the Territory or other Property belonging to the United States."

The Property Clause may sound like plenary power for the legislative branch, but it is not. Starting with George Washington, presidents have withdrawn land—excluding it from disposal—for the national interest. The executive's purview over federal properties comes from Article II, which names the president commander in chief and also chief negotiator of treaties. In the republic's first century, president after president made ad hoc land withdrawals as necessitated by foreign policy: war against Indians and diplomacy with Indian nations. War demanded forts for Army soldiers; diplomacy demanded reservations for tribes. In addition, presidents strategically reserved waterfalls for power sites, peninsulas for lighthouses, timber stands for naval ship masts, and lead deposits for munitions. Congress occasionally provided statutory authority for such actions, but mainly acquiesced to executive action, thus interpreting separation of powers through practice. Property powers, like war and military powers, are in practice held concurrently, not exclusively.

Over the long nineteenth century the federal government increased its landed authority through new roles: arbiter of competing private land claims; purchaser and conqueror of trans-Mississippi territories; and owner-in-trust of tribal reservations.[14] Complexities notwithstanding, the guiding principle of federal land policy in the long nineteenth century was expropriation and disposal. The best demonstration of the government's property powers was the disposal of so much land. The state worked to extinguish Indian title, then alienate that "public domain" (minus any reservations) to private owners through congressionally approved methods like auction, land scrip, land bounty, land granting, and homesteading. "Public" was meant to be a transitory state.

By the 1890s momentum to privatize the public domain slowed for two main reasons. First, not enough homesteaders could be enticed to make claims on inarable land throughout the mountainous and arid Far West. Second, more and more conservationists argued for government stewardship of timber and water supplies, and sites of outstanding scenery and wildlife. Congress gave new statutory powers to the executive to prevent certain uses (i.e., *withdrawing*) and to prioritize certain uses (i.e., *reserving*). A congressional act of 1891 included a sentence that allowed the president to reserve "any part of the public lands wholly or in part covered with timber or undergrowth."[15] Grover Cleveland and Theodore Roosevelt flexed this authority to create the national forest system, despite the objections of western newspapers, business interests, and senators. When Congress passed the Antiquities Act of 1906, western senators felt mollified that this new withdrawal authority applied to "the smallest area compatible with proper care and management" of "objects of historic or scientific or interest."[16] Designed to safeguard ancestral Puebloan ruins in the Southwest, the Antiquities Act was almost immediately used by Roosevelt to withdraw and reserve over eight hundred thousand acres at the Grand Canyon—a precedent-making power grab subsequently affirmed by the Supreme Court.[17]

Of equal legal consequence, Roosevelt created a new class of game reserves using neither statutory authority nor the implied authority derived from the presidential realm of foreign relations. Although T. R. didn't care much about Indian reservations—most of which were, at the time, being pulverized through privatization—he worried about reservations for America's migratory birds. In 1903 he created the first of dozens of national wildlife refuges, citing no authority but his own. Through words and deeds (such as the second Public Lands Commission), Roosevelt asserted a general stewardship role for the presidency that rose to the level of the national interest, like war and diplomacy. "I declined to adopt the view that what was imperatively necessary for the Nation could not be done by the President unless he could find some specific authorization to do it," he recalled. "My belief was that it was not only his right but his duty to do anything that the needs of the Nation demanded unless such action was forbidden by the Constitution or by the laws."[18]

His successor, William Howard Taft, acted with greater circumspection. In 1909, Taft made a temporary withdrawal of 3.6 million acres of oil and gas land in Wyoming and California, concerned that a key fuel source for the Navy would fall into private hands. The Mining Act of 1872 had not anticipated the problem of fossil fuels. Roosevelt had reserved tens of millions of acres of coal lands until a leasing system could be established, and now Taft wanted to do likewise with oil reserves. However, the White House doubted the legality of its withdrawals, and so sent a message to Congress in 1910 asking for clarification of executive authority.

The resulting General Withdrawal Act of 1910—better known as the "Pickett Act"—was meant to reassert congressional supremacy over western land and to contain future action by the executive. The Pickett Act permitted the president to "temporarily" withdraw lands from sale and entry and to reserve them for "public purposes." Withdrawn lands would remain open to "metalliferous" (i.e., hardrock) mining claims; the power to restrict all mining seemed excessive, even to conservationists. Legislators skirted the legality of Taft's oil reserves and all other prior withdrawals, leaving that issue to the courts. The Pickett Act stipulated that new reservations would remain in force until revoked, suggesting the possibility of an indefinite term. Floor debate indicated that Congress intended a short time frame, several years at most. However, by not explicitly defining "temporarily," conservationists in Congress created a legal gray area that would be exploited by future presidents. An act meant to check executive power would in the long run serve to magnify it.[19]

In the meantime, Taft's oil withdrawals had their day in court, resulting in a Supreme Court decision in 1915. *United States v. Midwest Oil* marked a victory for Hamiltonians in government. The court majority arrived at the opinion that President Taft's action, though not empowered by statute, was legal. The justices provided historical evidence that the executive had, without express authority, withdrawn federal land hundreds of times, going back to the earliest period of US government, with occasional specific support of Supreme Court rulings and attorney general opinions. Interior Secretary Henry M. Teller in 1881 had described "an existing undisputed power too well settled ever to be disputed." As of 1915, the Court enumerated 99 Indian reservations, 109 military reservations or accessory sites, and 44 bird refuges. Such withdrawals were, according to the justices, acts of exigency for the public weal (*existe ex necessitate rei*). Given that the legislative branch had never repudiated such executive actions, the Court derived a textbook formulation: "Its silence was acquiescence. Its acquiescence was equivalent to consent to continue the practice until the power was revoked by some subsequent action by Congress."[20]

U.S. v. Midwest did not technically contradict the Pickett Act. Whereas the Court ruled retrospectively, Congress had acted prospectively. Commonsense legal and historical reasoning provided a straightforward harmonization: in 1910 a constitutionally implied power had been revoked and replaced by a more limited congressionally delegated power. Nonetheless, an alternative legal interpretation remained open. For apologists of executive authority, the "acquiescence doctrine" articulated by the Supreme Court was a historical gift that could keep on giving. After 1915 an activist president could unilaterally exercise any number of unenumerated powers and, unless specifically reprimanded by Congress, claim post-facto legal authority for those actions based on the precedent established by *Midwest Oil*.

Franklin Delano Roosevelt, no less than his predecessor Theodore Roosevelt, used western land conservation to expand the scope of the US presidency. On November 26, 1934, with dust storms in the news, FDR exercised the authority of the Pickett Act to an incredible magnitude, temporarily withdrawing all the "vacant, unreserved and unappropriated" land in the twelve western states.[21] This one executive order affected eighty million acres and complemented the recently passed Taylor Grazing Act, officially "an Act to stop injury to the public grazing lands by preventing overgrazing and soil deterioration." In a process known as "classification," Interior Department officials would determine the "most useful purpose" of each section of all this unbought and unreserved land, with the expectation that most of it would be leasable for grazing, albeit under new regulations. The Taylor Grazing Act and FDR's associated mega-withdrawal (raised to 142 million acres in a subsequent order) were governmental admissions that the post–Civil War project to alienate the western public domain to homesteaders had sputtered long before all the available property had been privatized. Moving halfway from a policy of land disposal to a policy of land retention, the government created a custodial agency, the Grazing Service, to manage the leasable districts. Henceforth, the term "public land" generally referred to such leftover acreage—not forest land, not park land, not refuge land. Most of this public land was in the Great Basin and other western deserts.[22]

In land policy as in most realms, presidential power begets more power. By the end of its second term, the FDR administration asserted its right to withdraw public land permanently and absolutely—including the nullification of mining laws that appertained—something disallowed under an impartial reading of the Pickett Act. The executive might have asked Congress for such power; instead, it pursued the matter internally, and thus conservation bled into war. The legal test case was seemingly innocuous, being related to the conservation goals of the Taylor Grazing Act. The Interior Department requested that the Justice Department approve an "absolute" withdrawal in eastern Oregon for a Grazing Service experiment station used by range scientists at Oregon State University. Knowing that this local application of maximal power would have profound implications for presidential prerogative, Attorney General Robert H. Jackson reviewed the legal material with care and in July 1940 wrote an opinion that rejected the proposed executive order.

Before the opinion could be published, objections rolled in. The Navy judge advocate and the secretary of war each communicated to Jackson, requesting a reversal. Clearly this matter transcended rangeland science. Henry L. Stimson put it bluntly: The military desired "free and unrestricted use of its reservations" without possible "embarrassment and inconvenience" of mining claims. Secretary of the Interior Harold L. Ickes, a maximalist and interventionist in every sense, objected to Jackson's opinion in a long, lawyerly memorandum. Ickes argued that the president enjoyed not one but *two* legal authorities: (1) statutory power given in 1910 by Congress to temporarily withdraw land, excluding hardrock mining rights; and (2) residual implied power affirmed in 1915 by the Supreme Court to indefinitely or even permanently withdraw land, including all mining rights. In Ickes's view, the three hundred or so nonstatutory land withdrawals executed since the Pickett Act without subsequent contestation by Congress had demonstrated the "presumed inherent general withdrawal power" in the presidency. The executive possessed such power because people acted in the belief that such power existed. For legal ammunition, Ickes creatively mined *Ozawa v. United States* (1922), in which the Supreme Court had cited "legislative acquiescence" to the "popular" definition of "white person," regardless of original statutory intent. "In any event," concluded Ickes, "30 years of repeated and consistent administrative practice are eloquently persuasive."[23]

Jackson initially stood his ground, communicating in April 1941 that he felt "constrained to adhere" to his opinion. Soon enough he caved to partisan pressure, including pushback from his own Office of Solicitor General. In June, days after FDR had declared an unlimited national emergency, Jackson buried his actual opinion—never published and not made public until 1968—and issued an antithetical one for the record. In the published opinion, Jackson did not reference *Ozawa*, nor did he mention any military ramifications, sticking to the narrow question at hand. Grasping for legal precedent, the attorney general quoted from a predecessor's 1930 opinion that the ad hoc national wildlife refuge system had been allowed by the Pickett Act, even though no specific reservation authority had been enumerated by Congress.[24] This logic may have pained Jackson. A decade later, from his seat on the Supreme Court, he would vote to curtail presidential seizure power in the landmark case *Youngstown Sheet & Tube Co. v. Sawyer* (1952). In his influential concurring opinion, Justice Jackson described the "zone of twilight" between express and implied authority that could be exploited by activist presidents. He did not reveal his own murky history of widening the twilight zone.[25]

Read in isolation, the June 1941 opinion and resulting executive order about Squaw Butte Experimental Station seem wholly unrelated to the conduct of war. But context means everything. As published, Jackson's party-line opinion was expedient because the White House had, starting in 1940, begun withdrawing public land for the indefinite use of the War Department using the absolutist language "including the mining laws." Jackson thus provided legal cover for a domestic, territorial expression of wartime before any declaration of war.

On December 8, 1941, by signing the congressional declaration of war against Japan, FDR unlocked maximal Constitutional powers. In regard to public lands, however, the change was apparent in speed, not size or kind. In early 1942, after the secret authorization of the Manhattan Project, the White House approved another pair of large withdrawals as part of a fast stream of land orders. First, FDR reserved 1.2 million acres in New Mexico—Alamogordo Bombing and Gunnery Range, the precursor of White Sands Missile Range—again claiming statutory authority from 1918. The boundaries of the "general bombing range" included private property (3 percent of the total acreage) and New Mexico state property (21 percent), not to mention public land under grazing lease by local ranchers, plus White Sands National Monument, previously reserved by Herbert Hoover. Roosevelt's order included a vague promise that affected public lands would be returned to the administration of the Interior Department "when they are no longer needed for the purpose for which they are reserved."[26] White House lawyers appended the same boilerplate language to another order the next month that created a chemical warfare range in Utah adjacent to the big bombing range. For this wartime act Roosevelt simply invoked "the authority vested in me as President."[27]

As the war escalated in 1942, the White House decided to relieve the president of the burden of processing military requests for land withdrawals. By means of another executive order, FDR delegated authority to the Secretary of the Interior, formalizing an interpersonal power dynamic with Ickes that had been established before the war.[28] Unlike Theodore Roosevelt, FDR did not take great personal interest in western lands and generally deferred to Ickes, who had turned Interior into his empire. After April 1942 public land orders from the office of Ickes served in lieu of executive orders. One year later, FDR extended Ickes's purview to properties newly acquired by the federal government (in addition to unpatented public land).[29] Step by step, the interior secretary had become the third most important member of the military cabinet after the secretaries of war and Navy.

Even after the formal entry into war, absolute withdrawal remained the fastest, easiest way for the military to gain full control of public land, but it was hardly the only available land acquisition method. Consider the history of

Japanese-American detention. Once the War Department declared the West Coast a military exclusion zone, this vast exclosure demanded multiple small enclosures—"reception centers" and "relocation centers," to use the euphemisms of the time. For its ten main carceral camps, the War Relocation Authority relied on four land acquisition methods. In Arizona the Department of the Interior relinquished Indian reservation land to the War Department through memoranda of understanding. In one case (Poston), members of the Colorado River Indian Tribes objected to uncompensated taking of their trust land; in the other case (Gila River), the Pima tribe received nominal lease payments. The second acquisition method was an interagency memorandum of understanding. At Tule Lake (California), Minidoka (Idaho), and Heart Mountain (Wyoming), the Bureau of Reclamation agreed to lease public lands previously reserved for irrigation projects. For the two camps in Arkansas (Jerome and Rohwer), the Farm Security Administration, a branch of the US Department of Agriculture, agreed to similar leases. The third method, purchasing private land through the US Army Corps of Engineers, was used at Granada (Colorado) and Topaz (Utah). The fourth method was condemnation as empowered by the Second War Powers Act of 1942. At Manzanar (California) the federal government seized land owned by the City of Los Angeles.[30]

The Manhattan Project, authorized in early 1942, demanded its own western land acquisitions. At Hanford the government used the Second War Powers Act to acquire private land through condemnation and purchase. For the project's research center, the military decided to go through the National Forest Service because its land had already been reserved from public entry. To gain exclusive access to the property that became Los Alamos, Henry L. Stimson simply sent a letter to the secretary of agriculture asking permission to occupy the Pajarito Plateau "for so long as the military necessity continues." The small private inholdings within the boundaries of the so-called "demolition range" were then condemned through the Second War Powers Act. Because Hanford and Los Alamos did not involve any "public land"—that is, residual public domain administered by the Grazing Service—their post-1945 transition to Cold War permanence would be straightforward.[31]

Military land acquisition was not geographically restricted to western states. At the height of World War II the War and Navy departments had access to 52.7 million acres, compared to 2.6 million in 1940. Of the wartime total, 33 million acres were already federally owned or administered. Of that subtotal, the military gained partial use of roughly 20 million acres through temporary special-use permits and full use of roughly 13 million through indefinite public land withdrawals. The remaining 17 million acres largely came from private property in eastern and southern states, where the military displaced—through lease, purchase, or condemnation—tens of thousands of farm families. In the South the military built on earlier New Deal programs of retiring submarginal agricultural land from production.[32]

In western states military operations affected seasonal grazing more than year-round farming. In South Dakota the Oglala Sioux watched in helpless anger when the Interior Department, which managed the Pine Ridge Indian Reservation in trust, gave nearly nine hundred thousand acres of "badlands" to the War Department for an aerial and gunnery range.[33] Compared to Lakotas on reservation land, white ranchers on public land had somewhat greater political voice. In Utah and Nevada local stock growers registered their irritation when their grazing leases were suspended by the War Department. In 1942, Congress amended the Taylor Grazing Act to stipulate that losses resulting from cancellations of leases due to military land withdrawals would be compensated to a "fair and reasonable" degree.[34] In New Mexico, meanwhile, many private ranch owners resisted the condemnation orders that followed the designation of the Alamogordo Gunnery and Bombing Range.[35]

During the war, Senator Pat McCarran of Nevada presided over a series of hearings about the administration and use of public lands, giving white rural westerners opportunities to vent about the Taylor Grazing Act, eastern bureaucrats, and executive overreach. McCarran was a model powerbroker for the wartime West. Out of one side of his mouth he defended the customary rights of freedom-loving ranchers against the tyranny of big government; out of the other he sweet-talked the military to make sure Nevada got as many bases and government jobs as possible. In similar fashion Utah's elected leaders welcomed the War Department even as they castigated the Interior Department. As part of the McCarran hearings, the Beehive State's delegation helped prepare a Senate report in 1945. The Utahns blasted the feds for one withdrawal in the Uintah Basin that benefitted Ute Indians and inconvenienced Mormon graziers; and another near Moab—potash-rich lands reserved for a National Fertilizer Program—that shut out prospectors and miners.

These two temporary withdrawals—with their New Deal connections to the Bureau of Indian Affairs, the Grazing Service, and the Soil and Conservation Service—enraged the leadership of Utah. Politicians stoked fears of an impending socialistic takeover of southern Utah by the National Park Service that would remove public land from "beneficial use." Military land withdrawals in western Utah, which generated thousands of defense jobs, elicited no such anti–New Deal alarm. Besides, in 1945 any criticism of defense facilities would have seemed unpatriotic. While the McCarran committee exhorted Congress to recapture public land withdrawal, to restore the meaning of the Pickett Act, and to curtail the abuses of executive authority, it softened its tone in reference to military lands: "Obviously, the job has had to be done hurriedly and by a large number of officers and employees, most of whom were new to undertakings of this kind."[36]

II. Wartime Continuation

The planning for post–World War II land use in the US West began at a time when the Cold War and the national security state were not yet inevitable. In February 1945, anticipating the end of hostilities, FDR issued a proclamation that amended fifty-four executive orders and fifty-nine public land orders.[37] President Roosevelt declared that six months following the termination of the unlimited national emergency, thirteen million acres of public lands would return to their former jurisdictions, though remain withdrawn until otherwise ordered. This proclamation implied that absolute withdrawals for military use had been emergency actions made in a moment of exception, and hinted that wide application of Robert H. Jackson's published opinion might not bear legal scrutiny. Roosevelt's proclamation even applied to the big bombing ranges in Utah, Nevada, and New Mexico reserved under the presumptive authority of the Army Appropriations Act of 1918. Even more remarkably, the affected withdrawals stretched back in time to spring 1939—a tacit admission that the nation had entered wartime, or at least martial time, before Hitler's blitzkrieg, and even before FDR's limited national emergency.

Whatever Roosevelt's personal intentions, "peacetime" or "normal time" was not forthcoming in 1945, due to the death of the president, the onset of the atomic age, and the deterioration of US-Soviet relations. During Harry S. Truman's years in office, the White House, the military, and both parties in Congress struggled to find a balance between national security and the social contract.[38] This awkward balancing act resulted in congressional laws that both contained and normalized militarism: the Atomic Energy Act of 1946 transferred the military's Manhattan Project to the civilian Atomic Energy Commission (AEC); the National Security Act of 1947 established the DoD and the Central Intelligence Agency (CIA); and the Selective Service Act of 1948 instituted the modern draft system.

In these changed circumstances, the DoD had no incentive to let go of World War II land withdrawals. A standing military needed a standing dominion. Congress helpfully amended the Taylor Grazing Act in 1948 to allow the cancellation of grazing permits on public lands needed for "war *or national defense* purposes."[39] With those three words, wartime on the range could continue beyond (or without) any specific war. As of the Korean War, the Pentagon controlled approximately twelve million of the thirteen million acres withdrawn by FDR. At the fine level, many small changes had occurred since the surrender of Japan: bases deactivated or reactivated; lands transferred from the Army to the Navy; boundaries adjusted; mining claims revoked; grazing rights suspended or canceled or liquidated; and so on. For example, in 1950 the acting secretary of the interior, claiming no specific authority, withdrew Dugway Proving Ground at twice the size (279,000 acres) for continuation of the Army's chemical weapons program.[40] Further expansions followed, leading to financial losses for the Deseret Live Stock Company, Utah's largest sheep operation. In Nevada the AEC initiated nuclear testing in 1951, building on prior tests at Bikini Atoll.

Because of the race to nuclear armament—including hydrogen bombs—FDR's unlimited emergency continued long after VJ Day. In spring 1952 the Senate ratified the Treaty of Peace with Japan, and Truman used this opportunity to end his predecessor's limited *and* unlimited emergencies. However, his termination order specifically exempted his own 1950 proclamation that the threat of "world conquest by communist imperialism" had created a *new* national emergency "requiring that the military, naval, air, and civilian defenses of this country to be strengthened as speedily as possible."[41] In other words, all three concurrent emergency orders had been in effect when the United States entered the Korean War without a war declaration from Congress. Truman's residual anticommunist national emergency would remain active through the 1970s.

Nonetheless, when Truman terminated FDR's pair of emergencies, a countdown began. In one-half year, public land withdrawn during World War II was set to revert to the jurisdiction of the Interior Department. Six months later, October 28, 1952, nothing changed. The demilitarization of the public domain did not happen—by design. In May, Truman had signed an executive order delegating to the secretary of the interior not just the power to withdraw land, but to modify existing withdrawals. Truman cited the authority of the Pickett Act—that is, Robert H. Jackson's wartime interpretation of the act. A

Progressive Era conservation bill meant to restrict the president to limited, temporary withdrawals now allowed the continuation of absolute withdrawals. Truman's order also authorized the interior secretary to "redelegate" the power of withdrawal to his assistants.[42] Congress acquiesced to the bureaucratization of national security. In August the legislative branch passed a bill permitting the president to grant executive powers to agency-level heads.[43] With multiple layers of legal cover, the Interior Department on October 27 sent subcabinet correspondence to the Pentagon, permitting the military to continue its occupation of public lands "for an indefinite period" beyond the following day's deadline.[44]

In New Mexico and Nevada, at the two largest World War II reservations, the Truman administration additionally made specific moves to facilitate the status shift from transience to continuance to permanence. In 1952, through a new public land order, 2.4 million acres in New Mexico's Tularosa Basin, double the size of the original Alamogordo Bombing and Gunnery Range, was withdrawn indefinitely and reserved specifically for use of the Department of the Army. The Army redoubled its efforts to suspend remaining grazing leases and condemn remaining inholdings (a coercive process portrayed in Edward Abbey's 1962 antistatist cowboy novel *Fire on the Mountain*). The Army had been testing long-range missiles in New Mexico since 1945, starting with V-2 rockets seized from the Nazis. When the executive rewithdrew the Tularosa Basin for the soon-to-be-renamed White Sands Proving Ground, it could no longer claim to be reserving an "aviation station." Instead, the public land order simply cited the all-purpose authority of the Pickett Act.[45]

Similarly, in Nevada a large portion of the Las Vegas Bombing and Gunnery Range was repurposed into the Nevada Proving Ground—actually first, legally second. Back in December 1950, President Truman had approved the selection of southern Nevada as the "continental test site" for atomic weapons. The AEC selection committee had considered it mandatory—for reasons of efficiency, security, and public relations—that the site be "available," by which it meant already under military control.[46] In 1952, more than a year *after* nuclear testing had commenced, the secretary of the interior, through a simple public land order, transferred some 435,000 acres from the management of the Air Force to the AEC.[47]

The militarization of the arid West peaked during the presidency of Dwight D. Eisenhower, former five-star general. In 1953 the secretary of the interior signed a public land order creating a new cluster of Navy bombing ranges in central Nevada.[48] In 1955 the president personally set aside a top-secret base in southern Nevada—called Groom Lake, or Paradise Ranch, or Area 51—for the CIA's U-2 program. Officially, this test-and-training base did not exist. To this day, it remains absent from the National Map. According to a recently declassified history, Eisenhower reserved this "strip of wasteland" as an extension of the Nevada Proving Ground without the legal nicety of a public land order.[49] Later that year, Eisenhower reserved the air above the entire test area under the clear authority of the Air Commerce Act of 1926, which allowed the executive to create "airspace reservations" for national defense. Once the vertical space was legally withdrawn, the legality of the land withdrawals beneath it was a moot point—if all the warning signs, fences, and security checkpoints weren't sufficient already.[50]

Emboldened, the Pentagon made new plans. In 1955 the DoD requested thirteen million *additional* acres from the Department of the Interior. This imminent doubling of military land withdrawals came to the attention of California representative Clair Engle, Democratic chairman of the House Committee on Interior and Insular Affairs, who requested a pause from the interior secretary pending congressional research. After years of consent or silent acquiescence, the legislative branch decided to revisit the executive's property powers.

The facts obtained by Engle's committee were staggering. As of 1956, the Army, Air Force, and Navy controlled 27.6 million acres nationwide. As Engle liked to say, that was equivalent to a strip of land 14.5 miles wide from San Francisco to New York City. Of this total, 16.9 million acres (more than 60 percent) were public land withdrawals. The Air Force controlled most of this subtotal, 14.4 million acres. Speaking to Congress, Engle described the procedure of military capture: "The Air Force would simply make out a slip of paper . . . asking for an area perhaps 100 miles long and 50 miles wide, and send it over to the Secretary of the Interior saying it was absolutely necessary to their operations, and that area was set aside for those military operations and put into what could be regarded as a legal icebox."[51] When called before Engle to testify, an Air Force official confirmed: "We have never had a turndown." The Air Force even admitted that "five-million-some-odd acres" were in excess of its needs for bombing and gunnery ranges. Even so, it wanted to keep almost all this "excess" for other purposes, including unknown future purposes. During hearings, military officials emphasized how the intercabinet withdrawal process allowed for flexibility in a time of rapidly changing military technology. The arms race required constant adaptation, they said. A gunnery range today might not serve the needs of guided missiles tomorrow. A cushion of land boosted national security.[52]

Coming before Eisenhower's 1961 farewell warning about the "military-industrial complex," Engle's hearings received perfunctory interior-page coverage in the *Washington Post* and *New York Times*. There was no national constituency for BLM lands. Tellingly, when Engle wrote an opinion piece, his best available audience was the membership of the National Parks Conservation Association. *National Parks Magazine* was an odd fit, for Engle was less concerned about scenery and wildlife than about miners and hunters being "locked out." Using language familiar to white rural westerners, Engle decried how "land hogs" in the DoD had "grabbed" western land.[53] Engle's committee spent an inordinate amount of time investigating alleged hunting abuses by military officers. Sounding not unlike commoners protesting the gentry's privilege to hunt in the forest, committee members reprimanded the military for allegedly creating private game reserves—"lands without law"—where high brass could take weekend junkets to slaughter trophy bucks at will. The committee also worried that the military would arrogate the riparian water rights of rural westerners. Most of all, Engle hoped to reassert Congress's Article IV authority over public lands. He wanted to break the habit of acquiescence that had followed the attorney general's opinion of 1941.

The legislative result was a partial success, which is to say a partial failure. As signed by Eisenhower, the Defense Withdrawal Act of 1958—subsequently known as the "Engle Act"—was the biggest check on presidential property powers since 1910.[54] It thus represented a small but noteworthy corrective to the "constitutional dictatorship" or the "imperial presidency."[55] Henceforth, any absolute withdrawal for national defense purposes that exceeded five thousand acres required approval from Congress. But the law had only one side of teeth. Its statutory purview was prospective, not retroactive. It specifically exempted all the expired World War II "emergency" withdrawals that remained in military use with the concurrence of the Department of the Interior. One BLM official explained to the committee this version of limbo: "The use of those lands so far as the terms of the public land order are concerned are void now, that is, the order is not in effect as to the military use. But the lands remain withdrawn."[56] Engle's investigation left unresolved the issue of "vertical needs" for airspace, restricting itself to the "horizontal" question of military use requirements.[57] For new withdrawals the bill required the Pentagon to specify a period but did not set a temporal limit. Moreover, the law became void in future "times of war or national emergency." Even as western lawmakers tried to correct the excesses of wartime, they could barely think beyond the temporality of war.

A historian interested in narrating failure can point to instances in the late twentieth century when state national guards—not covered by the Engle Act—avoided legal scrutiny on requested land withdrawals, or when the US military attempted to circumvent Congress by claiming exemptions on land co-used with state guards.[58] Other times, the military simply ignored the law. For example, in 1978 the Air Force added a buffer zone to Area 51 by restricting access to an adjacent mountain range in the public domain. Las Vegas Representative Harry Reid objected, as did Governor Richard Bryan, who declared: "The day is past when the federal government can look at Nevada…as an unpopulated wasteland to be cordoned off for whatever national purpose seems to require it."[59] The Air Force responded by preparing an after-the-fact environmental impact statement, then asking the Hill for a formal withdrawal, which Congress duly provided in 1988.

The Engle Act was neither by design nor effect an anti-militaristic measure. The well-publicized 1980 cancellation of the MX missile program (including a proposed mega-withdrawal in Utah and Nevada) belied the post-Engle militarization of the Great Basin.[60] In particular, the Air Force increased its use of airspace for low-level and supersonic test flights. Chuck Yeager bragged about it in his bestselling autobiography: "You feel so lucky, so blessed to be a fighter pilot. Nearly one hundred of us are testing our skill and courage by leaving prop marks on the dirt roads, stampeding grazing cattle (a few angry ranchers even take pot shots at us), and raising the shingles off ranch houses."[61] The same kind of coalition that worked against the MX—ranchers, sagebrush rebels, outdoor recreationists, urban environmentalists, Native Americans—could not stop the Air Force from obtaining Saylor Creek Bombing Range in southwestern Idaho via congressional withdrawal in 1999. Today, more than half the "vertical" Great Basin is designated by the Federal Aviation Administration as restricted areas or military operations areas—airspace designations that have terrestrial effects on land use and wildlife.[62]

Even so, the Engle Act can be narrated as a success, for it anticipated a series of congressional land policies in the 1960s and 1970s: the Classification and Multiple Use Act (1964), the Public Land Law Review Commission Act (1964), the Public Land Sale Act (1964), the Wilderness Act (1964), and the landmark Federal Land Management and Policy Act of 1976 (FLPMA). Taken together, these laws determined that the federal government would permanently retain a vast public domain to be managed by the BLM under a "multiple use" mandate—though some portions would be sold off for future urban growth, and other portions would be studied for possible inclusion in the national wilderness system, outside the traditional meaning of "use." FLPMA also reasserted congressional authority over withdrawals, repealing the Pickett Act and repudiating *Midwest Oil*. Building on the Engle Act, FLPMA authorized the executive to administratively execute withdrawals smaller than five thousand acres, while demanding congressional approval for anything larger, with a twenty-year limit.

To harmonize the Engle Act with FLPMA and the key environmental laws of the 1970s, Congress passed the Military Land Withdrawal Act (MLWA) in 1986.[63] At that point, six large military bases contained public land in the legal gray area, including two bases dating to the Second World War: Nellis Air Force Range in Nevada (2.9 million acres) and Barry M. Goldwater Air Force Range in Arizona (2.6 million acres). Nellis could not be grandfathered in like the Utah Test and Training Range because its boundaries had been adjusted so many times after the war, including a formal takeover of one third of the overlapping Desert National Wildlife Refuge. The MLWA withdrew Nellis and Goldwater for fifteen years, stipulating cooperative management with federal and state natural resource agencies, and requiring input from citizen stakeholders. However, when Congress proactively reauthorized the six bases in 1999, Republican Senator John McCain of Arizona inserted language that exempted the Goldwater range from comanagement, transferring jurisdiction to the DoD. McCain also sought an indefinite withdrawal for the bombing range. In the end, he settled for twenty-five years instead of a renewal of the original fifteen.[64]

By 2016–17, Republicans in Congress had completed a full retreat from the spirit of the Engle Act. In the name of efficiency, Representative Rob Bishop of Utah, who occupied Clair Engle's former committee chair, quietly proposed jurisdictional transfer of the other five bases covered under the MLWA, plus permanent withdrawal. After the Obama administration expressed opposition to the bill, Bishop inserted similar language into the House version of the annual National Defense Authorization Act.[65] Although Bishop failed to get his complete wish list into the final bill, signed by President Obama in December 2016, he succeeded in enlarging the Utah Test and Training Range, adding 700,000 acres to FDR's withdrawal of 1940.[66] Local environmentalists decried this "land grab," but their opposition barely made local news, much less national news.

For his part, Bishop expressed his outrage over the "land grabs" of Presidents

Obama and Clinton, each of whom had reserved a large national monument in southern Utah. After Donald J. Trump stormed into the White House in 2017, Bishop and his Republican colleagues from Utah formally asked the forty-fifth president to rescind Bears Ears National Monument (2016) and shrink Grand Staircase–Escalante National Monument (1996), despite no statutory authority for such abrogations. Within his first one hundred days in office, Trump obligingly ordered a deauthorization review of all national monuments over one hundred thousand acres created in the previous twenty years. Standing next to Utah's highest-ranking leaders, Trump incongruously bragged that he had just signed "a new executive order to end another egregious abuse of federal power" and feigned anger at the executive's "abusive practice" and "unlimited power" to "lock up" land. Strikingly, Bears Ears National Monument had been supported by a multistate consortium of tribal nations. In his comments about this "massive federal land grab," Trump did not use the term *public land*, preferring "our land," leaving it to the listener to decide the identity of the "we" in "our."[67]

From an "America First" perspective, the public domain is a strategic reserve—of fossil fuel, and of deployable space. In a future national emergency a president could unilaterally withdraw additional acreage. This is specifically allowed under the Engle Act and FLPMA, though the White House must now abide by the National Emergencies Act of 1976—another congressional response to executive abuses during the Cold War. Whether this check on power means anything remains unclear. When Congress faced its first major enforcement test, it reverted to acquiescence. On September 14, 2001, President George W. Bush proclaimed a state of national emergency.[68] Subsequently, as required by Congress, President Bush transmitted annual notices stating the continuance of that emergency for another year. Each year, Congress chose not to exercise its power of termination. President Obama inherited this emergency, found it useful, renewed it eight more times, and bequeathed it to his successor.[69]

The post-1945 ossification of military land withdrawals can be attributed to both active and passive forces. Politicians, agencies, and corporations that supported the national security state—and financially benefited from it—pulled levers of power to continue war games on the range. In an example of agency capture, the Interior Department did the bidding of the Pentagon. But "capture" sometimes just means going with the flow. A bureaucratic pathway, once established, enables inertia, ignorance, incompetence. The larger the bureaucracy, the greater the inertia. A 1985 legal review of Barry M. Goldwater Air Force Range revealed that the DoD had tenuous jurisdiction over the land, and that the BLM had equally tenuous grasp of the law.[70] Congress clarified the situation with the MLWA in 1986—another victory for the World War II status quo.

Inertia affects all branches of government: consider how long Executive Order 9066—a straightforward and shameful proclamation—eluded termination. Not until 1976, when Gerald Ford proclaimed that the US bicentennial required a reckoning of the nation's "mistakes" alongside its "great events," did the executive disown the legal justification for Japanese-American incarceration. The Ford administration argued that the authorization for E.O. 9066 had in fact expired on December 31, 1946, the official cessation of World War II according to previous proclamation.[71] Regardless of when the specific power ended, the general power remained dormant for another forty years, long after Congress approved reparations, and President Reagan issued an apology. In 2018 the Supreme Court finally repudiated *Korematsu v. United States* (1944) in an ironic sidebar to a five–four decision that preserved Trump's xenophobic travel ban. The next year, when Trump declared a nonwar national emergency in service of a war cry, "Build the Wall," he ensured a future case before a high court that now contained two justices of his choosing.[72]

III. Legacies and Contingencies

The foregoing narrative uses the Second World War as a marker of continuity as well as change in the American West. Rapid and extensive land militarization from 1940 to 1955 rested on a nineteenth-century legacy of undisposed federal land—a legacy of conquest.[73] Likewise, wartime bombing ranges followed an established legal precedent of executive-order withdrawals for Indian reservations and nature reserves. Despite pushback from Congress before and after World War II, the executive's property powers were "facts on the ground."

Unlike national monuments, military reservations rarely get highlighted on maps. How are cartographers—and the public—supposed to make sense of lands that are undisposed but nondisposable? They are, in BLM terms, unclassifiable—they cannot be zoned for land use. Test-and-training bases exist in status quo limbo. The withdrawal of this vast terrain was not by itself exceptional, merely the expedient amplification of presidential power. Indeed, the most exceptional World War II land units—carceral camps for Americans of Japanese ancestry—were small and temporary. The extraordinary thing about the proving grounds has been their continuance. The extension of their durational status was part of the normalization of the "state of exception."[74] By persisting on the National Map, these special-use reserves have become spatial and territorial expressions of war-related powers. My term for these post-1945 properties is *executive domain*.

This descriptor is legalistic. It does not fully capture the environmental, social, and moral dimensions of military land retention in the US West. Here the language of landscape has more power. Although the military prefers the neutral term "range," antimilitaristic commentators have used a variety of polemical terms: "dark geography," "classified landscape," "purloined landscape," "nuclear wasteland," "American Ground Zero," "Tainted Desert," "Ugly West," "Dead West."[75] The most common moral descriptor is "national sacrifice area." This term originated in a different context—the Arab oil embargo and the greater "energy crisis"—when a group of experts from the National Academies wrote a report at the behest of the Ford Foundation on the rehabilitation potential of western coal lands available for strip mining. Their 1973 report created a probability schema for a range of rehabilitation objectives, from "complete restoration" to "abandon the spoils." In the nation's "desert zone," only one objective had a high probability of success: call a strip mine a "national sacrifice zone," and simply abandon it when done.[76] This expression of candor quickly escaped the policy realm and became a rallying cry for rural Americans who felt that Big Coal had come to rape their land. The key phrase appeared most frequently in connection to the high plains of Montana and Wyoming, the Four Corners region, and Appalachia. In the two western areas tribal peoples as well as white residents utilized the language.[77]

Applied categorically to military reservations, the phrase simply isn't accurate—especially for the period since the 1963 Partial Test Ban Treaty. "Sacrifice" in this context suggests continuing waste or permanent abandonment. Incongruously, two major waste remediation acts—the Resource Conservation and Recovery Act of 1976 and the 1980 "Superfund" (Comprehensive Environmental Response, Compensation, and Liability Act)—both extend to DoD facilities. The same is true of landmark environmental laws of the 1970s. Can installations that employ offices of waste rehabilitation, environmental compliance, and wildlife conservation be considered sacrifice areas?[78]

Western environmentalists have learned to live with the military, for the DoD has, in the long run, proven to be an acceptable manager of land and wildlife—or no less acceptable than the "Bureau of Livestock and Mining," as detractors sometimes call the BLM. Many defense installations are critical habitat, and some may yet become national wildlife refuges if they follow the trajectories of Rocky Flats, Rocky Mountain Arsenal, and the Hanford Reach. The ongoing endangered species recovery program for the Mexican gray wolf (*Canis lupus baileyi*) has been facilitated by White Sands Missile Range—and the military's prior removal of ranchers, livestock, and fencing.[79] Today, in the age of fracking, when most BLM lands are open to oil and gas exploration, military land withdrawals, along with congressionally designated wilderness areas, are uniquely protected from the deleterious effects of mining. Wilderness and war have compatibility in their exclusivity. In the view of the RAND Corporation, wilderness designation can be a "useful tool" for preventing "encroachment and incompatible development" near Air Force test and training ranges.[80]

In the US West, military land retention complicates the usual alliances and antagonisms over public land. Historically, many rural westerners have opposed national parks, national monuments, and wilderness areas because these designations "lock up" the land and "lock out" certain users. For many westerners the ability to freely use public land remains essential to their lived experience of American liberty. However, since World War II, the safeguarding of liberty, as defined by the national security state, has demanded the closure of vast stretches of federal and state properties, including the inverse condemnation of school trust lands.[81] If laissez-faire Republicans ever realize their dream of disposing the BLM's unreserved lands, military land withdrawals would ironically become the final "public domain." Given the benefits that come with defense facilities, libertarian opposition to military land retention tends to be situational and hyperlocal.[82] DoD reservations are job creators in job-poor areas; they add to the local tax base. Tellingly, active bases do not figure into the Payments in Lieu of Taxes Program by which the federal government has, since 1976, compensated western counties for lost property taxes related to nontaxable federal lands within their boundaries. By this calculus military land may be the most productive public land.[83]

Even if one makes a moral judgment that certain lands retained by the military have been sacrificed, one must acknowledge degrees of sacrificial killing. Asia's southern rim constituted the Cold War's "killing fields," where US-Soviet-Sino proxy wars took the lives of millions of civilians, leaving legacies of toxins and landmines.[84] During the era of atmospheric and underground nuclear testing, the Soviet Union used up areas of Kazakhstan with less legality and more lethality than the Nevada Test Site.[85] In Nevada, Yucca Mountain Nuclear Waste Depository may yet become an eternal no-man's-land—if and when it finally goes on line. To the north, in the Carson Sink, on land originally reserved for the Bureau of Reclamation for a showcase irrigation project, the Navy has bombed Bravo-20 to the point of oblivion. In Richard Misrach's famous photography this looks like land sacrificed to Moloch. But Bravo-20 is not representative of all military land withdrawals. Although untold acreage has been ravaged and contaminated, a greater total area has been managed as multiple-use public land—minus the public. In some cases, the airspace is more important to the DoD than the terrestrial space, so long as the land has been emptied of unauthorized persons.

Military reservations exclose and enclose: they keep some things out, other things in. As exclosures, they repel cattle, ranchers, hunters, antiwar activists, recreationists, UFO chasers, and terrorists, while letting in workers and wild horses. As enclosures, they have been less successful at containing sonic booms, not to mention radiation and chemical agents. During the all-too-hot Cold War, toxins blew downwind, sickening livestock and people, and contributing to long-term cancer clusters.[86]

In 1990 the federal government belatedly acknowledged certain externalities of the executive domain. The Radiation Exposure Compensation Act—a lump-sum cash program that followed government evasions, and class-action lawsuits—applied to three populations: atomic veterans of the Nevada Test Site, downwinders in southwestern Utah, and uranium ore workers in the Four Corners. This four-state region, which includes the Navajo Nation, was radically altered by the "U-boom" of the 1950s, which brought government-subsidized roads and government-incentivized mines. Most of these uranium operations were "dog holes" with no ventilation. Even after the AEC collected evidence on the hazards of uranium mining, it did nothing to regulate or warn. Many miners died prematurely from lung cancer. Even worse, thousands of Diné on their reservation now lack potable water because of contamination from abandoned uranium mines. The 1990 act compensated for past individual harm; it did nothing to address ongoing holistic harm. Unlike the DoD the Navajo Nation does not have easy access to federal funds for environmental mitigation and rehabilitation.[87]

To adapt the formulation of Traci Brynne Voyles, Diné land was selectively "wastelanded" in service of a weapons program that made "productive use" of Numic land in the Great Basin.[88] The Nevada Test Site comprises unceded Western Shoshone land recognized by federal treaty.[89] But in the final judgment of the Indian Claims Commission in 1979, Western Shoshone title throughout Nevada had been extinguished by a legal convenience called "gradual encroachment."[90] For this historic taking, the government agreed to pay compensation. When Western Shoshone litigants refused the settlement, and tried to revive treaty claims, the US Supreme Court ruled unanimously against them. The tribe had no further recourse because the government, its trustee, discharged its obligation when it deposited the damages into a trust account.[91] Unbowed by this loss, Western Shoshone activists have since contributed to the postponement of Yucca Mountain, and the cancellation of a major weapons test at the Nevada Test Site, using the language of sovereignty and sacredness.[92] Their local treaty-based activism challenges the still-dominant national media portrayal of the Great Basin as a wasteland—a natural repository for waste.[93]

In Utah, members of a related Numic group, the Goshutes, made a different choice in a similarly impossible situation. Historically, outsiders did not covet their homeland, for they lived on the edges of the Great Salt Lake Desert, among the most challenging landscapes in North America. Eventual encroachment by ranchers motivated the executive to delimit two tiny reservations, effectively designating two tribelets, in the 1910s. Then, in the 1940s, the Skull Valley Band of Goshutes abruptly found its reservation surrounded on three sides by aerial bombing ranges and chemical testing grounds. Due to military impacts, the reservation lost economic potential. As of 1997, some four-fifths of the band's give-or-take 125 members had left Skull Valley. That year, in a last-ditch but well-considered move, the Skull Valley Goshutes entered into contract with a private firm representing a consortium of energy utilities. The band—with the blessing of the DOE and the BIA—planned to build a temporary storage facility for nuclear waste on the reservation. In response, the political leadership of the State of Utah—the same elected officials who gave unwavering support to the highly contaminative Utah Test and Training Range—declared war against the sovereign tribe's economic enterprise, citing public safety concerns. The governor's oppressive efforts to create a "land moat" around the reservation failed in court, but they succeeded in slowing down the regulatory process. Then, Utah's antienvironmentalist, antistatist delegation, led by Rob Bishop, cynically partnered with urban environmentalists to pass a bill that gave strict wilderness protection to one mountainous area in western Utah that just so happened to cover the BLM-approved route of the rail spur that would deliver the waste to Skull Valley. Forced by Congress, the BLM canceled the right-of-way; and the BIA, under pressure from Utah, reversed its approval of the contract.

Frustrated by delays, the utilities pulled the plug in 2012. In the end, the Skull Valley Band had nothing to show for its initiative.[94]

As this ugly example suggests, the Indian reservation system is the lost fraternal twin of the military reservation system. Military forts and Indian reservations shared the same legal parentage in the early republic, but in the twentieth century the progeny separated. Thanks to political and legal clarifications related to World War II and the Cold War, every dimension of a military reservation—including subsurface, surface, and air rights—clearly belongs to the executive, as managed by and for the Pentagon. A military reservation is a kind of federal property, whereas an Indian reservation is a legal regime that encompasses various forms of title subject variously to tribal, state, and federal laws. Historically, the federal government had three mechanisms by which it could cede land to Indian tribes: statute, treaty, and executive order. Today, the boundaries of an Indian reservation may include private (fee-simple) land as well as federal (nonfee) land. The private land may be owned by tribal members or tribal corporations—or by non-Indians or nontribal entities. The federal land is held in trust by the BIA on behalf of individual tribal enrollees (including fractional owners) or for the tribe as a collective. Despite the sovereignty promised by territoriality, tribes don't (yet) enjoy enough self-determination to release their reservations from federal paternalism. In short, American Indian property has become ever more complicated and contradictory, while the executive domain has become simplified and unambiguous.[95]

Another crucial difference: military reservations support general concepts like "national security" and "national good" rather than specific rights granted by treaty to tribal communities. When the BIA, as trustee, decides (or defers) property questions on an Indian reservation, it must, for better and usually worse, determine what is best for tribes and tribal members on ancestral lands. By contrast, the DoD can manage military reservations without thinking of permanent on-site residents, much less multigenerational inhabitants. Perhaps the defining social characteristic of military bases is the impermanence and placelessness of the personnel. In a bureaucratic sense, military bases without true occupants are ideal sovereign lands. The history of the US military in the Atlantic, Pacific, and Indian oceans demonstrates the strategic importance of such uninhabited—or depopulated—locations.

For this overseas dimension there is another prewar day that lives on without infamy: September 2, 1940. That was the date FDR informed Congress about a deal the White House executed on its own with Great Britain. By the terms of the "destroyers-for-bases" agreement, the United States traded fifty "overage" naval ships for long-term leases on military bases in multiple territories in the western Atlantic. For his authority FDR claimed that "preparation for continental defense" was "an unalienable prerogative of a sovereign state." The immediate context was Hitler and fascism, but for his precedent Roosevelt referenced Jefferson and expansionism. "This is the most important action in the reinforcement of our national defense that has been taken since the Louisiana Purchase," the president told Congress.[96]

By referencing the founding act of the imperial presidency (an emergency action made, ironically, by a great Anti-Federalist), FDR illustrated the interplay of legacies and contingencies. World War II, a contingent event, enabled an expansion of military land withdrawals in the US West and a matching explosion of US military basing overseas. Contingencies are most consequential when they redirect legacies—in this case, federal properties in the Caribbean and the Pacific as well as the trans-Mississippi West. From 1803 through 1898, as the United States grew from a continental to a semiglobal power, it annexed numerous guano islands and more traditional colonies like American Samoa, Guam, Hawaiʻi, the Philippines, and Puerto Rico.[97] From this imperial foundation the United States could in 1945 take immediate advantage of its superpower status by establishing bases across the globe—by right of victory and by persuasion of power.

Here it is important to make a connection—and draw a distinction—between the US military's sovereign and *extra*-sovereign dominion, both of which were critical to the establishment of the post-1945 order, and the nation's "forward presence" from the Cold War through the War on Terror. Sovereign dominion requires federal title. It includes military bases in the US South (mainly used for basic training), military reservations in the US West (mainly used for weapons and equipment testing), and more than a dozen insular areas, both incorporated and unincorporated. By contrast, extrasovereign dominion comprises some eight hundred "base sites" leased from foreign countries. These sites appertaining to the United States constitute the "leasehold empire" (C. T. Sandars), or the "networked empire" (Ruth Oldenziel), or the "pointillist empire" (Daniel Immerwahr). In countries that the United States defeated, or occupied with permission, these leased sites are extensive and semipermanent. Defense installations in Germany, Italy, Japan, and South Korea have functioned as spatial complements to military reservations in California, Nevada, New Mexico, and Utah. Meanwhile, in oceanic zones, military lands (leased or owned) do not require great size to host intensive basing or testing—or torture. For examples, consider the respective histories of Bikini Atoll, Diego Garcia, and Guantanamo Bay. Unincorporated military lands can also facilitate large-scale conservation. In one of George W. Bush's final acts as president, in a transparent attempt to salvage a Rooseveltian legacy, he deployed his executive authority to set aside Pacific Remote Islands Marine National Monument, which covered a surface area more than one hundred times that of Yellowstone National Park. President Obama later added to this ocean reservation, made possible by US ownership of strategic locations like Wake Island.[98]

The 1940s base-building campaign at home and abroad was, in retrospect, a moment of peak US influence, when the future of abundance, and the promise of liberalism, seemed limitless. The global footprint of this imperial idealism outlasted the Cold War. But after the triple disasters of the George W. Bush presidency—two reckless wars and one financial crisis—the national mood changed, as Donald Trump intuitively recognized. President Trump is hardly an anti-imperialist, but his rhetoric rejects globalism in favor of (white) nationalism; and stresses hard limits for some rather than endless horizons for all.[99] In the tumult following the 2016 election, the "American Century" (i.e., building bases) rhetorically shrank to "America First" (i.e., building walls). Even so, the US military has not yet retreated from its forward posture: its dual dominions persist, comprising a vast concretion or, in DoD language, "base structure." Going forward, however, the leasehold empire will inevitably contract. This contraction may make federal lands like Guam and the Utah Test and Training Range all the more strategic.

Where is American empire is also a temporal question: *When* has the United States acted imperially? In 1793, when James Madison made his prescient comment about executive aggrandizement in wartime, he could not have foreseen that the new republic—now the oldest constitutional democracy in the world—would scarcely go any year of its existence without being in a state of war, or a state of emergency, or both. The history of US expansionism—continental, then extracontinental—is a war-filled record of land grabs that unfolded deliberately, and opportunistically, and also accidentally. The US entry into World War II did not finally occur until one empire made a surprise attack on its rival empire in the Pacific. The coordinated Japanese strikes on US bases in federal territories (Hawaiʻi, Guam, the Philippines) on December 7/8, 1941, set into motion a series of contingencies that eventually produced US bases on Okinawa Island.

American territoriality and American temporality have global and epochal dimensions. The year 1945, the pivot point for military land withdrawals, was also the takeoff of what environmental historians—and geoscientists—call the Great Acceleration. The post-1945 period brought a step-function increase in the human impact on the planet as measured in land use, water use, and energy use.[100] The US military helped to defend and export the high-use "American way of life"—a process that generated as many long-term detriments as short-term benefits. The awareness that humans and nations (some more than others) have planet-changing capabilities owes much to US military planners who, during the Cold War, developed environmental scenarios about World War III.[101] Now, seventy-five years after the conclusion of World War II and the introduction of postwar wartime, the DoD is an anomaly: a branch of the US government, dominated by Republicans, that accepts climate science and makes contingency plans for global warming as a national security threat. If, as some Democrats hope, a future president declares climate change a national emergency, the US military would have strategic interest to respond with alacrity. In the coming decades, as the Earth system crosses thresholds and enters feedback loops, the executive domain may become newly important to the national good—assuming the commander in chief still governs as a constitutional executive.

2

ENLISTING THE LABORATORIES

Science, Defense, and the Transformation of the High-Tech West

DANIEL J. KEVLES

On the eve of World War II new high technologies were emerging among the palm and eucalyptus trees in southern and northern California—in Pasadena, with explorations of rocket propulsion and flight at the California Institute of Technology; and in Berkeley, with the cyclotrons in the Radiation Laboratory at the University of California. Caltech aerodynamics, which encompassed the rocket project, and the Berkeley laboratory, which was part of the physics department, had both originated in the early 1930s. By the end of the decade, both had achieved world-class distinction and formed a crucially important part of a nascent high-technology West.

What made for their success was a match between the dynamism of their leaders and their patrons' ambitions for California's industrial future. The chief leaders were unabashed captains of science and technology—at Berkeley, the physicist Ernest O. Lawrence, and at Caltech, the aerodynamicist Theodore von Kármán along with his upcoming lieutenant, a graduate student named Frank Malina. All were recent migrants to California, drawn by its frontier West prospects of new, innovative beginnings in science and technology. All joined entrepreneurial energy and talent with bold technical vision and an iconoclastic willingness to pursue it by breaking conventional academic arrangements. They gravitated naturally to cross-disciplinary modes of thinking and practice, combining engineering and science, including its theoretical forms, to devise pathbreaking technologies. Caltech was institutionally designed to encourage such approaches, and Berkeley, recognizing the merits of Lawrence's innova-

FIGURE 2.1 Ernest Lawrence examining the vacuum chamber of the 37-inch cyclotron, c. 1935. *Source*: © 2010 The Regents of the University of California, through the Lawrence Berkeley National Laboratory.

tions for its standing in science, willingly accommodated his insistence upon increasing mold-breaking independence for his cyclotron laboratory.

The patrons, both public and private, saw in science and technology the keys to commercial and cultural power for the region in the new age of automobiles and airplanes, electricity, radio and radioactivity. Significant funding for the programs at Caltech and Berkeley came from philanthropic foundations and wealthy individuals, their personal fortunes of recent and often western origin. Additional money was supplied by the state's burgeoning high-technology industries, including electrical utilities, which needed knowledge and experts to build and control high-voltage generators and transmission lines; and aircraft companies, which, as they moved into the era of all-metal, enclosed planes capable of carrying passengers and mail across the continent, required knowledge and expertise in fields ranging from metallurgy to communications to engines and fuels. The state legislature also opened its purse for the support of scientific research at Berkeley.

These three scientists—von Kármán, Malina, and Lawrence—all intended their innovations to enable the discovery of new basic knowledge, but after 1939 they adapted them to the ends of national defense. During the war von Kármán and Malina established a jet-engine program intended to assist heavy-bomber takeoff that was adapted during the war to boost fighter takeoff from carriers and then transformed into the Jet Propulsion Laboratory for the development of guided missiles. Lawrence turned the Berkeley cyclotron laboratory from explorations in nuclear science to the realization of a prototype technology for the production of fuel for one type of atomic bomb and, building on a discovery in his laboratory, spawned the sprawling reactor complex at Hanford, Washington, to generate the fuel for another type. All three laboratories flourished after 1945 as instruments of Cold War science and technology. All contributed robustly to the high-tech industrial clusters identified by Gavin Wright in his chapter in this edited volume, to the growth and economic transformation of the postwar West.

Caltech and the Birth of Rockets

In 1926, Robert A. Millikan, the head of Caltech and the nation's second Nobel laureate in physics, obtained support from the Daniel Guggenheim Fund for the Promotion of Aeronautics to establish a program in the field. Millikan, who had been the principal mobilizer of civilian scientists and engineers during World War I, was well acquainted with the swiftly evolving technologies of aircraft. He saw a rich opportunity for Caltech in aeronautics with its proximity to the region's rapidly emerging aircraft industry. Southern California's balmy climate and open spaces made it an appealing venue for the development, testing, and production of airplanes. During the 1920s the state drew Donald Douglas, John K. Northrop, and Alan Lockheed, among others, who established the companies that would become mainstay names in the aircraft industry.[1] Millikan aimed to establish Caltech as a vital center of research and teaching in aeronautics that would advance the field, serve the region's budding aircraft enterprise, and in turn attract support from its corporate firms.[2]

To these ends, Millikan recruited von Kármán in 1929 to head Caltech's new Guggenheim Aeronautical Laboratory. The product of a cultivated and cosmopolitan family in Budapest, von Kármán was at the time head of aeronautics at the Technical Institute in Aachen, Germany, and one of the leading aerodynamicists in Europe. He was literate in much of modern physics, including relativity and quantum mechanics, and counted among his friends Max Born, Albert Einstein, and Nils Bohr. He had established his reputation in aerodynamics in 1911, while a postdoctoral fellow at Göttingen University with a major analysis of the vexing topic of vortices, swirling motions that arise in fluids at their boundaries with surfaces in motion and that can generate oscillations and instabilities.[3]

Appointed to his aeronautical professorship and directorship in Aachen in 1912, at age thirty-one, von Kármán centered his research on problems in fluid dynamics, including those that figured in the transition from the cloth-and-wood biplanes of the Wright era to the all-metal, single-wing aircraft coming off the drawing boards in the 1920s.[4] He was known for his commitment to research and teaching that combined theoretical analysis from first physical principles with experimentation and application to the real-world engineering problems of flight. In 1930, von Kármán joined the Caltech faculty, partly to escape the palpable anti-Semitism and xenophobia in Aachen, partly because Millikan offered him a level of salary and support he could hardly refuse. Adding to the financial attractions was the trend in aeronautics at Caltech toward a theoretically oriented curriculum and a wind tunnel that had been designed to von Kármán's specifications that generated air flows in excess of two hundred miles an hour, making it the most powerful in the western United States.[5]

At Caltech, von Kármán established fluid dynamics—theoretical, experimental, and applied—at the center of the research enterprise, including his own.[6] With the aid of his colleagues, especially Millikan's son Clark, a like-minded aeronautical engineer, von Kármán strengthened Caltech's ties with the southern California aircraft industry, providing key companies with expert consultation, well-trained graduates, and the use of its high-powered instrument for testing airplane designs. As Gavin Wright notes in his chapter in this volume, the emphasis of the lab at Caltech (by then known as GALCIT, the Guggenheim Aeronautical Laboratory at Caltech) on fluid dynamics and its wind tunnel provided the nascent industry with far more of a comparative advantage than did the region's climate and open spaces. When Douglas was developing its DC-3 ("C" stood for "commercial")—a twin-engine plane that reliably transported twenty-one passengers across the continent and that in 1940 would carry some 80 percent of US airline traffic, von Kármán had directly solved a troublesome problem of turbulence in the plane's design by climbing into the wind tunnel one day and applying a fillet of clay to round the intersection of the wing and the fuselage. The fix, which came to be known as "Karmans," was adopted throughout the world.[7]

At Aachen, von Kármán had breached the social and hierarchical barriers common in German academia, especially between teachers and students. Now, in Pasadena, he similarly integrated his professional and domestic lives, hosting a seemingly boundless range of friends and acquaintances, including Einstein, Bohr, and Enrico Fermi, Bela Lugosi and the Gabors, and countless other actresses along with screen writers, priests, engineers and aircraft executives.[8] He was no less hospitable to students, inviting them to his study at home, where they jointly worked through technical problems across a glass-topped wicker dinette table. He granted special encouragement to students who thought independently and generated novel ideas, so long as they subjected their imaginative conceptions to the intellectual constraints of the fundamental sciences, mathematical analysis, and the realities of empirical data.[9]

Frank Malina was such a student. A native of Brenham, Texas, he was the son of a passionate Czech nationalist, a graduate of Brenham High School, where his father directed the band, and of Texas A&M, where he majored in engineering. In 1934, Malina enrolled for graduate work in mechanical engineering at Caltech and discovered the exciting field of aeronautics.[10] He had brought to Caltech a dreamy curiosity about space flight that had been inspired by a boyhood reading of Jules Verne. The dreaminess turned into a concrete interest in rockets when during his first year he heard a speculative but engineering-rich talk about them by a guest in Clark Millikan's seminar. The guest also gave a public talk on the subject. Two young men from Pasadena read a newspaper account of it, showed up at Caltech asking for advice about rockets, and were directed to Malina. One was John Parsons, a self-taught, knowledgeable chemist with a strong interest in explosives, a propensity for mysticism and the occult, and the family means to indulge his hobbies. The other was Edward S. Forman, a skilled engine mechanic. Impatient to build and fly rockets, they had been conducting experiments to that end in the backyard of Parson's posh family home.[11]

Malina, intrigued, began working with Parsons and Forman, decided that he wanted to write his doctoral dissertation on rocket engines, and asked Clark Millikan for authorization to do so. Most aerodynamicists of the day considered rockets impractical, the stuff of science fiction. In the United States, Robert H. Goddard, with funds from the Guggenheims, was investigating the development of rockets, but he was secretive, shared his data with virtually no one, and helped foster the impression that rockets fell in the purview of oddballs and mystics.[12] Whatever Millikan's views about rockets at the time, the topic of propulsion was not part of the GALCIT program. He rejected Malina's dissertation proposal, suggesting that he finish his masters' degree and find a job in the aircraft industry. Malina remembered the occasion as "a rather bleak day."[13]

Desperate, Malina turned to von Kármán. A talented artist and draftsman, he was getting to know von Kármán because he was illustrating a text von Kármán was coauthoring. Malina was aware that von Kármán was inclined to encourage students with unconventional ideas, but he was also aware that von Kármán expected lines of proposed experiments to be framed in theoretical assessments of their prospects. In March 1935, Malina went to see von Kármán, a written proposal in hand and Forman and Parsons in tow. The report laid out the theoretical and experimental parameters of the project, including calculations of the rocket's engine dynamics, fuel, thrust, and lift. The aim was to produce a sounding rocket—that is, a vehicle capable of reaching the upper atmosphere to collect data on phenomena such as cosmic rays and weather patterns.[14]

Impressed by the proposal's technical merits and by the hardheadedness of Malina's goal, von Kármán offered Malina and his two compadres, all in their mid-twenties, off-hours' use of space in GALCIT (even though Forman and Parsons had no connection with Caltech) and moral support, but he had no money to give them. Rather than expressing a starry-eyed ambition for reaching the moon, their goal was to send a rocket to high altitudes to collect scientific data. If it would open a new line of work at GALCIT, so much the better. In the following months, Malina, Parsons, and Forman spent their spare time and whatever cash they could afford scouring Los Angeles for parts and materials, designing a rocket motor, and planning its first test. They roughed out a test area in the Arroyo Seco, an uninhabited canyon northwest of downtown Pasadena in the foothills of the San Gabriel Mountains, about three miles above the Rose Bowl football stadium. In October 1936, in a first trial, their engine, fueled by a combustible mixture of liquid oxygen and methyl-alcohol, fired for several seconds. In January 1937, using an improved version, the fuel burned for forty-four seconds.[15]

At von Kármán's insistence, Malina, assisted by two fellow graduate students—Hsue-shen Tsien, from China, and Apollo M. O. (Amo) Smith—produced a theoretical demonstration that linked the likely power of the engine to the dynamic requirements for flight. In April 1937, von Kármán, his enthusiasm for the project rising, granted Malina's group regular experimental space in

FIGURE 2.2 Frank Malina's rocket research group (Malina third from left), in the Arroyo Seco before a motor test, 1936. *Source*: Courtesy of the Archives, California Institute of Technology.

GALCIT.[16] Malina was ecstatic, but by early spring 1938 his group was stalled, not least because they were running out of what little money they had been able to raise. Malina earned his keep by assisting von Kármán in the wind tunnel with a soil conservation project funded by the US Department of Agriculture, which was interested in wind erosion but not rockets.[17]

Lawrence and the Cyclotron

While Malina struggled, some four hundred miles to the north Lawrence at Berkeley was on the verge of winning the Nobel Prize for his cyclotron. The idea for the cyclotron had occurred to him one evening in spring 1929 while reading a journal in the Berkeley library. The next afternoon, hurrying across campus, elation written all over his uncomplicated face, Lawrence yelled to a colleague's wife: "I'm going to be famous."[18]

Lawrence had been speeding toward accomplishment since his boyhood days in Canton, South Dakota, where his father, a progressive-minded educator, was twice elected state superintendent of public instruction. Hard work and success, Lawrence told his younger brother, John, were the greatest things in life. At the University of South Dakota, where Lawrence studied engineering, a professor persuaded him that another great thing was physics. He earned a PhD in the science at Yale, remained as an instructor, courted the daughter of the former dean of the medical school, and quickly developed a national reputation for his ability to conceive ingenious experimental devices and an uncanny knack for making the devices work. Yet Lawrence's ambitions were outsized for Yale, then conservative in its institutional structure and limited in its vision.[19]

In the 1920s, Berkeley physics was on the make, hungrily and—with the willing support of the state—successfully driving to achieve a rank in science coequal to that of its sister institutions in the East and Robert Millikan's new Caltech. In 1928, Berkeley recruited Lawrence to an associate professorship despite his youth—he was twenty-seven—and relative lack of experience, providing him with a research allowance, promising as many graduate students as he wished, and tacitly pledging to back him in whatever he wanted to do. Not long after arriving in California, Lawrence noted: "Not the least homesick for Yale (remarkable thing). I have a relative importance which I never could have attained at Yale in years."[20]

At the time, physicists were searching for a means of probing the structure of atomic nuclei by bombarding them with high-energy particles. The cyclotron did the trick by moving the particles in a circle inside two hollow semicircular electrodes (two "Dees"), the straight edge of one facing that of the other but separated to form a gap, across which an oscillating voltage was imposed. The particles were accelerated every time they crossed one of the gaps, and they were kept in orbit by the force of a magnetic field that ran perpendicular to their plane of motion. In January 1932, with the indispensable help of a graduate student named M. Stanley Livingston, Lawrence obtained a sizable flux of protons at an energy of more than 1 million volts, with only 4,000 volts on the gaps. From the million-volt machine, which was 11 inches in diameter, Lawrence pressed ahead to a 27-inch edition, then to a 37-inch, and on to a 60-inch.[21]

With the end of paying for the cyclotrons and the operations of the laboratory, Lawrence promoted the overarching dream that the disintegration of nuclei under accelerator bombardment might eventually point the way to the practical release of the energy contained in the atomic nucleus. He spotlighted the payoffs that the cyclotron was already yielding—notably the production in abundance of neutrons and radioactive isotopes useful in medical research and cancer therapy.[22] The mixture of atomic dream and medical reality gained Lawrence support for his laboratory from individuals, corporations, and foundations, from the state of California, and from the federal government, notably the National Advisory Cancer Council, the grant-making arm of the National Cancer Institute, which Congress had established, in 1937. He explained to the Danish physicist Niels Bohr, "I must confess that one reason we have undertaken this biological work is that we thereby have been able to get financial support for all of the work in the laboratory. As you know, it is much easier to get funds for medical [than for physical] research."[23] When the 60-inch cyclotron began operating in 1939, generating 16 million electron volts, it served not only medical purposes but also, by design, as an instrument for the testing of nuclear theory.[24]

By then, Lawrence was planning to build a colossus of a cyclotron—a machine that would accelerate particles to an energy of 100 million volts. The physicist Hans Bethe, a recent émigré to the United States from Germany and one of the most respected theorists in the world, had argued that because of the relativistic increase of mass with speed, cyclotrons could not accelerate particles to such an energy; long before reaching it, the beam would become unfocused and fly off in multiple directions. Lawrence put a few of his theoretically able young colleagues to work on the problem raised by Bethe; they concluded that the relativistic focusing difficulty could be overcome. Bethe should realize, Lawrence confided to a fellow physicist, that there are "many ways of skinning a cat."[25]

But the skinning of that particular cat awaited the resolution of the technical problem in laboratory fact rather than in just theory on paper. The building and operation of the 60-inch machine required collaborations among engineers and physicists, theorists and experimentalists, and a new breed of staff, the cyclotroneers—specialists who kept the machine in good repair and adapted it to particular scientific inquiries.[26] Lawrence's laboratory was big in physical size (it now occupied a cluster of buildings on a hill above the campus); big in number of staff, which exceeded forty; and big in budgetary demands. All promised to become bigger still if Lawrence was to achieve the 100 million-volt machine. Lawrence's lab might be operating on a vastly larger scale than Malina's makeshift enterprise in Pasadena, but they had in common the need for funds to realize their large-scale, technology-dependent scientific ambitions.

Taking Off

In Pasadena, one day in May 1938, about the time that Lawrence was figuring out how to skin his 100-million-volt cat, General Henry H. ("Hap") Arnold of the Army Air Corps paid von Kármán a surprise visit at GALCIT that led to putting Malina back on his rocket track. Arnold was well acquainted with both Caltech's chief executive and its leading aerodynamicist. He had gotten to know Robert Millikan in Washington, DC, during World War I, in connection with Millikan's involvement with aircraft research and development (R&D). During the early 1930s, when he commanded March Field, near Riverside, California, Arnold provided Millikan with the use of a bomber to conduct cosmic ray experiments aloft and he sometimes visited Caltech and von Kármán in his wind tunnel.[27]

Serving in the Austro-Hungarian army early in the century, von Kármán had spent much of World War I in aeronautical research for the government. He was comfortable with the military. So was Millikan, who remarked in 1934 to a military gathering that defense research ought to be "a peacetime... and not a war-time thing.... [It] moves too slowly to be done after you get into trouble." Arnold, Millikan, and von Kármán were all worried about the rising threat that Hitler and his Luftwaffe posed to the rest of Europe. All three men were of like mind that the strength of the Army Air Corps depended on a strong R&D program that linked basic civilian science to the practical needs of military aviation.[28] Theodore von Kármán also likely saw an advantage for GALCIT in Arnold's enthusiasm for basic science. By the late 1930s companies far and wide were using—and paying for—the wind tunnel so much that all "independent research," as Clark Millikan put it, "had to be abandoned in spite of a seventeen-hour daily operating schedule." Some degree of independent research might be restored with support from Arnold's Air Corps.[29]

Early in 1938, at Arnold's urging, Louis Johnson, then acting secretary of war, asked the National Academy of Sciences, the US government's official scientific adviser, to form a committee to evaluate the prospects of several ideas for advantageous aeronautical technologies that included the de-icing of aircraft and the jet-assisted takeoff of fighters and bombers. Thus, when Arnold appeared at GALCIT, he was excited to learn about Malina's rocket project, seeing in it a potential enabler of jet-assisted takeoff.[30]

Arnold became commander of the Army Air Corps on September 29, 1938, the same day that Britain, France, and Italy signed the Munich Agreement with Hitler that ceded the Sudetenland to Germany. At his urgent request the

National Academy of Sciences speeded up the organization of its committee and scheduled its first meeting in Washington, DC, for December 27 and 28. Called the Committee on Army Air Corps Research, the high-powered group included Millikan and von Kármán as well as several comparably prominent scientists and engineers from industry and academia in the Northeast and Midwest. Its chair was Max Mason, a physicist and former head of the Rockefeller Foundation; he was then at Caltech supervising the construction of the Palomar Observatory and happened to learn about Malina's work. In early December, Mason, Millikan, and von Kármán asked Malina to prepare a report on the potential payoffs for aviation of the Caltech rocket project and present it to the National Academy of Sciences committee when it met in Washington.[31]

Most of the committee was at the meeting, and so was Hap Arnold and an assortment of other high-ranking military officers. For some reason von Kármán was not there, leaving Malina, then twenty-six and still a graduate student, to present the promise of the rocket project on his own. He marched with sober and authoritative lucidity through the current state and possibilities of "jet propulsion"—the term that he and von Kármán had agreed he should use instead of "rockets" because it was the strong preference of the Air Corps and because they wanted to avoid associating their initiative with *Buck Rogers* fictions.[32] Malina laid out the principles and workings of the two types of jet-propulsive engines available (liquid-fuel and solid-fuel); detailed how each might be used to power airplanes; and focused on the most immediately achievable: liquid-fuel devices to assist the takeoff of large, heavy aircraft such as bombers, and solid-fuel "propulsors" for the same purpose with fighters, each to be mounted under the aircraft's wings. He outlined the need for experimental research on both the liquid-fuel and solid-fuel fronts and pointed to evidence that jet propulsion research programs were under way in France, Germany, Italy, and Russia.[33]

In January 1939, von Kármán having now weighed in, the Air Corps authorized the National Academy of Sciences committee to award Caltech one thousand dollars from funds it had in hand from the service for a study of the technical prospects of jet-assisted takeoff and the preparation of a research plan to achieve that purpose. It was to be carried out by Malina under the supervision of Clark Millikan and von Kármán, to be delivered by mid-June.[34] The study proceeded rapidly, combining theoretical analysis with experiments at GALCIT. In spring 1939 a test-firing engine exploded. No one was hurt, but the event forced the engine-testing branch of the effort off campus, back to the

Arroyo Seco, in the area where Malina, Parsons, and Forman had conducted their first joint experiments. Only the theoretical and light experimental work remained at GALCIT.[35] Progress was sufficient enough to convince the Corps to provide ten thousand dollars to the Academy committee for the Caltech project through the twelve months ending on June 30, 1940.[36]

Von Kármán took active charge of the enterprise, which was now called the Air Corps Jet Propulsion Research Project. Malina, Parsons, and Forman comprised the central research staff. They made progress on liquid-fueled rockets, but they encountered persistent trouble in the solid-fuel effort. A workable solid-fuel rocket had to burn slowly enough so that its charge of powder would provide thrust for at least ten to thirty seconds. To achieve that end, Parsons, the group's principal chemist, tried different mixtures of powders and oxidizers and different shapes for the mixtures. But on firing, the results were similar to what rocket enthusiasts had seen for centuries: the fuel either burned rapidly, lasting only a few seconds, or it exploded. "We need to show we are more clever than others have been," Malina remarked in December 1939.[37]

Unswervingly supportive, von Kármán came to be regarded by Malina as a second father. Malina relished his hospitality and flair as well as their shared interest in the arts and in world affairs. While engaged in a politically left-leaning discussion group with several other scientists and engineers, Malina had been recruited into the Communist Party's Professional Unit 122, which had been established by Frank Oppenheimer, was based in Pasadena, and was mainly devoted to music, talk, and local activism on labor and racial issues rather than to planning, let alone carrying out, revolution. Malina had been reluctant to work on rockets for war, but he was persuaded by the fascist threat to the democracies in Europe to give up the goal, at least for the time being, of sending rockets into the high atmosphere for science.[38] Von Kármán, with his wide contacts in Europe and his own experience of anti-Semitism in Germany, no doubt reinforced Malina's willingness to do research for defense. With the Nazi Blitzkrieg swallowing up Western Europe, the slow-burning problem took on increasing urgency.[39]

One evening in April or May, von Kármán invited Malina to his home for a skull session. They chatted for a while, von Kármán with a drink in hand. Then his face lit up, as though in response to an epiphany. He arrived in the laboratory the next morning with a paper on which he had written four differential equations describing the output of an ideal slow-burning engine. He asked Malina to solve them, saying that if the solution showed that the engine was stable, they would be in business. If not, they would give up.[40] Malina's solution pointed to stability. The key to building a practical solid-fuel engine was to maintain a constant pressure in the combustion chamber, a goal that could be achieved by keeping constant the ratio of the cross-sectional area of the exhaust nozzle's throat to the burning area of the propellant. Parsons proceeded to devise and test arrangements of powders and oxidizers that conformed to the dictates of the theory.[41]

Toward mid-June 1940, buoyed by a progress report from von Kármán, the Academy requested that the Army Air Corps provide twenty-nine thousand dollars—roughly half a million dollars in 2019—for Malina's group to continue its work on both solid-fueled and liquid-fueled rockets during the next fiscal year. Arnold approved the request on June 17, 1940, just after the fall of France, telling Malina that in light of recent events in Europe, he anticipated that the Air Corps would have no trouble obtaining the money for a contract that would go into effect on July 1.[42]

A few days later, Vannevar Bush, who in 1938 had left a distinguished career in engineering at MIT to become the president of the Carnegie Institution of Washington, prevailed upon Franklin Roosevelt to issue an executive order establishing the National Defense Research Committee (NDRC). FDR gave the new agency the power independent of the military to mobilize civilian science for national defense and the authority to obtain funds for the purpose from Congress. Hap Arnold, wondering whether the NDRC would take over the rocket project, put the Air Corps contract on hold. Bush, however, had no confidence that rockets could be developed into a working technology, certainly not in time for use in the war. He left the rocket project to the Academy committee and Arnold's Air Corps.[43]

Von Kármán was formally appointed director of the project and Malina, its chief engineer. With the contract money the project erected a few boxlike corrugated metal huts on six acres in the Arroyo Seco leased from the city of Pasadena for five years, and it paid salaries to Malina, Forman, and Parsons. The Arroyo site was designated: "Experimental Station of the Air Corps Jet Propulsion Research Project."[44] In the following months, with an eye to the von Kármán–Malina theoretical criterion for slow-burning, the group tested hundreds of combinations of black-powder fuels and nozzle shapes. By the spring of 1941 the results were promising enough to design an engine and schedule a trial with an airplane. On August 12, at March Field, near Riverside, the Caltech group strapped three solid-fuel rockets, each shaped like a long bottle, under

FIGURE 2.3 Ercoupe, assisted by six jets under the wings, leaves the Piper Cub still taxiing, August 12, 1941. *Source*: Courtesy NASA/JPL-Caltech.

each wing of an Ercoupe, a small single-engine plane with one of von Kármán's former students at the controls. Alongside it was a standard Piper Cub piloted by Clark Millikan. The two aircraft started and roared down the runway together, but when the Ercoupe's pilot ignited his rockets, the plane left the Piper Cub in a trail of smoke and shot up into the air, clearing a fifty-foot banner set at a calculated distance down the strip. The rockets had cut the normal takeoff distance by nearly half and the normal time to get airborne by some 40 percent.[45]

The triumph was marred, however, by the discovery that after being in storage for several days, the fuel used in the rockets deteriorated, causing the motors to explode on ignition. Malina recalled how fortunate it was that March Field was only about an hour's drive from Pasadena, which had meant that the rockets that accelerated the Ercoupe could be safely fired shortly after they were charged with propellant.[46]

With the Ercoupe success in his pocket, von Kármán requested another twenty-nine thousand dollars for the GALCIT project for fiscal 1942. Part of the funds would be used to find a sustainable solid-fuel propellant and to aim

FIGURE 2.4 Calculating on the Ercoupe wing, August 1941, Theodore von Kármán (center) and Frank Malina (to his left). *Source*: Courtesy of the Archives, California Institute of Technology.

for the design of a jet motor that would weigh 60 pounds and produce a thrust of 1,000 pounds for sixty seconds. The Air Corps granted the funds, but the National Academy of Sciences asked to be relieved of the responsibility for overseeing the grant. It simply did not have the resources to manage the staff, accounting, and myriad details required for so large a task. On July 1, 1941, the Air Corps assigned the jet-propulsion contract to Caltech directly.[47]

In the succeeding months, the effort on liquid-fueled rockets proceeded apace, and in the early spring of 1942 a takeoff-assist engine was ready for test with a heavy bomber. On April 15, at Muroc Field in the Mojave Desert, the engines were mounted on the wings of a Douglas A-20 bomber that weighed 20,000 pounds. The plane rumbled down the runway and, when the rockets were fired, it rose, Malina noted, "as though scooped upward by a sudden draft." Its takeoff distance had been cut by a third. Malina exulted to his parents: "We have been struggling for this event for six years. We now have something that really works and we should be able to help give the Fascists hell!" The event, as von Kármán saw it, was "the beginning of practical rocketry in the United States."[48]

All the while, the Caltech group had spent months trying to devise a fuel that would withstand long-term storage in weather conditions ranging from those in Alaska to Africa. Malina recalled that they were stymied until June 1942, "when Parsons, no doubt after communing with his poetic spirits, suggested trying a radical new propellant"—a combination of potassium perchlorate as an oxidizer together with the common asphalt used on roads. The asphalt would serve as both a fuel and a binder and could be cast into the shape of a combustion chamber. Parsons's flash of inspiration solved the problem. Malina later reflected that Parsons's idea together with the von Kármán–Malina proof that a stable slow- and long-burning rocket motor was possible constituted "two of the most important discoveries in the long history of solid rockets."[49]

The engines tested at March and Muroc fields and then with the asphalt-based propellant were prototypes. Arranging to have them produced in large quantities to the military's specifications was a crucial next step. Late in 1941, von Kármán tried to persuade several aircraft companies to undertake production of the new technologies, but he failed. The firms were already bursting with orders and doubted rockets had a future. In March 1942, von Kármán, Malina, and several other project members decided to form their own production company: the Aerojet Engineering Corporation. Each invested two hundred dollars in the firm, and the lawyer who organized the company invested two thousand dollars. The company was incorporated in Delaware but opened a branch—its operating facility—in a small space on East Colorado Boulevard in Pasadena.[50]

Its start was financially rocky. The Air Corps discovered that it could construct runways sufficiently long to obviate the need for assistance from rockets when its bombers took off. The founders kept the company afloat with personal loans and donations of time. However, it found a better client in the Navy, which early in 1942 had asked the GALCIT project to develop rockets with sufficient thrust to assist planes taking off from aircraft carriers. In 1943 the rockets—the Navy gave them the name that stuck, "JATOs," for "jet-assisted-takeoff"—were ready, and the Navy gave Aerojet a large contract to produce them.[51] All the while, the GALCIT project grew, reaching a staff size of eighty-five in mid-1943 and a budget for the coming fiscal year, of 1944, of $650,000. Its outcroppings in the Arroyo Seco now comprised a small office building, two laboratories, several auxiliary structures, and several firing pits lined with railroad ties cut into the side of a hill. Staff reached the site along a bumpy dirt road awash in the rainy season.[52]

But in mid-1943, alarming intelligence arrived from the Allies that von Kármán helped interpret and that would dramatically transform the enterprise in the Arroyo: the Germans were preparing to launch rockets across the Channel. In November 1943, in a report generated at the suggestion of two Army officers stationed at GALCIT, von Kármán and Hsue-shen Tsien proposed that the Caltech project adapt its JATO motors to the development of a series of successively longer-range missiles capable of carrying progressively heavier explosive loads. They designated the report "JPL-1," the first use of the acronym and of the title Jet Propulsion Laboratory.[53]

In 1943 the Army Air Force—which the vastly expanded Air Corps had turned into—rejected the JPL-1 proposal, doubting that it would produce immediately useful technologies. Army Ordnance, however, was decidedly interested. It had tried to obtain support for research on guided missiles from Vannevar Bush. In June 1941, Bush had obtained a second executive order from FDR that incorporated the NDRC into a new Office of Scientific Research and Development (OSRD). Like the NDRC, the OSRD was an independent agency backed by the president's authority and the congressionally authorized appropriations to pursue not only research in the new technologies of war but also their development toward production. But Bush wanted no part of guided missiles now just as he had shied away from rockets in 1940. He considered guided missiles too inaccurate to be worthy of support and expected that a missiles project would divert too many technical people from the immediate war effort.[54]

Army Ordnance thus regarded GALCIT's eager willingness for a project on guided missiles as a welcome gift. It authorized a comprehensive program at GALCIT for research and development not merely on rocket engines but on a complete guided missile system that would include the manufacture of prototypes for production. The Caltech trustees approved the initiative in February 1944. In June, Army Ordnance provided $1.6 million and pledged another $3.6 million on a cost-plus-fixed-fee contract for another eighteen months. On July 1, 1944, the guided missile program began officially under the auspices of the "Jet Propulsion Laboratory, GALCIT."[55] The ultimate goal was a missile capable of delivering a 1,000-pound load 150 miles away within an accuracy of 3 miles. The goal was to be achieved with the development of successively more powerful rockets—the first called "Private," the second "Corporal," and the third

FIGURE 2.5 Frank Malina with the WAC corporal rocket, at White Sands Proving Ground, October 11, 1945. *Source*: Courtesy of the Archives, California Institute of Technology.

"Sergeant." At that point the designations would halt because, von Kármán joked, Sergeant was "the highest rank that works."[56]

In December 1944 von Kármán left GALCIT, taking extended leave from Caltech to assist the Army Air Force. Caltech replaced him with an executive board that included Clark Millikan, who was also GALCIT's new acting director. JPL's acting director was Frank Malina, now thirty-two. It had been only six years since he had been thrilled to receive the one thousand dollars from the National Academy of Sciences committee to develop a proposal for research in rocket engines. In 1945 he found himself in charge of a multimillion-dollar operation that comprised a rapidly expanding physical plant—the Army invested three million dollars in the construction of facilities in the Arroyo, including a supersonic wind tunnel—and that encompassed R&D not only in engines but also in the aerodynamics of missiles and systems for their guidance and control.[57]

Fueling A-Bombs

In December 1938, the same month that Malina presented his case to the National Academy of Sciences committee, a trio of scientists working in Berlin with just desktop apparatus discovered nuclear fission. News of the discovery immediately gave rise among physicists on both sides of the Atlantic to imaginings of nuclear-generated electrical power and of nuclear-fueled explosives. Refugee physicists from Europe worried that their brethren who remained in Germany would build an atomic bomb for Hitler. In the summer of 1939, Albert Einstein in his subsequently famous letter to Roosevelt, apprised the president of the discovery of fission and its implications. The letter gained the president's attention but at the time prompted little action and the release of no money for a nuclear weapons project.[58]

Ernest Lawrence was too absorbed with the business of his laboratory to jump on a nuclear bandwagon. His Nobel came in the fall of 1939, when the Swedish Academy of Sciences announced that Lawrence had won the year's Prize in Physics for the invention and development of the cyclotron. The machine's "greatest significance," the spokesman for the Swedish Academy said, was the production in large quantities of radioactive isotopes for "biological and medical purposes."[59] In 1940 the Rockefeller Foundation granted Lawrence $1,150,000 to construct a cyclotron 184 inches in diameter that would generate 150 million electron volts, a power half again greater than what Lawrence had wanted for his next machine. In a world plunging into war, the president of the foundation justified the 184-inch cyclotron as "an emblem of the undiscourageable search for truth which is the noblest expression of the human spirit."[60]

Yet after the fall of France, in Berkeley as in Pasadena, the search for truth increasingly gave way to arming for war. Well connected like von Kármán with scientists abroad, Lawrence was a pro-Allied advocate of national preparedness in science and technology. In the summer of 1940, he helped the NDRC get under way a laboratory at MIT for the development of microwave radar (the technologies it devised would prove to be among the most important for the Allied war effort). It was named the Radiation Laboratory, after Lawrence's in Berkeley—the idea being that the name would mislead people into thinking that it was engaged in something that seemed so impractical at the time as nuclear physics.[61] By then physicists in the United States and England had learned a good deal about uranium fission. Uranium occurs as a mixture of two isotopes—U-235, which fissions, and the slightly heavier U-238, which does not. On fissioning, an atom of U-235 releases one or more neutrons and a quantity of energy. In principle, the daughter neutrons would stimulate other uranium atoms to fission, thus producing a chain reaction. If the reaction proceeded slowly, it would generate heat for a power plant. If it proceeded rapidly, it might produce a sudden cascade of energy—and thus an enormous explosion.

In natural uranium, U-235 comprises only 1 in every 140 atoms, only about 0.7 of a percent of the total; the rest are U-238. Reaching a "critical mass"—the minimum material necessary for a self-sustaining chain reaction—required separating away enough U-238 from the natural uranium to produce a mixture of the two isotopes containing a proportion of U-235 far greater than the natural ratio to its sister isotope. Various estimates had it that a critical mass of adequately enriched uranium would amount to no more than 100 pounds.[62] But it was not at all clear how to separate the two isotopes so as to achieve the enrichment. Both isotopes share the same chemical characteristics; they cannot be separated chemically. The only way to separate them is with some physical process that exploits their slight difference in weight.

By early 1941 several separation methods were under discussion, and Lawrence conceived a bold one of his own—a method that employed the electromagnetic forces that controlled the circulation of the beam in his cyclotron. It depended on the fact that, if uranium atoms were sent through the magnetic field of a cyclotron, the ions of U-238, being slightly heavier than those of U-235, would move in an arc of slightly larger diameter than those of the fissionable isotope. The two beams would thus separate somewhat, allowing for the collection of a mixture enriched in U-235 ions. While neat in concept, the scheme struck a number of scientists as unlikely to succeed in practice. However, Lawrence, his gusto for the impossible intensified by the war emergency, thought he could skin this new type of cat by using the powerful field generated by the new 184-inch magnet. It would be strong enough to bend the beams of the two isotopes apart as they accelerated through the semicircle of a cyclotron "Dee" from entrance to collector.[63]

Lawrence turned to the OSRD for authorization and funds to mount an electromagnetic isotope separation project in Berkeley. The Uranium Committee had been under Bush's authority since mid-1940, having then been transferred to the NDRC; and in mid-1941 it was organized under the OSRD as Section S-1. To Lawrence's frustration, neither the committee, which had focused on nuclear power, nor S-1, which had expanded the scope of its inquiries to encompass research into the possibility of a nuclear bomb, appeared to treat the subject with any sense of urgency. Neither did Bush. He did not dismiss an atomic bomb the way he did rockets. He was simply reluctant to initiate an expensive bomb production effort while the way forward remained unclear. Even should Lawrence's proof of concept succeed, producing enough fissionable fuel for a critical mass would require a virtual factory of expensive cyclotrons, not just the one in Berkeley. At a meeting in New York, in March 1941, Lawrence had browbeaten Bush to move the bomb effort into high gear, whereupon Bush dressed him down, bluntly declaring that he was in charge and that if Lawrence didn't like it he could go elsewhere.[64]

During the summer and fall, authoritative reports arrived from Britain that a bomb could be made with as little as 25 pounds of enriched uranium and that such a quantity could be produced within three years using a separation technology called gaseous diffusion that was then under development. Lawrence agitated again for a stepped-up bomb project, now joined by several of the highest-ranking physicists in the United States and Britain. All stressed that, should an atom bomb prove to be possible, it was imperative that Hitler not be allowed to get it first.[65]

In October 1941, Bush asked the National Academy of Sciences to appoint a committee to report on the prospects of producing a nuclear weapon. While the committee investigated, Bush fully briefed FDR on the state of affairs and obtained his authority to proceed. In November the Academy committee endorsed the project and urged that S-1 pursue in parallel the several methods proposed for separating U-235 from U-238, including Lawrence's electromagnetic approach.[66] Combining funds in the laboratory with four hundred thousand dollars from the OSRD, Lawrence adapted the 37-inch cyclotron to prove the merits of his concept. By March 1942 his laboratory managed to enrich the natural uranium by a factor of five, bringing the portion of U-235 it contained up to 3.5 percent. Now the laboratory turned to developing technologies and methods to speed the separation; many were tested using the 184-inch magnet. Lawrence called the full prototype of the separation cyclotron "Dee" an "alpha calutron," signifying that it comprised the first stage in the process and was a product of California.[67]

Late in 1940, the bombardment of uranium with neutrons in the Berkeley cyclotron produced an unknown radioactive material. By February 1941 it had been identified by Glenn T. Seaborg, a young nuclear chemist in the laboratory. Seaborg and his collaborators demonstrated that the material was a new element, with an atomic number of 94. It was created by two successive transmutations that started with U-238. Drawing on the then-prevailing convention of naming new elements as they were discovered or made in accord with the order of the outer planets, Seaborg christened element 94 "plutonium." Berkeley scientists soon demonstrated that plutonium fissions, giving off energetic neutrons that, like those from the fissioning of U-235, could be harnessed to generate a rapid chain reaction, an explosion.[68]

Plutonium promised to be far less difficult to produce in quantity than enriched uranium. If natural uranium was organized into a suitably arranged pile, its U-235 would emit neutrons, inducing fission, and hence a chain reaction, among its neighboring atoms of U-235. The neutrons would also stimulate the successive transmutations in the U-238 that resulted in the creation of plutonium. The plutonium, being a different element, could then be chemically separated from the remaining uranium and purified into fuel for a nuclear weapon. An essential requirement of the process was to control the pace of the chain reaction and to keep the pile cooled, so that the reactor would not melt down. In January 1942, S-1 established what it called the Metallurgical Laboratory at the University of Chicago. Enrico Fermi and a team of other physicists settled in to design a reactor to test the feasibility of plutonium production in a controlled chain reaction. Chemists under Seaborg, using micrograms of plutonium obtained from the cyclotron at Washington University, devised production techniques for the chemical separation of plutonium from the uranium retrieved from a reactor.[69]

In June 1942, given a final green light by President Roosevelt for a full-scale effort to build a bomb, Bush concluded that the operation would require an enormous effort in industrial production, of a magnitude far beyond the managerial capacities of the OSRD. He helped arrange for the consolidation of S-1's now multiple parts into a new Manhattan District of the Army Engineers. In September command of the Manhattan Project was given to Brigadier General Leslie R. Groves. Groves was the son of an Army chaplain and the husband of an Army daughter. His upbringing gave him a Calvinist-flavored sense of self-discipline and obligation to excel. He graduated fourth in his West Point class and opted for the Engineer Corps, an elite cadre within the Army. At the outbreak of the war, he headed the construction division in the Quartermaster Corps, overseeing billions of dollars' worth of projects, including munitions factories, camps, and the Pentagon. He had the knowledge and experience to manage the huge production job that was as essential to the Manhattan Project as the scientific research that enabled it. Brusque, supremely self-confident, and single-minded, Groves also had the temperament and drive to barrel through any obstacle that stood in the way of achieving the project's purpose.[70]

Like Hap Arnold and von Kármán, Groves and Lawrence found themselves advantageously compatible. But what initially bound Arnold and von Kármán was a shared commitment to advancing scientific knowledge related to flight; Groves and Lawrence were joined by a ferocious, no-holds-barred determination to build an atomic bomb. Lawrence recognized in Groves a tough-minded ally in the cause of electromagnetic separation. Groves, who had his doubts about the method, nevertheless admired Lawrence's imaginative resourcefulness and capacity for organization. He steadfastly supported Lawrence's plans to turn his method from a laboratory prototype into full-scale production of enriched uranium.[71]

Groves acquired fifty-nine thousand acres along the Clinch River in the vicinity of Oak Ridge, Tennessee, as the site for both the gaseous diffusion and the electromagnetic separation plants. Lawrence's plans entailed the construction and installation of five sets of ninety-six calutrons, each set gathered in an arrangement called an Alpha racetrack. (The number of Alphas eventually grew to nine.) The magnet for each racetrack would consume one hundred times the power anticipated for the 184-inch cyclotron. Lawrence drove his staff day and night to perfect the design of the calutrons' multiple parts, including vacuum tanks, ionization apparatus, magnets, and collectors of U-235. Groves and Lawrence skipped the testing of pilot-plant versions of the calutrons. There was no time. The construction of the racetracks at Oak Ridge proceeded directly from the Berkeley designs.[72]

When the racetracks first went into operation, in late 1943, electrical shorts and vacuum leaks erupted everywhere. By then, Robert Oppenheimer, now head of the bomb design lab that he and Groves had established at Los Alamos, New Mexico, told Lawrence that the fuel for a uranium bomb would require an enrichment of 90 percent, which meant that the portion of U-235 atoms had to be bumped up from the natural proportion of 1 in 140 to 126 in 140.

FIGURE 2.6 Industrial-scale nuclear physics: Ernest Lawrence (far right), Brigadier General Leslie R. Groves (to his right), and officials from the Tennessee Eastman Company at the magnet for the 184-inch cyclotron, 1943. *Source*: © 2010 The Regents of the University of California, through the Lawrence Berkeley National Laboratory.

Berkeley scientists designed a supplementary set of racetracks—they were designated "Betas"—intended if needed to intensify the enrichment of the products from the Alphas. Groves, taking no chances, ordered the installation of six Betas, each containing thirty-six calutrons, at Oak Ridge.[73] All the while, breakdowns continued to plague the system. Lawrence, made physically ill by the pressure, spent the end of 1943 in a hospital. In 1944 he brought squads of scientists and technicians from Berkeley to troubleshoot the equipment. The racetracks would work, he assured Groves. At one point, Groves remonstrated:

"Dr. Lawrence, you know your reputation's at stake." Lawrence retorted, "No, General, my reputation is made. Yours is at stake."[74]

In December 1942, Fermi's experimental reactor, built in the center of Chicago under the stands of Stagg Field, the university's abandoned football stadium, went critical and achieved the world's first controlled nuclear chain reaction. In 1943 physicists and chemists left Chicago for Oak Ridge, where they designed and built an experimental pile and separation facilities; at the end of the year the equipment yielded the first milligrams of plutonium. Among the Oak Ridge staff was Eugene Wigner, who came up with the basic design for a plutonium reactor and processing works.[75] Groves specified a number of criteria for a suitable plutonium production site, aiming to reduce the expected radiation hazards. He defined safety by distance from either a reactor or a separation plant: for the laboratory at least eight miles away; the employees' villages, no less than ten miles upwind; any town of at one thousand people or more, at least twenty miles; and any highway or railroad, at least ten miles. Groves declined to locate the plutonium production facilities at Oak Ridge, thinking it too close to a population center.[76]

Instead, Grove chose a large tract of land—some four hundred thousand acres—on the Columbia River, near Hanford, Washington, about thirty-five miles north of the Oregon border. The site was mostly desert, thinly settled, and isolated. It offered abundant materials for construction, electric power from the Grand Coulee Dam, and water from the river for cooling the reactors. Most of the tract was owned by the federal government; the rest of it by some twelve hundred farmers and Native Americans. The government bought them out, in a number of cases over their strong objections by, as Jared Farmer explains in his chapter in this volume, invoking the Second War Powers Act of 1942. This enabled the government to acquire private land by condemnation and purchase.[77] Groves enlisted the DuPont Chemical Corporation to manage the Hanford works. The company's executives at first refused the job, not least because they feared being popularly charged once again, as their predecessor had been during the mid-1930s for having supplied munitions in World War I, with acting as cold-blooded "merchants of death." Under pressure from Groves, DuPont accepted the task but, to forestall a repeat indictment, on the condition that it be paid only one dollar a year above costs.[78]

Applying the strategy he employed throughout the Manhattan Project, Groves counted money no object in reaching for success. He authorized the construction of not just one but of three full-scale reactors. If one or two failed, the third would be available. The chain reaction in the reactors was to be moderated by the insertion of graphite control rods. He added in a plant to produce heavy water, also a moderator, in case the rods failed. Concerned that raw Columbia River water might not sufficiently cool the reactors, Groves ordered the construction of a water de-ionizing plant, just in case.[79] The first reactor, called the "B reactor," was started up in September 1944; the other two were then nearing completion. The first separation plant was finished in December 1944. DuPont said that it would be able to produce one kilogram a month of weapons-grade plutonium. Groves found the schedule far too slow and demanded that DuPont speed things up. The company's staff complied.[80]

Lawrence's racetracks enabled the production of most of the enriched uranium that formed the 64-kilogram core of the bomb dropped on Hiroshima on August 6, 1945. Hanford's three reactors and three plutonium processing facilities produced the fuel used in the Trinity atomic test at Alamogordo, New Mexico, on July 16 and in the bomb that was dropped on Nagasaki on August 9. The two explosions, each requiring 6.1 kilograms of plutonium, totally depleted the 12 kilograms that Hanford had shipped to Los Alamos, but the lab predicted that it could send enough additional material between August and December to supply seventeen more atomic bombs.[81]

By then, Hanford was a booming nuclear complex, the third most populous region in the state, its plutonium-making installations sprawling across the landscape. The Berkeley Radiation Laboratory now occupied several large buildings in the hills above the university that housed the 184-inch magnet, a forest of auxiliary equipment, and a staff of more than a thousand.[82] The creation of the one, the enormous expansion of the other, and the embrace of guided missile development at the Jet Propulsion Laboratory had together transformed the high-technology West in multiple ways that the uneasy post-1945 peace would quickly reveal.

Legacies, Post-1945

The regional transformation expressed a comparable change in the relationship of civilian science and technology to the national government. The war had taught policymakers a series of salient lessons—that in general national security would henceforth depend upon technological superiority; that technological prowess would in turn require support of research in multiple fields of basic science, even those seemingly remote from military purpose, and of the production in abundance of scientists and engineers; that much of the research and all of the training was to be conducted in academia, the main locale of fresh thinking and activity on the technical frontiers; and that policymaking in the development of weapons systems and planning for their potential use had to include advice from civilian practitioners at the cutting edges of their fields.[83]

After 1945 the federal government fostered these ends through the creation of a series of new agencies and programs. It largely accomplished the task by the end of the Korean War, in 1953, making the government the country's principal patron of R&D. Military purposes dominated the support through this period and well beyond, with the new Department of Defense and the new defense-oriented Atomic Energy Commission accounting for 90 percent of the federal R&D budget.[84]

The high-tech West helped promote these national developments, and between the end of the war and 1953 they combined with regional circumstances, interests, and ambitions to expand and strengthen the region's own transformation. The change was manifest in multiple dimensions: the empowerment of the West's protagonists in policymaking at both the national and local institutional levels; its capture of sizable portions of the largesse available from Washington, DC; the growth of the region's economy and the enlargement of its employment, especially, as Gavin Wright notes in his chapter, in aerospace, missiles, and microelectronics; and withal, in some respects, its troubled engagement with the exigencies of national security.

A major source of the boom in microelectronics was Stanford University, in Palo Alto, which had played virtually no role in the field during the war, but generated it after 1945 thanks to Frederick L. Terman, the dean of engineering.[85] He was a son of Lewis Terman, the Stanford psychologist famous for his pioneering of IQ testing in the United States. If he needed a model of how to make a difference in the world through building an academic research program, his father provided it. During the 1920s Terman had earned a doctorate in electrical engineering under Vannevar Bush at MIT and had then joined the Stanford faculty, ambitious to make the university "the research center for electrical engineering." [86] His vehicle was a program in communications that emphasized cooperative cross talk between engineering and physics, and between the university and local start-up companies.

Terman spent the war running the radar countermeasures laboratory at Harvard. In 1945 he returned to Stanford, bringing with him a number of his countermeasures colleagues, plans to establish an Electronics Research

Laboratory (ERL), and expectations of handsome funding from the Office of Naval Research (ONR) to put Stanford on the map as a major center of microelectronics. ONR money arrived in increasing abundance, and so beginning in 1947 did support from the Army and Air Force; the combined patronage reached five hundred thousand dollars in 1950. At the onset of the Korean War the budget tripled in size. All the work was conducted on campus by faculty and graduate students. A sizable part of it was for directly practical military purposes, was classified, and was conducted under the auspices of the Applied Electronics Laboratory. With the lines between the ERL and this laboratory growing increasingly blurred, Terman combined them into the Stanford Electronics Laboratory (SEL). He counted the SEL a jewel in Stanford's academic crown, declaring Stanford "the most important center of electronics among American universities."[87]

So it was. Collaborating closely with physics, the SEL pursued groundbreaking work in nuclear physics, high-power microwave tubes as well as laser physics and transistor engineering. From the beginning, it encouraged productive ties with existing electronics companies. In 1951 one of them, Varian Associates, founded in 1948 by several of Stanford engineering's longtime collaborators, became the first tenant of the new Stanford Industrial Park, a shrewd venture pioneered by Terman and the Stanford Treasurer. Other companies followed Varian onto the Park along with start-ups by Stanford faculty and students, while still others—for example, Motorola, Sylvania, and Litton Industries—created research centers nearby, drawn by Stanford's powerhouse expertise in microelectronics. Together with Stanford, all established the San Francisco Bay Peninsula as a thriving agglomeration of high-tech companies and helped lay the foundation for what became Silicon Valley.[88]

All the while, the GALCIT leadership in Pasadena and Lawrence in Berkeley were also promotionally busy.[89] In 1944, Hap Arnold recruited von Kármán to come to Washington, DC, for an extended stay to form and chair an Air Force Scientific Advisory Group. Its immediate purpose was to lay out a long-term plan for R&D bearing on the new defense technologies, particularly microelectronics, radar, jet propulsion, and rockets. Its ongoing job was to provide technical advice to the Air Force on its current programs. Civilian scientists had been essential to the technological prowess of the Army Air Force during the war, Arnold told General Carl Spaatz, the commander of the service in Europe. "We must not lose these contacts."[90]

In 1946 the advisory group was succeeded by the Air Force Scientific

Advisory Board, which von Kármán also chaired, and, after a rocky start engendered by the budgetary cutbacks of demobilization, fostered a broad, long-term program of R&D for air power, with an overall budget that skyrocketed during the Korean War, more than doubling, to $523 million just in the first year of the conflict. Just after World War I, von Kármán had had a bellyful of communism when he worked briefly in Budapest for the government of Bela Kun; he was an unquestioning Cold Warrior, not to mention an avid friend of high technology in southern California. He no doubt did not find it objectionable that Air Force funds went in sizable amounts to GALCIT, Aerojet, Douglas, and the state's other aircraft companies.[91]

Army Ordnance, ranking guided missiles second in importance only to nuclear weapons, asked in September 1945 that JPL be made permanent under Caltech's management. The key ordnance officer assured both Caltech's and JPL's leadership that the lab would be free to focus on basic research. In von Kármán's absence, an oversight committee chaired by Clark Millikan had been made responsible for JPL, and Malina was the lab's acting director. Malina had little taste for military-oriented research now that the war was over. He wanted to return to the kind of work that had produced the Malina–von Kármán equations and would enable rockets to study the upper atmosphere. He worried that if JPL continued under the Army, its program would be skewed toward practical work and closed off from the world by security restrictions. With von Kármán's support he urged the Caltech administration to integrate the lab into the campus, where classified research was prohibited. It would be run by faculty and free to pursue open and "completely unfettered research."[92]

Clark Millikan had no discomfort with militarily purposeful research. He urged that Caltech continue to operate JPL for Army Ordnance as a "special national defense laboratory supported by government funds." He argued that by signing on for the missile work in 1944, Caltech had made "a certain moral commitment" to doing so. Besides, the JPL facilities were highly valuable, the Army had promised that the laboratory could focus on basic research, and it was difficult to see how Caltech could raise the money for a comparable facility on campus.[93] The Caltech administration sided with Millikan. In March 1946, bowing to institutional interest, so did Malina and von Kármán. Malina recalled that he then traveled often to Washington, DC, to meet with Army, Navy, and Air Force officers thinking ahead to "the next war." He found himself increasingly "disturbed" and would break into "a cold sweat," hating the idea of "planning to use all this for bombarding people." In December 1946 he took a leave of absence from Caltech to work with UNESCO in Paris for a two-year stint that turned into an ongoing new job.[94]

However, Malina had been under FBI surveillance for his communist associations since 1942. Jack Parsons had first fingered him, and in 1950 his successor as director of JPL, Louis Dunn, an arch conservative from South Africa, had informed the agency that Malina might have conducted espionage. In 1950 the US government refused to renew his passport and in 1953, faced with the Truman administration's international crackdown on Americans held to be security risks, Malina quit UNESCO. He was saved from being a man without a salary and without a country when shortly thereafter his Aerojet stock made him suddenly and unexpectedly rich and the French, in recognition of his wealth, granted him residency. Malina turned to a career as an artist, remained a resident of Paris, and eventually earned an international reputation as a pioneer in the genre of kinetic art.[95]

As director of JPL, Louis Dunn, another student of von Kármán's and an avid poker player, was wily, shrewd, and practical. Dunn kept the laboratory focused on the task at hand: the program of developing successive missiles—Private, Corporal, and Sergeant—that von Kármán had originally outlined. The R&D yielded important new designs for solid-fuel rocket charges, the achievement of flights to unprecedented heights, and the pioneering of methods of inertial and electronic systems for guidance and control. However, during the War in Korea the lab oriented itself almost entirely to rockets for war, with an eye to arming them with tactical nuclear warheads. JPL turned into what neither Malina had wanted nor the Army had promised—a weapons lab. Its investment in basic research declined to 30 percent of the total allocation and its connections with the campus, where classified and weapons research remained prohibited, all but dissolved. The lab spent much of its energies on development and testing. In 1953, JPL's budget was $11 million and it employed 1,061 people.[96]

Like Malina, Lawrence wanted to return his laboratory primarily to basic research, but (unlike Malina) he possessed the power and prestige to accomplish his purpose. After the Trinity test in the New Mexico desert, Lawrence's expectations of support mushroomed in magnitude, like the cloud of the bomb exploding in the desert. In September 1945, Robert Sproul, the president of the University of California, gave Lawrence license to seek whatever he wanted, telling him that he was "unwilling to yield this field [atomic energy], in which we are now preeminent, to any other institution."[97] Lawrence energetically lobbied Groves for the support of his grand plans. Groves was happy to accommodate him, holding that funding the Radiation Laboratory was "in the best interest of the government." At the end of the war, a physicist at Lawrence's laboratory named Edwin McMillan had figured out how to skin the cat that Bethe had concluded stood in the way of accelerating charged particles to 100 million volts in a cyclotron. McMillan's scheme was an accelerator called a "synchrocyclotron." In 1945, Groves authorized the funds to complete a 184-inch synchrocyclotron that used the workhorse magnetic the Rockefeller grant had enabled the lab to obtain and that had been diverted during the war to the testing of the prototype calutron. He also authorized the construction of an electron synchrotron.[98]

In the postwar years the federal government largely replaced the corporate and philanthropic sources of support that Lawrence had successfully cultivated before the war. The new Atomic Energy Commission, which shouldered responsibility for all the country's accelerators, not only took over the funding of Lawrence's synchrotrons but declared in 1947 that it considered his facilities a national laboratory. By then the 184-inch synchrotron was producing a beam and the laboratory was in the vanguard of the emerging field of elementary particle physics. Lawrence aimed to widen its lead. In the late 1940s the staff was beginning to explore the design of an enormously powerful proton synchrotron—the Bevatron, so named because it would accelerate particles to the energy of 10 billion electron volts.[99] The Bevatron, which started regularly accelerating particles in 1954, enabled experiments that would win two Nobel Prizes in Physics by the time Lawrence died, in 1958, at the age of fifty-seven (the lab was soon thereafter renamed the Lawrence Radiation Laboratory). His death arose from the usual overwork, but this time in service of trying to help negotiate a nuclear test ban.[100]

High-energy physics was remote from direct connections with national security. Between 1946 and 1949, less than 30 percent of the Radiation Laboratory's contracted activities involved military subjects, and most of those that did concerned work in the Crocker medically oriented laboratory on the decontamination of radioactive ships.[101] Lawrence's laboratory remained a world center of unclassified research in elementary particles, but Lawrence himself was by no means unfriendly to the development of ever more powerful nuclear weapons. Although in June 1945 he had urged a demonstration of the atomic bomb, Lawrence had in the end supported its use against Japan and had no later regrets. After the Soviet explosion of an atomic device in mid-1949 and the outbreak of the Korean War less than a year later, Lawrence endorsed the physicist Edward Teller's urgent lobbying for a crash program to build a hydrogen bomb.

FIGURE 2.7 Hanford reactors complex along the Columbia River, 1960, with the B Reactor in the distant background. *Source*: US Department of Energy.

To this end, Lawrence proposed to build two linear accelerators, the first a trial model, which would produce polonium for radiological warfare; and a far more powerful second, which would produce tritium, an isotope of hydrogen that could fuel a thermonuclear explosive. No doubt drawing on his own experience, Lawrence argued resourcefully, "One never knows when a new process of military importance will demand the existence of an accelerator. In fact, the mere existence of such a machine may easily influence the thinking of scientific and technical men along lines which they would otherwise dismiss at the outset as absurd."[102]

The accelerators were to be located at Livermore, California. The project was canceled when it proved to be unnecessary for the hydrogen bomb, but in 1952 Livermore was established as the site of a second laboratory for nuclear weapons to satisfy Teller, who, distrustful of the commitment for the new bomb at Los Alamos, held that the Livermore Laboratory would offer Los Alamos healthy competition. Berkeley shifted the remainder of its classified work to the new installation. At the end of the Korean War, California was the home of two major national laboratories sponsored by the AEC—one in Berkeley devoted to open, basic research; the other, at Livermore, for the classified development of thermonuclear weapons.[103] The Livermore Laboratory contributed little to the first hydrogen bombs, but by the time of Lawrence's death its prowess in designing nuclear and thermonuclear weapons was on a par with that of the Los Alamos laboratory.[104]

The drive to produce both nuclear and thermonuclear weapons heightened the demand for uranium (a fission explosion figured in the hydrogen bomb as the trigger for the explosive fusion of the hydrogen atoms). Hanford steadily expanded its capacity to produce plutonium. Between 1945 and 1965 it would add six more reactors, two more processing plants, and several major laboratories.[105]

Beginning in 1952, the AEC encouraged the expansion of a domestic uranium supply by offering prospectors a ten-thousand-dollar bonus for each discovery of a uranium lode and guaranteeing to purchase ore production for ten years at a certain minimum price. The inducements helped to stimulate a boom in uranium prospecting, mining, and production in the Colorado Plateau, the dry, unforgiving region where Arizona, Colorado, New Mexico, and Utah conjoin.[106] Hanford boosted the economy of its region, bringing in hundreds of millions of federal dollars and, for most of the period, employing between nine thousand and fourteen thousand people. JPL, Lawrence's laboratory, and Livermore all enlarged opportunities for increasing numbers of technical and support staff as well as demand for materials from local suppliers. To be sure, women were in general not welcome in science and engineering positions, and security and loyalty restrictions limited or barred employment to anyone with politically suspicious views or affiliations, even in the distant past.[107]

JPL along with GALCIT helped enable the enormous growth in southern California and elsewhere in the region in the aircraft and now also the missile industries. The complex was a magnet for thousands of scientist and engineers, including an increasing number of Jews and Chinese Americans as well as white male products of state universities and small colleges, like Malina's. The technical achievements of JPL, the Lawrence Laboratory, and the Stanford Electronics Laboratory combined with their impact on the economic development of their respective regions speak to Richard White's tantalizing conceptualization (in the afterword) of the Great Acceleration. A salient downside of the acceleration comprised the security suspicions and constraints that suffused the Lawrence laboratory, the SEL, and JPL in the 1950s. They upended many lives and ruined some, including those of Malina's friends in Unit 122.[108] After the creation of the People's Republic of China, Hsue-Shen Tsien wished to return home. Although he said that he was not a Communist, the authorities barred him from leaving the United States because he knew too much about rockets; they excluded him from access to classified information and finally allowed him to leave the country in 1955, when they counted what he knew as insignificant to national security. He is widely believed among knowledgeable analysts to have then played a significant role in China's development of an intercontinental ballistic missile.[109]

Yet some number of employees were glad to be part of the security-classified complex, believing that they were paying dividends to the nation in nuclear deterrence and more. In 1989 a woman who had been working at Hanford for thirty-eight years explained to a historian: "We were pioneers. We were pushing back the frontiers of knowledge." During the 1950s the engineers and physicists at Stanford's SEL did not mind their engagement in on-campus classified work for the military, holding that their research would be no different if it were unclassified and sponsored by a civilian agency.[110] Still, the public health and environmental costs of nuclear deterrence were palpable even at the height of the Cold War. The Hanford Laboratory's hunger for natural uranium kept the mining companies looking for strikes on the Colorado Plateau, but the region turned into a kind of slot machine. If it enabled the making of fortunes overnight, it also produced a variety of losers.

Some—the lucky ones—lost only their shirts. Others comprised the uranium miners, many of them Native Americans, whose lungs were exposed to radon and its daughter products. In 1956 the first lung-cancer death cropped out among the miners. Over the years many more followed. AEC officials had been aware of the danger by a member of the US Public Health Service in 1952. They declined to publicize the information for fear that its release might jeopardize the production of uranium. A public health official called for the adoption of various safety measures in the shafts—notably improved ventilation—to reduce the radiation hazards. Some of the larger mines took ameliorative action, but most of the operators did not. The federal government did not set safety standards in the uranium mines until 1967.[111]

In 1964 the federal government judged that it had more than enough plutonium for weapons; by 1971 it had shut down all but one of the Hanford reactors, leaving it in place for the generation of electric power. But the Hanford facilities had long leaked radioactive and chemical wastes into the soil, air, and groundwater, jeopardizing the waters of the Columbia River and the health of the Native Americans in the area, notably the Nez Percé Tribe, the Confederated Tribes of the Umatilla Indian Reservation, and the Yakama Indian Nation.

The AEC and the Hanford operators knew about the leakage but kept the information secret until 1986, when it was revealed upon the release of nineteen thousand documents. In 1987 the last of the government's reactors was shut down, and two reactors undertaken by the Washington Public Power System were abandoned before completion. Hanford, one of the most contaminated sites in the world, ranks as one of the most costly and locally injurious legacies of the Manhattan Project and its projection into the Cold War. The federal government embarked on a cleanup program that was estimated to last several decades and cost an estimated twenty-nine billion dollars.[112]

Yet Hanford and the Lawrence Laboratory complicated the conceptual framework of the Great Acceleration. The reduction of Hanford's emphasis on plutonium production was paralleled by an increased emphasis on nonweapons research, notably energy and the environment, and the diversification of the local economy through investment by its contractors. The Lawrence Laboratory was later found to have leaked radioactive materials into ground soil in its site's so-called "Old Town" sector, the area where in the 1940s it deployed the 184-inch magnet to develop and work with the synchrocyclotron. In 2018 the Department of Energy completed the first of four cleanup phases of the site. It comprised only a little more than an acre and the effort aimed not only at purging the soil of radioactive contamination but also at razing several seismically deficient buildings and floor slabs so as to restore the area for future use. In the 1970s, long before the discovery of the Old Town difficulties, the lab had become its own watchdog, establishing research programs in energy and the environment.[113]

JPL marched in a direction that diverged even more substantially from the trajectory of the Great Acceleration. To be sure, after the Korean War, its fortunes climbed with the military's. Weapons work continued to dominate its research program, and it developed considerable knowledge and expertise in inertial and electronic guidance of missiles. But the military emphases were much to the dissatisfaction of a number of its staff and influential members of the Caltech Board of Trustees. The dissidents were cheered and relieved when in 1958, in the wake of Sputnik, the laboratory was transferred from Army Ordnance to the new National Aeronautics and Space Administration, a civilian agency.[114]

In succeeding decades, JPL played little role in military research programs, the principal exception being an engagement in research for the Strategic Defense Initiative during the 1980s, which the Caltech faculty resisted but grudgingly went along with. In the 1960s it developed formal methods for controlling hazardous wastes, but in the late 1970s federal environmental studies tentatively concluded that the laboratory had through the 1950s introduced carcinogens in the form of toxic industrial solvents into local groundwater. The laboratory cooperated with the city of Pasadena in getting to the bottom of the problem, and in 1991, with the support of NASA, it agreed to spend about a million dollars a year to decontaminate the water. In 1992 the government designated JPL a Superfund site. Yet unlike Hanford, JPL's environmental culpability did not involve long-lived radioactive materials, its officials made a point of dealing thoughtfully and empathetically with local health anxieties, and in 1998 a federal review declared the site free of contamination. In all, in the run-up to the twenty-first century JPL endured budgetary vicissitudes but with its public support largely undiminished.[115]

Its strength rested on its commitment after 1958 to what Malina had long hoped it would do—largely open, unclassified research into the characteristics of space, using its sophisticated knowledge of rockets, guidance, and control. JPL became the lead laboratory in the unmanned explorations of the moon and the planetary probes to Venus, Saturn, Jupiter, and Mars. It contributed decisively to the development of computer graphics programs that transformed the data arriving from the planetary fly-bys into dynamic, colored visualizations of space and the planets. The images enthralled millions of people around the globe and the methods of creating them were spun out into the production of films and television. They were the latter day expression of the imagined West as a frontier of new beginnings, yet they were also a feature of the actual high-tech West that opened the mind to wonder rather than chilled the heart with fear.[116]

3

WORLD WAR II, THE COLD WAR, AND THE KNOWLEDGE ECONOMIES OF THE PACIFIC COAST

GAVIN WRIGHT

World War II had enduring effects on the economies of the Pacific Coast but not necessarily in the ways most commonly adduced. In his classic *World War II and the West*, historian Gerald D. Nash suggests that the war transformed the region from a colonial "Third World" economy based on agriculture and mining into a modern, technology-driven manufacturing dynamo. The war did indeed generate a flood of new workers into the West, propelled by an unprecedented infusion of federal spending for military production. But wartime spending did not particularly favor the West over other regions. Most of these jobs were transitory; employment in such industries as aircraft and shipbuilding fell rapidly between 1945 and 1948. Thus, as some analysts have observed, it was if anything *postwar* federal spending policy that sustained high income levels in the Pacific states, "preventing a decline that might otherwise have mirrored the Midwest."[1]

Moreover, the prewar geographic remoteness of the West Coast did not imply impoverishment or backwardness. Because Southern California was already the nation's leading aircraft center by the 1930s, that region's prominence in wartime production was more a consequence of prior development than a cause. In Seattle, Boeing's production of seaplanes for military purposes dates from World War I, not World War II, and the company was already on its way to national competitiveness in the 1920s. Referring to the peninsula that later became known as Silicon Valley—famous for rags-to-riches success stories featuring impecunious inventors toiling in garages—historian Stephen

B. Adams has written that in reality the valley was "born on third base" in light of its tight connections to San Francisco's legal and financial networks and to an "abundance of supporting institutions" in the state of California.[2]

Despite the persuasiveness of these critiques, this chapter nonetheless maintains that World War II was indeed the triggering shock that set in motion chains of events whose outcome was the Pacific Coast economy as we now know it. There were many historical links between World War II and the Cold War, from global geopolitics to domestic political ideologies. The focus here is on the handful of "knowledge economy" clusters that dot the country's western coastline, and the main association is with the far-reaching change in national technology policy that came out of wartime experience. A famous landmark in that transition was the 1945 report to President Roosevelt by Vannevar Bush, titled "Science the Endless Frontier." The report reflected a national consensus that science-based technology had been crucial to winning the war and that investment in science and its applications would better prepare the country for future conflicts. But whereas Bush envisioned a single agency to support basic science for defense and nondefense purposes, as events unfolded, early federal support for research and development was overwhelmingly military in sponsorship. This new stream of technology-oriented funding was unprecedented in scale and qualitatively different from wartime patterns. In particular, it strongly favored establishments and research universities on the West Coast, building an enduring regional infrastructure in the process.

This chapter traces the institutional and economic evolution of four Pacific Coast knowledge-economy clusters from wartime to Cold War to commercialization: Los Angeles, San Francisco Bay Area, Seattle, and San Diego. Devoting primary attention to just these areas may seem limiting, but these were four of the top seven metropolitan-area recipients of prime military contracts in fiscal year 1960; and the largest counties in each comprised four of the top five counties nationally in that year. Three of these counties were among the top seven in 1980, 1990, and 2000.[3] Extreme geographic clustering is one of the hallmarks of the emergent high-tech economy of the twenty-first century, a consideration of far broader significance than can be adequately covered here.[4] Although the four areas have a common heritage in military support for research-intensive enterprise, they differed markedly in their responses to the dramatic cuts in military spending at the end of the Cold War. The Bay Area high-tech economy continued to thrive during and after the transition, so much so that its Cold War origins are frequently forgotten or denied. Los Angeles, in contrast, struggled for decades after the 1990s dismantling of the aerospace economy. Seattle and San Diego represent intermediate variations, cautioning against simple formulaic historical interpretations.

The Economic Impact of World War II

Unquestionably, wartime demands dramatically increased the population and scale of economic activity in the Pacific states. Despite departures for military service, the region's civilian population increased by 2.4 million (25 percent) between 1940 and 1945, primarily from interstate migration. Because the war pulled the region as well as the nation out of the Great Depression, civilian employment grew even more rapidly, led by a doubling of manufacturing jobs. Although California turned migrants away during the 1930s, by 1942 Henry J. Kaiser and other shipyard managers were scouring the country for workers, targeting southern and midwestern cities. By 1943 war authorities declared Los Angeles, Portland-Vancouver, San Diego, San Francisco-Oakland, and Seattle-Tacoma "congested production areas" and placed restrictions on new procurement in these metropolitan areas.[5]

Employment gains were greatest in shipbuilding and aircraft. The Pacific Coast accounted for 52 percent of all vessels produced during the war, and 46 percent of all aircraft. The scale of the project was massive, but two features deserve emphasis: these were industries in which the region had already established strong comparative advantage before the war; and most of the mobilization was transitory, the postwar employment cuts being even more rapid than the wartime buildup. A 1948 report by the San Francisco Federal Reserve concluded: "The distribution of workers among major industry groups is now not markedly different than before the war. Little trace remains of the wartime pattern of employment."[6]

Seeing the wartime experience in longer-term perspective is essential, but there is a danger in overstating the case and seeing the entire episode as fleeting and therefore inconsequential. For one thing, scale matters. Most migrants from other parts of the country chose to stay after the war, despite cutbacks in military employment. Drawing on insights from the New Economic Geography, Paul Rhode finds that "home-market effects" were significant for the postwar regional growth of "nonwar" industries, such as automobiles, rubber tires, petroleum, and chemicals. The larger population required housing, which in turn supported expanded job opportunities in residential construction, infrastructure, transportation, and trade. These trends were no doubt under way before the war, but the pace at which home-market thresholds were crossed clearly increased with the surge in population. In Los Angeles many war production plants were converted into peacetime factories, and new branch plants were opened by such companies as Sylvania Electric, General Motors, and Quaker Oats.[7]

For our purposes, the deeper and more lasting legacies of the war were institutional and political, reflections of what might be called a "ratchet" effect well-documented in both psychology and economics: the powerful impulse to *retain* a status or achievement that has already been attained, as contrasted with open-ended but less intense efforts to improve on the status quo. Historian Roger Lotchin has documented ongoing efforts by California cities to secure federal military dollars for plants, bases, and infrastructure, dating back to the preparedness debates before World War I. But he also shows that in the wake of unprecedented upheaval during World War II, the same cities were determined to hang onto what a state commission called "war winnings." San Diego established a postwar planning committee as early as July 1942, dedicated to retaining payrolls after the war and ensuring the city's future as a "navy-industrial city." The Los Angeles Chamber of Commerce opened an office in Washington, DC, during the war to help local small businesses secure government contracts. The Chamber's Military Affairs Committee was revived and reorganized in 1947, charged to act "in a liaison capacity between the nation's military establishment and local businessmen and industry and to assist the army in the solution of appropriate problems." San Francisco's postwar planning was less focused on naval or aircraft industries, but Bay cities like Vallejo actively lobbied to retain naval bases, and the area foresaw a large federal, defense-based role in hoped-for infrastructure investments. A Bay Area Council publication argued: "Close contacts between Federal and private business groups built up during the war should be continued and strengthened.... Government business—Federal State, and local—is a big business in the Bay Area and is a vital factor in its economy."[8]

What was true for cities held even more strongly for defense firms and universities: nearly all parties hoped to extend wartime economic relationships into the postwar era. It is perhaps not surprising that producers of aircraft, ships, and weapons for the war effort would actively seek defense contracts. Doing so typically required restructuring toward greater technological sophistication, but many firms were able to manage that transition. The leading aerospace firms of the 1950s all descended from major aircraft producers of World War II. They were joined by electronics companies entering aerospace and firms specialized in propulsion units for rockets and engines for aircraft.[9] Wartime experience undoubtedly helped in securing these contracts, but there is little indication that the contracting process itself was geographically biased. Nonetheless the geography of military contracts did shift markedly over time.

The most dramatic discontinuity associated with the war was in the relationship between the federal government and the country's leading research universities. As historians Roger M. Geiger and Creso M. Sa have written: "The mobilization of university scientists during World War II permanently altered the perception and the reality of academic research." It was not that federal military funding invaded and corrupted what had previously been an isolated ivory tower world. Responsiveness to market forces and engagement with private-sector interests have long been distinctive traits of American universities. Caltech in particular was a foremost aeronautical research center before the war, with close ties to aircraft companies, which in turn implied indirect funding from the War Department. Even before Pearl Harbor, the Institute's Kellogg Radiation Lab began work on rocket projectiles, primarily for the Navy. Eventually the rocket project became so big that it took over the Kellogg Lab, the optical shop, the steam plant, the astrophysics shop, Bridge Laboratory of Physics, the Astrophysical Laboratory, and several off-campus buildings as well, prompting the Institute's historian to call it "an educational institution in name only during the war." Afterward the Institute returned to its educational mission, but with a substantially increased role for federally funded research (especially including the National Aeronautics and Space Administration, founded in 1958).[10]

The most famous research mission was the Manhattan Project to develop an atomic bomb, often said to have ushered in the age of "Big Science." But many other projects were contracted to research universities, and wartime experience established many basic institutional arrangements that persisted afterward. Vannevar Bush, director of the Office of Scientific Research and Development (OSRD) during the war, understood that an important background objective was to strengthen the infrastructure of scientific departments and industrial labs, so institutional overhead rates were relatively generous. This policy was continued after the war, when for idiosyncratic reasons, the Office of Naval Research emerged as the primary provider of federal research funding. Although Bush himself pictured broad support for science in the interests of both national security and economic progress, the advent of the Cold War meant that defense funding led the way. Military historian Paul Koistinen has written: “Money flowing from the armed services was unlike anything academia had ever seen or imagined.”[11]

Nothing in this emerging policy was intended to support any one region more than another. Berkeley’s Radiation Laboratory (later the Lawrence Laboratory) was an important player in the Manhattan Project, but no more so than the MIT Radiation Laboratory or the Applied Physics Laboratory at Johns Hopkins. But the new orientation of US technology in a science-driven direction may reasonably be considered an effect of World War II, which ultimately did have important regional consequences. The regime change was sufficiently visible that even Stanford University, which played no important role in wartime research, understood that tapping into defense support was the key to future institutional success. Frederick Terman, then a rising Stanford engineer, spent the war years directing the Radio Research Laboratory (RRL, a spinoff of MIT’s Rad Lab) at Harvard, an experience that impressed upon him the importance of close interaction between scientists and engineers for institutions that aspired to elite status.

Pondering his personal plans late in the war, Terman wrote to his colleague Paul Davis: “The years after the war are going to be very important and also *very critical* ones for Stanford. I believe that we will either consolidate our potential strength, and create a foundation for a position in the west somewhat analogous to that of Harvard in the East, or we will drop to a level somewhat similar to that of Dartmouth, a well thought of institution having about 2 per cent as much influence on national life as Harvard.” In pursuit of this goal, Terman returned to Stanford as dean of engineering, bringing at least eleven former RRL members with him. Contacts with the ONR developed by Terman and his RRL colleagues also proved valuable, as this agency soon became Stanford’s largest funder.[12]

The Cold War and the Pacific Coast Economy

The postwar rise of the Pacific Coast economy may thus be seen as the intersection of two war-related but largely separate developments: regional population growth accelerated by the war, and the shift into science-based technologies coming out of wartime experience. But there was a third contingency, by no means independent of the first two but not historically inevitable: the intensification of the Cold War and consequent expansion of federal defense spending. Some observers have argued that this process was itself a reflection of a ratchet effect, as military agencies and their clients resisted budget cuts and actively lobbied for more resources. This perspective may well have validity, but it is undeniable that fears of the Soviet Union in the postwar era were real, punctuated by the 1948 Communist coup in Czechoslovakia, the Berlin Blockade of 1948–49, and the Soviet atomic bomb detonation in August 1949. According to economic historian Paul Rhode, West Coast business leaders in the immediate postwar years did not foresee military spending as a plausible long-term foundation for the region's economy. But such skepticism was swept away with the surge in spending after the outbreak of the Korean War in 1950. By that year, employment in defense-related industries such as aircraft and electronics (though not shipbuilding) exceeded wartime peaks; the same was true of defense R&D budgets.[13]

Even during the pre–Korean War years when defense spending was relatively stable, the development of Cold War institutional arrangements continued virtually without interruption. The Federal Airport Act of 1946, providing generous federal support for urban airport projects, was billed in part as a defense measure, foreshadowing the creation of the National System of Interstate and Defense Highways in the 1950s.[14] The ONR continued its cultivation of relationships with academic scientists and departments, supporting projects at two hundred institutions almost immediately after the war's end and interpreting the defense-related research mission broadly. Private industry had relatively little interest in direct support for academic science at the time, but firms responded eagerly to the prospect of drawing upon federal R&D funding, often with close ties to universities.[15]

Meanwhile, new organizational forms were taking shape to pursue mutual interests of defense agencies, universities, and private businesses. Project RAND was initiated in 1946 as a research arm of the Douglas Aircraft Corporation, with an infusion of funds from the Army Air Force, to consolidate scientific and technological research on air warfare. Because of conflicting interests among companies, the organization became an independent nonprofit corporation in 1948—one year after the Air Force itself became an independent military service. Primarily funded by the military, RAND made numerous technological contributions in such areas as orbital satellites, material science, airborne reconnaissance, and over-horizon radar, but subsequently broadened its scope to encompass complex systems, the cost-effectiveness of weapons systems, linear programming, and game theory.[16] The Stanford Research Institute, founded

TABLE 3.1 *Total military prime contract awards, by region*

	Annual average					
	World War II (1941–45)		Korea (1951–53)		1961	
Regions	US$ millions	US spending (%)	US$ millions	US spending (%)	US$ millions	US spending (%)
New England	3,701	8.9	2,573	8.1	2,334	10.5
Middle Atlantic	9,817	23.6	7,955	25.1	4,397	19.9
East North Central	13,468	32.4	8,696	27.4	2,606	11.8
West North Central	2,329	5.6	2,170	6.8	1,285	5.8
South Atlantic	2,988	7.2	2,382	7.6	2,345	10.6
South Central	3,640	8.8	2,028	6.4	1,812	8.2
Mountain	477	1.2	214	0.7	1,267	5.7
Pacific	5,102	12.3	5,680	17.9	5,951	26.9
Alaska and Hawaii	—	—	—	—	119	0.6
California	3,795	9.1	4,323	13.6	5,277	23.9
TOTAL	41,522	100	31,697	100	22,112	100

SOURCE: US Department of Defense, Office of the Secretary of Defense, "The Changing Patterns of Defense Procurement, June 1962," Tables I and III.

in 1946 with a large loan from the University, soon became a leading client of the ONR and consultant to such firms as the Chevron Corporation and the Disney Company. The Stanford Industrial Park opened in 1951. Early tenants included Varian Associates, General Electric Microwave tube division, Hewlett-Packard, and other electronics firms—nearly all of whom drew heavily on defense contracts.[17]

Although the preservation and expansion of military spending was in many ways a continuation of developments launched during World War II, the transition to the Cold War witnessed a remarkable change in the geographic distribution of these funds. The shift is succinctly summarized in Table 3.1, extracted from a report issued by the Secretary of Defense in 1962. Whereas the Pacific states received just 12.3 percent of military prime contract awards during the war, that share jumped to 23.9 percent in 1961, with California the largest gainer by far. While every other region experienced a decline in military contract awards across the three periods, funding in the Mountain and Pacific regions actually increased over time. Somewhat defensive about this regional imbalance, the report—issued in response to "many inquiries for information on the geographic distribution of defense contracts"—insisted: "Defense policy stresses awards on merit." Its summary explanation was as follows: "We have moved swiftly away from mass production into research, development and small quantity production as the normal character of major weapon system procurement. This phenomenon has created significant change in the military industrial base in many communities, states and regions. The report recommends no course of action. It should be recognized, however, that Defense must seek its needs where capability exists, in order to be responsive to the technological requirements of modern warfare."[18]

The report goes on to document the increase in contracts supporting "experimental, developmental, test and research work," especially the "vast expansion of missiles and electronics procurement."[19] Thirty years later, these themes were picked up and elaborated by economic geographer Ann Markusen and her collaborators in *The Rise of the Gunbelt*, which argued that the western military-industrial frontier featured a "new locational logic" in which the continual pressure to innovate to satisfy demanding technological standards reinforced tendencies toward agglomeration, clustering, and extreme geographic concentration.[20] Confirming the secretary of defense's 1962 observation that "a Region [*sic*] that gains a long head start in a new and expanding field of procurement is bound to enjoy an enduring advantage, especially when R&D is a primary element," these authors found that regional distribution maps of procurement and defense-related manufacturing were essentially stable from the 1950s through the 1980s. They warned, however, that regions dependent on specialized production for military demand were highly vulnerable to funding cuts, as occurred in the 1990s with the end of the Cold War.[21] Subsequent sections reconsider this prognosis with respect to the two main bases for technological clustering in the Cold War era: aerospace and electronics.

Aircraft and Aerospace

The Pacific region was already a major center of aircraft production prior to World War II. Between 1929 and 1939, California surpassed New York to become the leading aircraft state, as measured by employment, establishments, or value-added. In seeking to understand this pattern, one has to contend with the powerful retrospective impulse to see it as the inevitable consequence of geographic conditions—chiefly the mild climate and favorable terrain for flying. Rigorous analyses, however, almost always reject such natural advantages as decisive for aircraft production. Firms were located throughout the country in the prewar era, including such inclement areas as Buffalo (Curtiss-Wright) and Seattle (Boeing). Aerospace historian Peter Westwick has noted that "almost all aerospace work was, in the end, conducted indoors." In his classic 1951 study of the aircraft industry, economic geographer William Cunningham acknowledged a role for climate but identified the key characteristics of the main product: "The airplane is a nonstandardized product created largely for the military market. With such a product in such a market, performance, even above cost, often determines the allocation of contracts and the survival of firms." As early as 1927 through 1933, military sales accounted for two-thirds to three-fourths of sales for leading aircraft manufacturers.[22]

What drove Pacific Coast aircraft leadership in the interwar years was new technology originating in the West, specifically the "airframe revolution" that replaced wooden frames with metal and set new standards for speed and efficiency. Notable models included Lockheed's L-10 Electra (1933), Boeing's 247 (1934), and Douglas Aircraft's DC series, which dominated commercial sales by the late 1930s. An important individual figure was John Northrop, a committed Californian who worked for both Lockheed and Douglas before founding his own firm in 1932. Northrop's designs emphasized aerodynamic streamlining and stressed-skin metal construction, providing much of the technological basis for US leadership in the industry. This period also saw important regional developments in infrastructure, such as the founding of the Guggenheim Aeronautical Laboratory (forerunner of the Jet Propulsion Laboratory) at Caltech in 1929, under the directorship of Theodore von Kármán. Douglas provided instructors to the school to teach aircraft design, and in turn the firm made much use of the Caltech wind tunnel during the 1930s. Even Boeing arranged to use the Caltech wind tunnel from far-off Seattle, though that firm developed closer ties to aeronautical engineers at the University of Washington. One may also observe the prewar emergence of networks of subcontract shops and parts suppliers: in addition to its six major aircraft assembly plants, Los Angeles in 1939 featured thirty aircraft accessories and parts suppliers and three aeronautical instruments manufacturers.[23]

Prewar aircraft in the Los Angeles area thus displayed many features that later became prominent in Pacific Coast knowledge clusters: military demand for high-performance products, links between private firms and research uni-

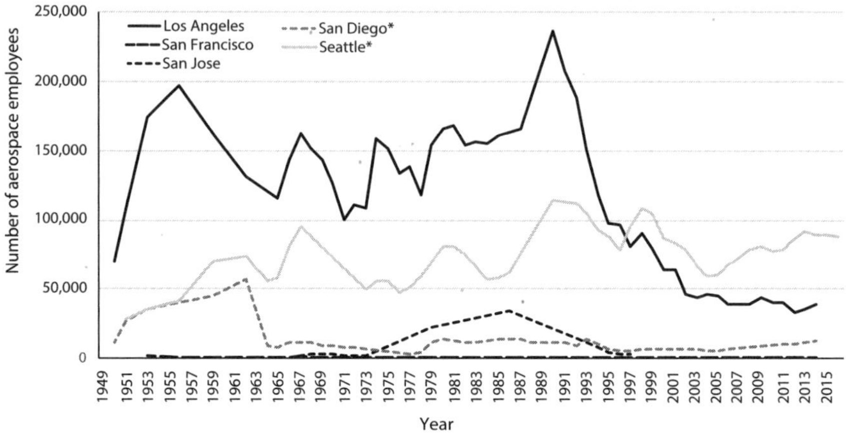

FIGURE 3.1 Aircraft and aerospace employment by metropolitan statistical area (MSA), 1949–2014. *Source*: County Business Patterns, various years. Seattle MSA 1990–2016 from Washington State Employment Security Department, Historical Employment Estimates. *Aircraft and Parts only.

versities, interfirm mobility of leading inventors, and local networks of specialized suppliers and skilled labor. The area's response to wartime demands certainly built on these strengths, though the war years actually saw a decline in the coastal shares of production. These features were accentuated in the postwar era by increases in scale and in the scientific sophistication of the industry.

Figure 3.1 shows the rapid growth of aerospace employment in the Los Angeles metropolitan area at the time of the Korean War. The industry employed more than 40 percent of manufacturing workers in Los Angeles County throughout the 1950s and 1960s, in an era when manufacturing drove economic growth for the region and state. Spreading into Orange County and further south and west after 1960, the metropolitan statistical area (MSA) accounted for 75 to 80 percent of aerospace employment in California. As pioneering aviation companies exited the midwestern cities in which they originated, the Los Angeles area seemed to exert a powerful gravitational force for profit-seeking firms in this fast-changing industry.[24]

From one perspective, the concentration of aerospace in the greater Los Angeles area can be seen as a direct consequence of federal policy choices, "a strong case of California-itis" on the part of key decisionmakers, particularly by the Air Force. The Army Air Corps looked west for advanced technologies throughout the war, continuing its support for rocket research at Caltech's Jet Propulsion Laboratory and in 1946 awarding a $1.9 million contract for a missile study to Consolidated-Vultee (Convair), then of Los Angeles. Hughes Aircraft of Culver City recruited Caltech PhDs Simon Ramo and Dean Wooldridge in 1945 to build capability in advanced aviation electronics, winning an $8 million contract to produce radar weapons control units in 1948. A watershed for regional aerospace was the report of the Strategic Missile Evaluation Committee, appointed in 1953 and chaired by John von Neumann, which endorsed development of an intercontinental ballistic missile (ICBM) with a nuclear warhead. The report led directly to establishment of an Air Research and Development field office on the West Coast and to the Western Development Division (WDD) and the Special Aircraft Project Office, both based in Inglewood, California. So committed was the Air Force to southern California for missile projects that it petitioned the Eisenhower administration for an exemption to the policy requiring that missile development as well as production be dispersed away from coastal areas. Although initially rejected, the exemption was granted by the secretary of the Air Force in 1955.[25]

The geographic preferences of Air Force officials, however, can hardly be attributed to idiosyncratic regional loyalties or favoritism. Taking a longer view, it seems clear that decisionmakers responded to already established capacity in key technologies, on the part of individual firms and even individual scientists and engineers. Air Force decisions in the early 1950s were undoubtedly central, but by the end of that decade there may have been little real choice, given the objective of developing complex systems with many interdependent components and the sense of urgency provided by the Cold War context. The Air Force philosophy of relying on private-sector expertise put a premium on identifying the most technically advanced firms and called for new organizational forms to supervise and coordinate the work—further enhancing the value of proximity. Thus the petition for exemption to the dispersal policy invoked the importance of avoiding delays in development schedules, and the waiver was approved so that the ICBM program would be "restricted only by technological considerations."[26]

These agglomeration economies tended to cumulate and become institutionalized over time. Both UCLA and USC established aeronautical engineering programs in the 1940s, and research laboratories, both corporate-sponsored and independent, dotted the landscape in the 1950s. More market-based forms of institutionalization were local networks of suppliers and service firms as well as a stock of skilled workers and engineers residing in the area. Empirical verification may be found in sociologist Allen J. Scott's 1993 book *Technopolis*, presenting survey evidence from the late 1980s. Scott documented a "dense local web" of transactions and subcontracting activity, especially among smaller establishments, featuring frequent face-to-face contact and site visits. Employee residences tended to cluster in island-type groups tightly defined by establishment size and journey-to-work distances. The survey question on previous employment revealed a "fair degree of shifting around," especially among younger workers, but the moves (including those of scientists and engineers) were primarily within the metropolitan area. Writing just after end of the Cold War, Scott was careful to note that this fine-tuned adaptation in one specialized sector left the area vulnerable to cutbacks in military spending.[27]

San Diego is sometimes included as part of a broader southern California supply chain, and that city enjoyed a dramatic but brief aerospace surge in the 1950s (see Figure 3.1), when Convair (now relocated to San Diego) recaptured a lead role in the first WDD prime missile contract, to build what became the Atlas missile. With the takeover of Convair by General Dynamics, the venture gained renewed vigor in its new location at the Kearney Mesa Industrial Park, created by the city in 1958 to house precisely such a project. After 1962, however, San Diego aerospace lost out to competition in both military and commercial markets, an early taste of the dangers of specializing in defense industries. But the city had a more stable economic base through its long-term association with the Navy, and more important, its broader scientific and technological infrastructure continued to develop across the decades. The Scripps Institution of Oceanography (SIO), whose origins predated World War I, established a vital research link with the Navy during World War II, culminating in the Naval Electronics Laboratory (NEL, a consolidation of two existing labs) in 1945. The NEL engaged in important research on precision radar navigation and electronic recognition systems, moving on to marine life issues such as the sudden disappearance of the California sardine fishery. The combined clout of SIO, Convair, and defense contractor General Atomic generated pressure for a San Diego campus of the University of California, which welcomed its first undergraduates in 1964. UCSD became the base for a world-class biological and health sciences complex by the end of the century.[28]

Seattle offers an instructive variant case: an aerospace center second only to Los Angeles in scale yet distinct in its domination by the Boeing Company. As early as the 1920s, when the company won big contracts from both the US

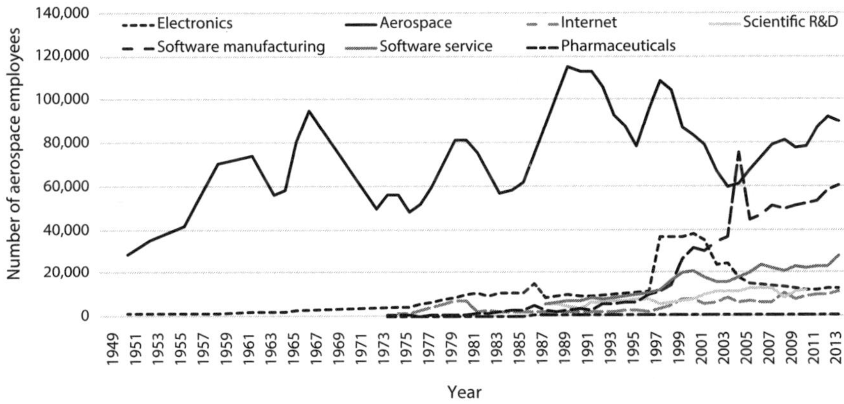

FIGURE 3.2 Seattle metropolitan statistical area (MSA) employment by industry, 1951–2015. *Source*: County Business Patterns, various issues. Aerospace for 1990–2015 is from Washington State Employment Security Department, Historical Employment Estimates.

Army and Navy, Boeing was distinctive among aircraft firms in building its own airliners and operating them over its own routes. Like other Pacific Coast cities, the Seattle MSA experienced rapid growth in both aircraft and shipbuilding during World War II but failed to develop the complex local supplier and labor market networks seen in Los Angeles. Figure 3.2 shows the roller-coaster character of Seattle aerospace employment, including devastating cutbacks in the 1970s associated with cancellation of the SST by Congress in 1971 and NASA's winding down of lunar exploration. Writing in 1991, economist Ann Markusen and colleagues called Seattle "a classic example of an ossified, single-sector economy, where one or a few firms dominate local resource markets."[29]

Domination by a single firm had its compensations, however, in that Boeing internalized many aspects of the MSA, serving as what one analyst calls a "surrogate university." Thus in 1970 Boeing formed a wholly owned subsidiary called Boeing Computer Services (BCS), which became the region's largest software supplier by the 1980s. Boeing also maintained a high-wage internal labor market, sponsoring programs at local high schools and colleges. The company itself became more stable after the huge losses of the early 1970s, emphasizing risk-sharing with contractors. Unlike other dominant firms, Boeing did not fight departures by employees launching their own companies; as many as thirty-seven Seattle start-ups in high-tech trace their origins to Boeing or

BCS. The area's fortunes may have been enhanced by the fortuitous loyalties of individuals: Seattle native Dr. William B. Hutchinson founded both the Pacific Northwest Research Foundation and the Fred Hutchinson Cancer Research Center in the late 1950s; Bill Gates and Paul Allen (both Washington natives) brought Microsoft to Seattle in 1979. But these moves would have been less likely and less successful if the area were not already congenial to high-tech enterprise. On all of these fronts, Seattle was better positioned than Los Angeles to respond to cuts in military spending in the 1990s.[30]

Computers and Electronics

The technologies now most closely associated with Silicon Valley represent a confluence of two earlier technological streams: computers, traceable back to the Jacquard Loom and Hollerith's punch cards, leading to the ENIAC computer at the University of Pennsylvania in 1946; and semiconductor electronics, coming out of wartime research on radar for submarine detection and the invention of the point contact transistor at Bell Labs in 1947. Neither of these originated on the Pacific Coast, and in both cases fundamental postwar developments took place in older parts of the country. Prior to the marriage of the two streams, it was widely believed that demand for giant vacuum-tube computers would be limited to less than one hundred nationwide. As with aerospace, the vast majority of semiconductor R&D was funded from the defense budget. Even at Bell Labs, nominally in the private sector, improvements on the transistor were driven by high performance standards demanded by the military: tolerance of extreme temperatures, resistance to radiation, and the ability to amplify high-frequency signals.[31]

Not only were core technologies in flux during the 1950s, but the division of labor between northern and southern California had not yet taken clear shape. Some of the earliest customers for computers were aerospace companies, because of the enormous computational requirements of aircraft design. Computer pioneers J. Presper Eckert and John Mauchly, lacking academic positions or financial support, signed a contract in 1946 with the Northrop Aircraft Company to design a digital computer to be used for guidance of the Snark missile, then under development for the Air Force. The Northrop computer group also contracted with a little-known Palo Alto firm named Hewlett-Packard to produce a series of digital difference analyzers for missile guidance. Hughes Aircraft made military computers until the mid-1950s, and the Rand Corporation built the JOHNNIAC computer (named for Von Neumann) in 1953.[32]

At the same time, the Bay Area had a long-standing tradition in aeronautics, also with strong military connections. Stanford had an aeronautical engineering program in the interwar years, supplying many of the top people at Lockheed and other southern California firms. After years of lobbying, the National Advisory Committee on Aeronautics opened its new aerodynamics laboratory (the Ames Research Center, later called Moffett Field) in Sunnyvale in 1939; with the Alameda Naval Air Station and the Army's Hamilton Field, the area had a place in the research and repair sections of the industry. Northern California largely missed out on the postwar aviation boom, but the Hiller Aircraft Company employed mechanics from East Bay shipyards and aerodynamicists from Stanford and Cal Poly to win many R&D contracts for helicopters in the 1950s. A major event for the peninsula was the move of Lockheed Missiles and Space to Sunnyvale and into the Stanford Industrial Park in 1956. Building on the peninsula's expertise in electronics, Lockheed won big missile contracts from the Navy, the Air Force, and the CIA, becoming the valley's largest employer by the 1960s.[33]

The main stream to Silicon Valley, however, was through semiconductor electronics, propelled by Cold War military support and demand. As in aerospace, there were prewar beginnings. Historian Christophe Lécuyer has recounted the early activities of William Eitel, Jack McCullough, and Charles Litton—Peninsula ham radio enthusiasts who became expert at making "power" vacuum tubes for long-distance transmission. Their expertise was sufficiently advanced that the Naval Research Laboratory and the Signal Corp Engineering Laboratories in New Jersey asked Eitel and McCullough in 1937 to adapt their tubes to the specific requirements of their radar systems. The firm mechanized production methods in response to wartime demands and expanded to thirty-six hundred employees by the summer of 1943. Litton was also interested in power tubes but found his niche making glass lathes and other equipment for tube producers. Both firms recovered well from the postwar crisis, becoming major manufacturers of microwave tubes. Litton in particular had strong ties to Stanford University, serving as lecturer and adviser to the new vacuum electronics program. Litton was also business mentor to David Packard and William Hewlett as they launched their electronic instrumentation company.[34]

Figure 3.3 shows the steady growth of electronics employment in the San Jose MSA after 1950, accelerating in the mid-1970s. The leading subcategories within this growth spurt were computers and peripherals, components, and communications equipment, all closely linked to the semiconductor economy.

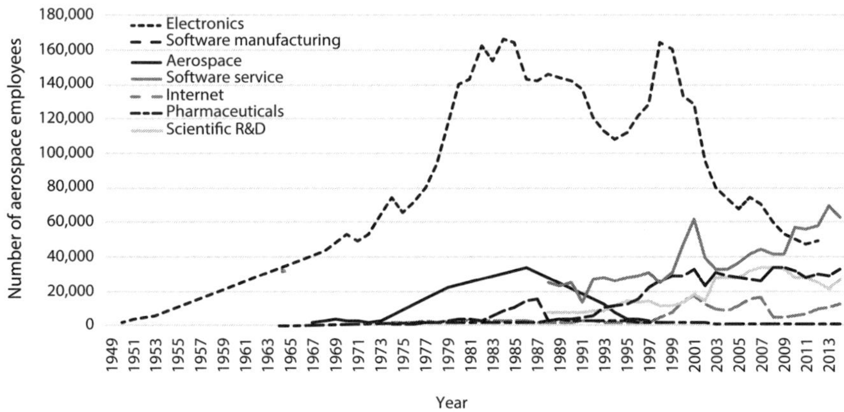

FIGURE 3.3 San Jose metropolitan statistical area (MSA) employment by industry, 1949–2014. *Source*: County Business Patterns, various issues. Industries shift from SIC (Standard Industrial Classification) to NAIC (North American Industrial Classification) codes in 1998.

On one reading, the rise of Silicon Valley represented an organic coevolution of technology and institutions, a "social process of bricolage…an unplanned iterative learning process" leading to a "regional recipe for creating and nurturing startups," in the words of scholars Martin Kenney and Donald Patton. A notable landmark in this narrative was the move of William Shockley (co-inventor of the transistor) to Mountain View in 1956—fortuitous because Shockley's mother lived in Palo Alto, where he himself grew up—but not strictly exogenous because Provost Frederick Terman had encouraged the inventor to locate his new firm near Stanford. When Shockley's despotic managerial methods led to the resignations of the firm's leading employees, this "traitorous eight" formed an alliance with Fairchild Camera and Instruments of Long Island, one of the first venture capital agreements on the West Coast. Fairchild Semiconductor soon became famous not just for pioneering the planar process and its commercial success, but for establishing the pattern of spinoffs and high mobility among technical people in the Valley. These economic arrangements and supportive entrepreneurial culture were celebrated by AnnaLee Saxenian in her 1994 book *Regional Advantage*, comparing the Valley's external-economy structure favorably to the internal economies of large, vertically integrated corporations on the East Coast. Historians differ on the relative importance of large corporations, start-ups, dense personal networks, venture capital, and

Stanford, but these are largely matters of emphasis on what is best seen as an interdependent coevolutionary process.[35]

If instead we search for ranges of plausible historical variation, however, it is difficult to escape the conclusion that the entire process would not have been launched, much less boosted to escape velocity, if it had not been for research funding from federal military sources, traceable to the Cold War and in turn back to World War II. As late as 1959, more than 85 percent of US electronics R&D was funded by the federal government, overwhelmingly from defense. In the early days on the peninsula, even local firms deploying practical skills and workmanship, like Eitel-McCullough and Litton, actively pursued military contracts at every opportunity, enjoying their most rapid growth during the Korean War. Military demand dominated early markets for transistors and then for integrated circuits, leaving a lasting impact on specifications and direction for these technologies. At Stanford, the Korean War doubled the size of the electronics program. When the Department of Defense through its Advanced Research Projects Agency (ARPA) sought to establish materials science as an academic discipline, alert responses by metallurgist Robert Huggins won contracts from the Air Force and the Navy, boosting the new department near the top of national rankings. The promise of rising support from military agencies loomed large at a time when support from private industry for university research was essentially stationary.[36]

What was so special about military funding? Defense agencies served as both investors and purchasers, with limited concern for price; sole-source contracts provided a market for new, complex components that were still too expensive for industrial or commercial markets. But the defense budget was by no means simply a gravy train for easy money. Military purchasers could be extremely demanding in terms of technical requirements and delivery times. Fairchild's high-frequency transistors did not initially meet the reliability criteria of the Minuteman ICBM. Adapting its technologies to meet these standards pushed the firm to innovate, first through the planar process and then the integrated circuit. The demands of military avionics impelled Fairchild to set up a Reliability Evaluation Division to appraise the dependability of transistors, logging millions of transistor-hours of testing, "orders of magnitude higher than those results from previous evaluations in the industry."[37]

The prominence of defense funding does not imply that firms' technological horizons were restricted to military objectives. Although large corporations like IBM were reluctant to invest large sums in risky projects in the 1950s, Thomas

Watson Jr., and other IBM leaders clearly saw electronic calculation as a path toward new commercial markets. The IBM research laboratory in San Jose, opened in 1952 to develop random-access disc storage devices, drew heavily on defense funding but also designed low-cost data processing systems for very small businesses. Retrospective remarks by Robert Noyce and Gordon Moore minimizing the role of defense funding for Fairchild seem amnesic, but there is little reason to doubt their recollection that the firm saw semiconductors as a general-use technology and actively pursued commercial applications from the beginning. Yet it was the scale of the defense market that drove progress down the learning curve, reducing costs and opening market possibilities.[38]

Because the military wanted to cultivate American technological capabilities, sponsors often promoted dissemination of information as broadly as possible. Early in the development of transistor, Bell Labs was tasked with holding a symposium featuring lectures and demonstrations to representatives from military services, universities, and electronics firms. A second conference for Bell licensees in 1952 distributed more detailed information, generating two substantial volumes that became known as "the Bible" of transistor technology. At Stanford's Applied Electronics Laboratory, part of the understanding with its military sponsors was that it would work closely with industrial firms, streamlining the transition from prototypes to deliverables. Defense-related procurement also facilitated entry of specialized semiconductor firms: in 1959 such firms received only 22 percent government R&D funds but accounted for 63 percent of sales to the federal government. When UC Berkeley opened its integrated circuits laboratory in 1962, they were assisted by Gordon Moore of Fairchild and by military contractors such as Westinghouse and Texas Instruments, who were instructed by the Air Force to share their semiconductor manufacturing expertise. Fairchild's founders actively encouraged technicians to establish their own equipment-supply firms, extending the Valley's start-up tradition.[39]

The End of the Cold War and the Civilianization of High-Tech

Military R&D spending fluctuated markedly across time. Figure 3.4 tracks the value of prime contracts relative to personal income, for California and for the nation. After a brief hiatus at the end of the Korean War, the launch of Sputnik in October 1957 led in quick succession to the creation of the Advanced Research Projects Agency (later DARPA) to execute R&D projects and the

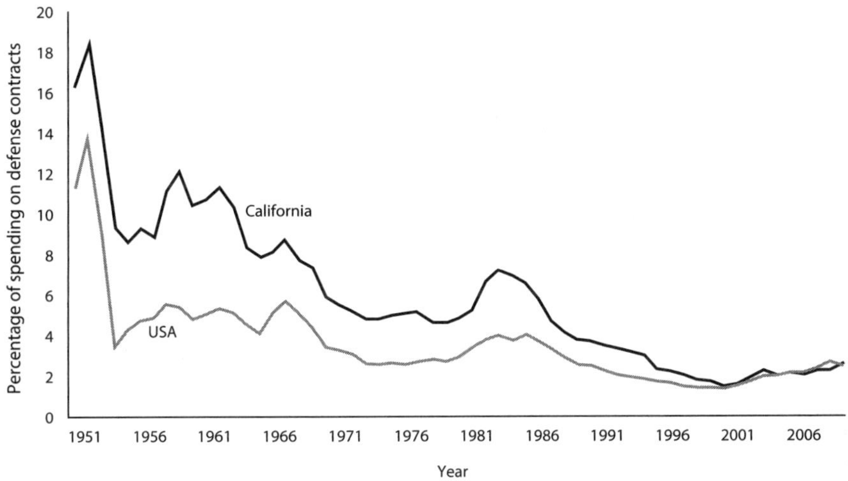

FIGURE 3.4 Prime defense contracts as a percentage of personal income, 1951–2009. *Source*: 1951–1964, 1975–1981, 1986–1988: Department of Defense, Prime Contract Awards by Region and State; other years Statistical Abstract of the United States, various issues.

National Aeronautics and Space Act creating NASA. Although NASA was a civilian agency, the space race was undeniably part of the Cold War. Vietnam caused another spending spurt in the 1960s, followed by a decade of steady decline. The Reagan buildup of the 1980s interrupted the trend, but cutbacks had resumed even before the fall of the Soviet Union in 1989. As Figure 3.4 shows, both expansions and long-term decline were magnified in California relative to the nation as a whole.

Despite the formative role of military R&D spending for the nation's scientific and technological infrastructure, by the 1980s distinctly different voices could be heard about the continued value of these programs. Observing competitive inroads in markets for advanced manufactured goods, critics complained that defense-oriented technologies put American producers at a disadvantage relative to countries like Japan and Germany, whose engineers could concentrate on "leading-edge technologies devoted to socially useful ends." Studies appeared with such titles as *The Militarization of High Technology*, *Military Expansion Economic Decline*, or *The Baroque Arsenal*. Writers sometimes grudgingly acknowledged a few transfers into civilian uses, such as computers, jet planes, and lasers, but these were considered rare and overly expensive when they did occur. As analyst Robert DeGrasse Jr. put it: "Using scientific and engineering talent to solve military problems is an inefficient means of stimulating scientific or commercial advancement." Such formulations seemed to take underlying national technological capabilities as a given, viewing deployment of these resources for military pursuits as "skewed" and "inefficient." With the end of the Cold War, defense analysts contended even more forcefully that because of the high degree of segregation between military and commercial activities, the "spinoff model" was outdated and inefficient.[40]

From this perspective, one of the worst aspects of a sophisticated, high-tech military was that whole communities became dependent on highly specialized economic pursuits and hence exposed to fluctuations in defense policy. In their portentous 1992 critique, economists Ann Markusen and Joel Yudkin wrote that the rise of the so-called Gunbelt "has led to increasing geographical segregation of military-industrial activities from other sectors in the economy, creating communities with pro-military cultures and greater vulnerability to downturns in the military spending cycle." The authors identified several major metropolitan areas as highly dependent on defense spending, listing Los Angeles and San Diego ("California is perhaps the most vulnerable, at least in absolute terms") and "Seattle as a one-company industrial city." At the root of the regional adjustment problem, according to defense industry surveys, is that firms committed to the military found it "difficult if not impossible... to make the transition to nondefense businesses." A spokesman for the Aerospace Industry Association said that "conversion is baloney... these [defense] companies use highly specialized technologies." Norman Augustine, CEO of Lockheed-Martin, said that "conversion efforts have been unblemished by success."[41]

In hindsight, we can now say that some defense-dependent metropolitan areas were more successful than others in the transition to civilian markets. The Bay Area was not included on the endangered-regions lists of the 1990s because well before that decade, many of its leading firms had achieved effective independence from military funding. Ongoing progress in semiconductor technology opened up major new markets in consumer electronics, such as microwave ovens, transistor radios, burglar alarms, and soon personal computers. So rapid was the transition that leading entrepreneurs came to minimize the role of military funding in their own histories. Robert Noyce claimed that Fairchild had "stayed clear of military involvement... because I thought it was an affront to any research people to say that you are not worth supporting out of real money," while his colleague Gordon Moore wrote that "from our perspective, the impact exerted by defense R&D was quite small." In fact, Santa

Clara County continued to be a leading recipient of prime military contracts throughout the 1990s, but these transactions did not deter prominent executives from a hands-off, antigovernment rhetoric that did violence to the historical record. One venture capitalist told the *New York Times* in October 2000: "I've worked in the valley since 1963... and I don't think government ever had a role in it." The vagaries of memory can be vexing to the historian, but their presence indicates that Silicon Valley saw its path of escape from the "defense trap" from an early point. Moving Fairchild's department of application engineering from R&D to marketing in 1961 was perhaps symbolic.[42]

The semiconductor industry stumbled in the 1980s, more from Japanese competition than defense cutbacks; but it recovered strongly in the 1990s, partly through accelerated technological change but primarily by shifting toward design-intensive product innovation. Market fundamentalists had their worldviews reinforced when NSF's 1994 announcement of plans to privatize the internet launched the dot-com boom of the late 1990s, centered in Silicon Valley. Despite the excesses of that half decade, the area emerged in the twenty-first century as the world's largest and strongest high-tech economy. The transition from military to commercial markets was as smooth as the transition from hardware to software (see Figure 3.3).[43]

The transition for LA aerospace was never that easy. In 1987, California had one in four aerospace jobs nationally, Los Angeles County alone accounting for one in ten. Within ten years of the end of the Cold War, aerospace employment had fallen by more than 50 percent, and by 2011 to less than one-third of its peak. Economists and policy analysts have debated the incidence of these cuts since the 1990s, with somewhat inconclusive results. Close industry observers such as Maryellen Kelly and Todd Watkins rejected the caricature of overspecialized military contractors, insulated from competition and out of touch with civilian technologies; they pointed to many examples of defense firms shifting into commercial production, such as ultra-lightweight insulation (Aerojet), satellite TV systems (Hughes), navigation gear for commercial aircraft (Litton), and laser machine tools for assembly lines (TRW). Many plants shut down, however, and according to economists Valery Ramey and Matthew Shapiro, their capital was highly "sector specific" and sold at steep discounts. Employees had more mobility than physical capital, but studies found that displaced aerospace engineers experienced long unemployment spells and a decline in earnings after finding new positions. The ultimate outcome for displaced workers is difficult to determine, however, because an estimated 60 percent of those who lost their jobs migrated out of the region. A study by UCLA geographers concludes: "After the end of the Cold War, Los Angeles never re-established its previous levels of focus in technology-related industry." The authors argue that the root of the area's problem was not the direct costs of defense cutbacks, but the failure to replace aerospace with a new technological focus. In other words, Los Angeles was not Silicon Valley.[44]

The contrast between the two metropolitan areas is multifaceted. One important factor is simply that defense aerospace is more specialized and less readily transferable between sectors than the diverse cluster of electronic and information technologies that characterize the Bay Area. Defense consultant James Hasik has noted that "the development processes for military and commercial aircraft are quite different, particularly because combat aircraft producers have not often profitably speculated on projects." Geographer Michael Storper and coauthors have shown that as late as 1990, Los Angeles and the Bay Area were comparable by such measures as patents granted in high-technology industries or net local patent citations—an index of intraregional knowledge synergies—but diverged markedly after that date. The authors attribute the difference to the Bay Area's early specialization in highly paid, nonroutine economic activities, and more deeply to better-developed networks of civic activism for the region.[45]

A simple theory of intrinsic sectoral properties is contradicted by the counterexample of Seattle, even more aerospace-centered than Los Angeles, but which managed a relatively smooth transition into a diversified knowledge economy. Boeing was one of the most diversified major defense contractors all along, adapting well to both domestic and export markets after 1995, so that overall aerospace employment in Seattle held up remarkably well (see Figure 3.2). Despite shifting its corporate headquarters to Chicago in 2001, Boeing over the years invested substantially in the area's infrastructure of schools, social services, and arts. The growth of Microsoft as a second "hub" also spawned generations of internet and software companies, the founding of Amazon.com by Jeff Bezos in 1994 being a prime example. The start-up culture now extends to commercial aerospace, merging the city's two lineages.[46]

Figure 3.5 compares per capita income in the four metropolitan areas, relative to the national average. Per capita income is an imperfect index of economic performance, yet the post–Cold War surges of the Bay Area and Seattle are evident, as is the decline of Los Angeles over the same period. San Diego represents an interesting variant (Figure 3.6). Without historic strengths in

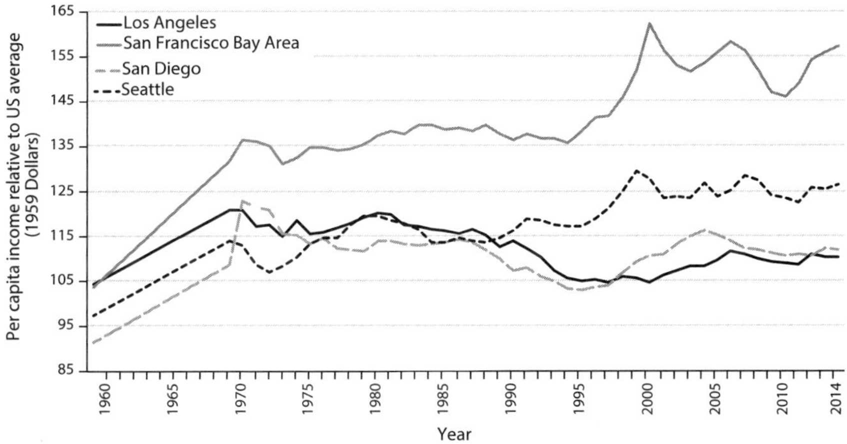

FIGURE 3.5 Per capita income relative to US average, four metropolitan statistical areas (MSAs), 1959–2014. *Source*: Hannah M. Anderson, ed., *Patterns of Economic Change by State and Area* (Lanham, MD: Bernan Press, 2016).

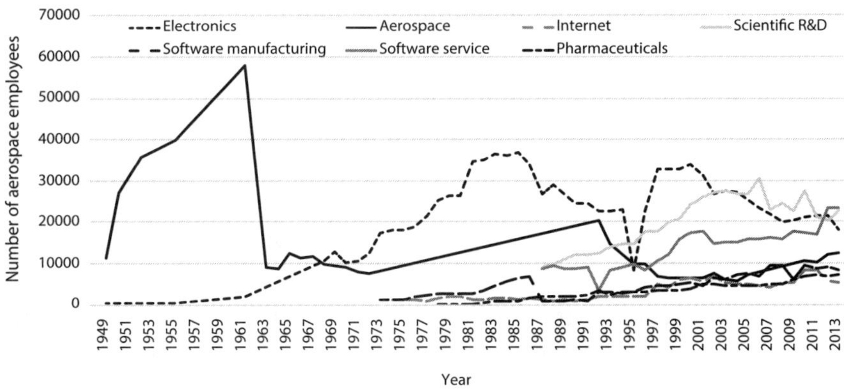

FIGURE 3.6 San Diego metropolitan statistical area (MSA) employment by industry, 1949–2014. *Source*: County Business Patterns, various issues. Industries shift from SIC to NAIC codes in 1998.

aerospace or electronics, and lacking a major university, the city was long seen as a lethargic "martial metropolis." But industry and civic leaders successfully pushed for a UC branch with a strong technology orientation, finding success in 1964. Chancellor Richard C. Atkinson, a former Stanford faculty member, consciously emulated the "Terman model" of university partnership with firms in telecommunications and biotechnology. In 1985 the area became home to telecommunications powerhouse Qualcomm, whose success led Forbes to declare San Diego the "World's Wireless City" in 2012. Infused by funding for health research, UCSD and the surrounding area attracted a new generation of "bioscientific entrepreneurs." Historians Mary Lindenstein Walshok and Abraham Shragge have written that "in little more than a decade, many of these companies gave rise to new commercial enterprises, which eventually found their way into the market economy even though their roots were in products of value to the U.S. Department of Defense or other federal agencies." San Diego's post–Cold War income spurt may be seen as a payoff to these investments, though both southern California MSAs were hard hit by the recession of 2007.[47]

Conclusion

This chapter argues that defense support for advanced technologies generated the infrastructure for knowledge-economy clusters in all four Pacific Coast metropolitan areas, comprising networks of firms, research universities, suppliers, and educated professionals. With the end of the Cold War, each of the four cases offers a different variation on the adjustment to civilian technologies and commercial markets. Silicon Valley was eager for commercialization early on, and its networks spread to encompass virtually the entire Bay Area. For Los Angeles, in contrast, the loss of government funding devastated the aerospace network, and the area high-tech economy has yet to recover. Seattle was equally specialized in aerospace, yet its metropolitan area has managed a relatively smooth transition into a diversified modern knowledge economy. The divergence between Seattle and Los Angeles reflects many factors: Boeing's unique balance between defense and commercial markets; its sponsorship of local infrastructure and tolerance of spinoffs; and the arrival of Microsoft in 1979, itself partially attributable to the area's attractiveness for high-tech enterprise. San Diego represents yet another path, gradually nurturing a high-tech community around a new university, while avoiding debilitating budget cuts in the 1990s.

The focus in this chapter has been on the performance of knowledge-economy centers as organic entities, not the implications of these developments for human well-being. On that larger topic, it should at least be noted that these robust clusters have contributed to the rise of inequality emphasized by historian Richard White in his afterword to this edited volume. That relationship was not constant throughout the postwar period. In the heyday of the Cold War, new technologies generated well-paying nearby jobs for blue-collar workers. In its 1978 report IBM proudly displayed the growth of the IBM San Jose family, within which employment in manufacturing actually outnumbered that in research, development, and programming laboratories. That link began to break down in the 1980s, through the combined effects of offshoring, import competition, and outsourcing of service jobs. But these distributional effects must be analyzed across wider geographic spaces. In successful knowledge-economy centers, rising property values effectively squeezed low-income people out, widening the gaps between metropolitan and nonmetropolitan areas. If Los Angeles had matched the Bay Area in the resilience of its post–Cold War knowledge economy, it is far from clear that the majority of its residents would have gained from this achievement.

4

THE POLITICS WROUGHT BY WAR

Phoenix, Seattle, and the Emergence of the Red-Blue Divide in the West, 1939–1950

MATTHEW DALLEK

What makes the political culture of one place become conservative and the political culture of another place become liberal? The forces that drove politics in Seattle and Phoenix in the 1940s shed some light on this question. During the years of World War II and the early Cold War, Seattle and Phoenix's distinct political cultures were seen in the way each city responded to the federal infusion of wartime resources and the rules that accompanied them. At the same time, it was the older political cultures of Seattle and Phoenix—the geographic and earlier twentieth-century institutions and culture—that influenced how each city reacted to wartime federal activity. As historian Richard White suggests in the afterword to this edited volume, the 1940s, rather than acting as a turning point, functioned more as a speed ramp as wartime federal interventions mobilized networks of conservatives in Phoenix and activated a progressive infrastructure in Seattle, pushing each city along distinct political axes.

That is not how political fault lines are typically understood. Historians stress the importance of cultural developments in the 1970s and after to explain how the so-called "red-blue" divide emerged in the United States. The South became a Republican stronghold in reaction to the civil rights movement, they conclude, and the advent of 24/7 cable news channels and social media exacerbated partisan polarization. Social issues ranging from abortion to gender to guns to gay rights emerged to sort voters into ever-more-polarized ideological and geographic camps, they assert.[1] Other historians have studied Orange

County's grassroots right-wing activists and the rise to power of Phoenix's "Sunbelt capitalism" in the post–World War II period to explain political divergence in modern America.[2] One 2018 book cited the 1950s as the beginning of the West's partisan divisions.[3]

These explanations all have some validity. Yet, as a comparison of Seattle and Phoenix in the 1940s reveals, the roots of the West's (and America's) political divisions were deeper than that, and there are good reasons to study these cities in a side-by-side analysis.[4] Seattle and Phoenix became two of the more populous cities in two of the West's more populous states. Suburban and rural Washington State residents denounced Seattle as a hotbed of left-wing activism, while liberals later vilified Phoenix as a locus of conservative mobilization. One historian has classified Washington State as one of only two solidly "blue" states in the West since 1950 (the other is Hawaii).[5]

The cases of Seattle and Phoenix underscore the ways in which the federal government became a daily presence in Americans' lives during World War II and accelerated each city's political development along distinct axes. From 1939 to 1945 the federal government drafted young men into the armed forces, raised income taxes, provided greater union protections, imposed wage and price controls, and entered into treaties and alliances that committed the United States to sustained international engagement in the postwar world. "As the larger trajectory of federal spending, revenue, debt, employment, and military deployment in the twentieth century makes clear, the Second World War, building on but also superseding the New Deal, was a critical turning point for the growth of the federal government within American society," historian James Sparrow has written.[6]

This dynamic was particularly true in Phoenix and Seattle. Federal investments funded military air bases and training centers, defense industries, and public housing, transforming Phoenix's economic base. Boeing, the Seattle-area suburban-based airplane manufacturer, saw its workforce rise more than tenfold thanks to an infusion of wartime federal dollars. Government funding was also responsible for invigorating Seattle's shipyards, while soldiers found housing and veterans later attended the University of Washington. At the same time as these federal investments were happening, the federal government's largesse interacted with three powerful issues—labor rights, civil rights, and anticommunism—that served to highlight the real differences in each city's politics. (There were other issues, of course, but these three were particularly salient and explosive.) In the process, Phoenix's anti-union and anti–civil rights political commitments deepened, and Seattle's pro-union and pro–civil rights traditions became more durable.

As the cases of Phoenix and Seattle illustrate, federal action in the 1940s combined with older political culture pushed the West to become arguably the nation's foremost region in the struggle between liberal action and conservative reaction. Although it took years for the impact of wartime mobilization to be fully felt, and although Seattle developed a strong identity as a defense manufacturer while Phoenix had some liberal dissenters, it was in the 1940s that each city solidified its place as a center of liberal and conservative politics, respectively. The combination of each city's political traditions and wartime federal investments established Seattle's and Phoenix's distinct politics—suggesting that America's modern political divisions were evident in two western metropolitan areas and traceable to developments that unfolded not in the second but rather in the first half of the twentieth century.[7]

Political Traditions: Prewar Seattle and Phoenix

Why did Seattle and Phoenix develop distinct political identities? Part of the explanation lies in each place's economic and social conditions before World War II. Seattle had an active African American community and a strong labor movement that at times checked the power of its timber, railroad, and shipbuilding industries. Geographic details also shaped Seattle's progressive identity. Coastal exposure to diverse ideas and peoples made the city's politics less monochromatic than Phoenix's, and its location turned it into a shipping and rail hub and helped ensure that its economic activity would be more diversified than Phoenix's; between 1890 and 1920, Seattle's population increased from around 40,000 to 315,000, reflecting the city's early industrial and trade economy. By the 1930s Seattle had become a "navy town" with its own defense industry, and two Seattle-based congressmen, Warren Magnuson and Marion Zioncheck, served on the Naval Affairs Committee.[8]

Pre–World War II Seattle also developed a network of left-wing activists, as Socialists, the Industrial Workers of the World, and the Knights of Labor shaped the city's civic affairs.[9] In 1902, Seattle voters approved a bond funding the nation's first municipally run hydroelectric facility, and the national Democratic Party soon adopted public power in its platform.[10] Seattle was in the vanguard of Progressive-era struggles to advance women's and workers' rights. In 1910, Washington voted to become only the fifth state to enact women's suffrage.

In 1926 the city elected the first woman mayor of any major US city. Popular-front coalitions such as the Washington Pension Union and the Washington Commonwealth Federation worked within electoral politics to promote labor rights and civil rights, raise Social Security and pension payments to the elderly, and pressure the city's Democrats to adopt more radical stands.[11] The New Deal employed thousands of Seattle residents and built airports, low-income housing, roads, bridges, parks, and recreation centers. The Works Progress Administration, for example, planned to hire more than two hundred men for a project designed "to improve the water distribution system in the Kenwood district, in Seattle," according to a government press release.[12] The New Deal agenda, according to one University of Washington geographer, loomed so large that by 1975 Seattle had become one of the most egalitarian cities in the United States.[13]

Seattle also had a more robust civil rights infrastructure than Phoenix had prior to World War II. Seattle's African American community, concentrated in the Central District's East Madison and Yesler-Jackson neighborhoods, made up no more than 1 percent of the city's pre-1940 population. In 1900, Seattle had 406 black residents; by 1940, it had 3,789 black residents. The existence of this relatively tiny population gave the black community more leeway than it had in other western cities. African American men in Seattle exercised their voting rights, won election to a handful of political offices, and enjoyed the kind of freedom of movement that made the city more racially tolerant than the Jim Crow South and much of the rest of the urban West.

At the same time, black men, shut out of nearly all industrial and crafts jobs, had few choices but to work as poorly paid cooks, waiters, barbers, and in other service jobs. Black women had even fewer options and often were forced to seek employment as maids. Although Seattle's black and Asian American residents had to compete for jobs and housing, in the prewar years they also occasionally formed coalitions to challenge the city's racial restrictions.[14] African Americans built a formidable network of organizations including local affiliates of the NAACP and the National Negro Congress. African American–run businesses dominated the city's Madison Avenue, while black leaders partnered with white communists and other left-wing organizers to combat housing and employment discrimination and helped block two proposals before the state legislature that would have barred intermarriage. Adding to this network of activism, Seattle's African American newspaper the *Northwest Enterprise* editorialized in favor of racial integration.[15]

Seattle's industrial economy gave birth to a labor movement that was far stronger than Phoenix's in the pre–World War II years. During World War I almost thirty-five thousand people worked in the city's shipyards and related industries, as more than one-fourth of America's war ships were built in Seattle.[16] In 1919 a five-day general strike highlighted the power of organized labor in the city.[17] Boeing, which was established in 1916, gave Seattle's suburbs including Tukwila and Renton a major industrial employer, and generally speaking, the Seattle area had a more dynamic industrial economic base, and during and after World War II the area never had to push as hard as Phoenix did to attract businesses. The Seattle area's relatively advanced industrial economy gave it an advantage over Phoenix after World War II had ended.[18]

In contrast, Phoenix's underdeveloped and extractive-heavy prewar economic base stifled the development of the city's progressive politics. The city's hot, desolate climate—"as close to Hell as you could be," quipped banker George Leonard—stymied economic growth, and its dependence on the four "Cs" (copper, cotton, cattle, and climate) "effectively placed the land and its people in a form of servitude to outside commercial cities," historian Elizabeth Tandy Shermer has observed.[19] Although Arizona had a statewide labor tradition, the lack of heavy industry in prewar Phoenix meant that the union movement there was relatively enfeebled. Phoenix's reliance on outside financial interests required the city's leadership to attract and keep businesses during and after World War II, in the hopes of putting Phoenix on a permanent industrial footing.

Between Arizona's passage into statehood in 1912 and the outbreak of war in Europe in 1939, Democrats dominated the city's politics. Yet Phoenix's politics were still not as progressive as Seattle's. Franklin Roosevelt's New Deal agenda did win some popular support in Phoenix. The federal government became Maricopa County's largest employer during the Great Depression, and the administration's Civil Works Administration built dams, roads, schools, and swimming pools, modernized the city's airport, and provided residents access to cheap electric power. By 1938 registered Republicans comprised only 14 percent of Arizona's electorate.[20]

Yet such appearances were misleading. Strong undercurrents of antiliberal sentiment prior to 1939 anticipated the city's more explicit rightward turn in the late 1940s. Predominantly white ranchers, mine owners, and their managers dominated the city's government and along with downtown business leaders opposed federal protections for workers, a guaranteed minimum wage, and other perceived threats to their financial interests.[21] Anglo business interests launched "the material and political work necessary to build an industrial metropolis," thus laying the ground for conservative politics to develop after the war, one historian has suggested.[22]

And few western cities were as racially segregated as Phoenix before World War II. In the early twentieth century, law and custom forced African Americans and Latinos to live in the dilapidated South Phoenix neighborhoods. "Public expenditures on water lines, sewage, paved roads and urban services were directed toward neighborhoods north of the downtown, while those south of the rail corridor did without," observed three Arizona State University scholars. In 1920 the Phoenix Chamber of Commerce sought to lure tourists with a report claiming the city had "the best kind of people" and only "a very small percentage [of] Mexicans, Negroes, or foreigners." Phoenix's laws mandated segregation in its schools, housing, and workplaces; during the Great Depression, South Phoenix had the highest child mortality rate in the country.[23]

In his book *Color-Coded*, historian Walter Nugent has argued that Arizona's conservative streak developed during the 1950s and 1960s, when business interests came to dominate politics, retirees moved to the state from Republican regions, and non-unionized high-tech firms brought engineers and technicians to the state. Phoenix's politics was a form of "business conservatism through and through," he asserts, and "not a Religious Right or social issues conservatism." Sunbelt capitalism indeed guided the city's approach to politics. At the same time, though, the federal infusion of resources and the rules that accompanied them in the 1940s helped thrust social issues from anticommunism to labor power to civil rights onto the public docket, mobilizing networks of conservatives in Phoenix, setting the city on its own distinct path.[24]

Federal Action: Phoenix and Seattle, 1939–1950

Federal investments mobilized Phoenix's bankers, lawyers, and retailers to get active in local politics and embark on pro-business policies that eroded the New Deal's social and economic protections. They helped transform Phoenix from being economically reliant on commodities into a hub of high-tech manufacturing and defense production. Phoenix experienced its first significant industrial activity during the war. Afterward, its business and political leaders decided to industrialize permanently, and businessmen's anti-union views became policy reality as postwar Phoenix prioritized pro-growth policies to lure factories and jobs to the desert. The city's economic fears of a postwar economic depression and business leaders' desire to make defense production a lynchpin of the economy gave new impetus to the city's antilabor, anti–civil rights, and anticommunist ideology. World War II, one historian has said, "led city leaders to rethink their understanding of the community's prospects." They now envisioned their city as a manufacturing hub and prioritized business needs ahead of workers' rights.[25]

Although federal interventions had a sizable impact on Seattle's economy, the changes the wartime government wrought in Phoenix were arguably even greater. Phoenix's geographic advantages made it attractive to federal officials seeking to strengthen America's military preparedness. Military officials eager to fortify the nation's aviation capabilities thought air power could prove decisive in any war against the Axis Powers, and Phoenix's arid, sunny climate made it ideal for flight training. The rural desert region's vast tracts of undeveloped land appealed to military planners who wished to build airfields and airplanes to meet the nation's urgent defense needs.

A symbiotic partnership between city business leaders and federal officials enabled Phoenix to win more than its share of defense dollars. The Phoenix Chamber of Commerce and Aeronautics Commission helped persuade the city to acquire and rent acres of land to the US military for one dollar per year. Goodyear's President Paul Lichtfield reasoned with federal officials that "much of the [aircraft-related] work could be done out-of-doors [and] planes could be flown and tested every day of the year. Arizona was far enough inland to be safe from enemy air raids, such as might threaten plants on the Pacific Coast."[26] Federal contracts turned Phoenix into a bustling center of aircraft manufacturing and flight training; the establishment of air bases such as Luke Field, Thunderbird Field, and Williams Field brought an influx of soldiers to the city and led to a housing construction boom and higher profits for downtown businesses.[27]

Federal military projects yielded big dividends. The Civilian Pilot Training Program funded the expansion of Phoenix's Sky Harbor airport, while government spending helped boost the Goodyear Corporation, which employed seventy-five hundred workers in its rubber-making factory, and make the Phoenix-based Aluminum Company of America the largest aluminum-making factory in the United States.[28] Phoenix Chamber of Commerce president Sylvan Ganz declared that Goodyear's expansion into Phoenix marked the city's rise as an "increasingly important . . . industrial center." Real estate tycoon Del

Webb said his construction business had become "a subsidiary of the federal government." A citywide consensus formed that held, as Sen. Ernest McFarland summed up, "we must develop industries."[29]

Business leaders feared that postwar demobilization and the resulting loss of federal support would trigger a return to economic depression. The war's end, they worried, would make Phoenix dependent on extractive industries again; the high-tech manufacturing future that federal action had helped bring to life would thus be stillborn. Another concern was that thousands of returning servicemen would lack access to housing and jobs in the city, creating mass unemployment and disrupting the social peace required for economic growth.

Federally funded economic growth in Phoenix also put issues of morality and corruption at the fore of city politics. Thousands of soldiers frequented downtown businesses, the city experienced a rise in prostitution and gambling, and the number of soldiers who contracted venereal disease also spiked. The military officer in charge of Phoenix's airfields responded by barring enlisted men from visiting downtown, thus damaging business revenues. Frightened city and state politicians worried that the city's inability to stamp out vice would imperil its economic revival. In a sign of desperation, Governor Sidney Osborn proposed imposing martial law on Phoenix, while the city manager suggested that officials inspect every inbound train for prostitutes. Lawyer and business leader Frank Snell urged city commissioners to replace the city manager, city clerk, and police chief, but after the commissioners acted, they inexplicably rehired all three within weeks.

This episode jarred Snell and his business allies into the realization that their city's economic future rested on having a dependable group of welfare capitalists in positions of power who could guard their business interests and eliminate social disruptions—whether vice, labor protests, or civil rights pickets. Keeping the social order stable became a prerequisite to industrial production and broader economic prosperity, they concluded. The Chamber of Commerce grew more and more politically active and helped elect four candidates to the City Commission in the war's last three years.[30] Retailing magnate Barry Goldwater, who would become a hero of the national conservative movement in the 1960s, declared that city business leaders ought to get engaged to "maintain and strengthen our system of free enterprise," take "a firm stand against evils which threaten our communities," and "become a model [of political mobilization] for the rest of the country."[31] The warfare state thus inspired business elites to head off an economic downturn stemming from military demobilization.

Such fears of a new depression turned politics in Phoenix on the right into an existential pursuit. When the federal government closed some military bases and withdrew some of its defense contracts, the city's business elite rallied to take control of all levers of government to defend their city's manufacturing, pro-growth policies, ensuring that industrialization would be the foundation of Phoenix's economy.[32]

During the 1940s federal action helped galvanize Seattle's most progressive residents and accentuated its progressive traditions. Although federal intervention in support of civil or labor rights seemed to most Phoenix residents a threat to their economic interests and social relations, some Seattle residents regarded liberal reforms as tools to fulfill the nation's war aims. It was the federal government that helped thrust unionization and labor unrest, civil rights, and the tension between civil liberties and national security into the center of each city's political debate. Federal action in the 1940s sharpened political divisions between two places that were already moving along distinct axes. (For another example of how an infusion of wartime government resources triggered progressive politics in some places, see Rebecca Jo Plant's chapter in this volume on the efforts by parents to defend public funding for nursery schools in postwar Los Angeles.)[33]

In Seattle, federal interventions ultimately generated greater racial diversity, inspired progressive grassroots activism, and spurred some residents to assert their free speech rights as part of the war against fascism. Thus Seattle became an even greater bellwether for progressivism in the 1940s. Federally funded economic transformations fueled demographic changes. "No major industrial area in the United States during 1940 and 1941 felt the economic impact of the war more intensely than did the Seattle region," Clark Kerr, the future University of California president, observed during the war. Just in those two years, Seattle underwent a greater expansion in manufacturing jobs and in migration than any major US city relative to its prewar employment and population size.[34] By 1942, Seattle had more than $1.5 billion in defense contracts (the third highest per capita of any American city). Washington secretary of state Belle Reeves pointed out that Seattle's "relationship of war work to normal activity has been about twice as great as for Los Angeles and four times greater than for San Francisco." Boeing's Seattle-based aircraft factories employed seventy-five hundred workers in 1940 and some fifty thousand by 1944, and the city's shipyards employed twenty-two thousand workers who helped to build forty-six US naval destroyers during the war.[35]

Demographic changes also bulked large. During the 1940s, 550,000 people migrated to Washington State. Seattle's African American population rose from 3,789 in 1940 to 15,666 in 1950, and the city's population increased from roughly 368,000 to 467,000 over the same decade. (Consider Seattle's population boom in contrast to two midwestern cities with large defense industries: in Detroit during the 1940s the population rose from about 1.6 million to 1.8 million, while Kansas City's hardly budged.)[36] Federal spending touched off economic and demographic changes. A growing clamor in the city followed. Supporters wanted expanded labor and civil rights and safeguards for civil liberties, while key civic institutions such as the University of Washington and its two leading newspapers *The Seattle Times* and *Seattle Post-Intelligencer* provided liberal causes with a voice that was missing in Phoenix.[37] Rather than see the 1940s as a fulcrum in each city's political development, the decade is better understood as pushing the pace of political development in both places.

Civil Rights

In Seattle, federal and military policies and the moral agitation of grassroots activists advocating on behalf of greater social equality helped tip the scales in favor of civil rights. Activists insisted that the war's aims were meant to provide equal opportunity to all citizens regardless of class or skin color. Despite a violent strain of anti-Japanese racism that peaked following the bombing of Pearl Harbor, Seattle's civil rights activists drew on America's antifascist war aims and the federal government's stated commitment to workplace equality to campaign against Boeing's whites-only Seattle-based workplace.

The struggle to desegregate Boeing and the International Association of Machinists (IAM) union local demonstrated how federal actions and residents' progressive traditions combined to accelerate liberal politics in the city during the 1940s. Boeing posed a formidable obstacle to racial progress. From its founding in 1917, the company had never had an African American factory worker, and the IAM union local had also prohibited African American membership. But labor shortages in the federally funded wartime defense industry gave African Americans more economic clout. A growing number of African Americans moving to Seattle with expectations of well-paid jobs provided the backdrop that helped make victory possible.

Led by reporter and former communist Hutchen R. Hutchins, in 1939 activists established the Committee for the Defense of Negro Labor's Right to

Work at the Boeing Airplane Company (CDNL). The CDNL began to encourage African American men to seek work at Boeing and to refuse to "take NO for an answer. If you are refused, learn why and who refused you." The African American newspaper *Northwest Enterprise* exposed Boeing's and the union's racist practices, while Hutchins invoked the war abroad to argue that "the most dangerous enemy facing Negroes [in Seattle] is jim-crowism and segregation masquerading under the banner of liberalism and progressivism in labor unions."

Federal wartime rules aided the cause. In June 1941, Franklin Roosevelt signed Executive Order 8802 establishing the Fair Employment Practices Committee (FEPC) and barring discrimination in hiring in companies with federal contracts. Roosevelt's order initially fell "on deaf ears in the far northwest," reported the *Northwest Enterprise*. But the order raised expectations that African American men would now have federal backing in their quest to break Boeing's and the IAM's whites-only policy. When an aircraft training school program that all Boeing workers had to complete before their jobs began expelled Eugene Beech, a black man, in September 1941, civil rights leaders urged Seattle Democratic Rep. Warren Magnuson and Washington Sen. Monrad Wallgren to pressure the FEPC to launch an investigation. The members of Congress sent the case to the Committee and asked the agency overseeing the FEPC to look into the matter. Eventually, federal officials ordered Beech reinstated and promised to eliminate "bans against qualified negroes in both training and employment." The NAACP also filed complaints with the FEPC that ultimately helped force the union local to admit African American members.

The Roosevelt administration's actions failed to end all racial discrimination in the Boeing workplace, and segregated bathrooms and lunchrooms remained the norm for the war's duration. Yet the FEPC's intervention, African American organizing that drew on the city's civil rights tradition, and government aims (equality and democracy) in the war against fascism combined to alter the balance of power and help grant African Americans access to jobs at Boeing for the first time. Indeed, by 1944 approximately sixteen hundred African American men and women held jobs in Boeing's Seattle-area factories. The activists' "constant agitation and relentless fight" made victory possible, in the words of the *Northwest Enterprise*.[38]

The story of resettling Japanese Americans and Japanese nationals in Seattle toward the war's end underscored the US military's clout in the city's racial politics. In 1945 the Army announced that the internal threat of enemy subversion had abated and with aid from the civilian War Relocation Authority, the government began to disband the internment camps. Military and civilian officials ordered that internees be allowed to return to the communities in which they lived prior to Pearl Harbor, which essentially reintegrated Seattle's neighborhoods. The announcement stirred racist rage among some of the city's white population. One resident vowed to "burn the house down the minute the white people move out, and to beat up the Japs and send them to the hospital," and Washington's governor opposed resettling internees in Seattle's communities.[39]

An outbreak of anti-Japanese racist violence, which had transpired after Pearl Harbor, was therefore a live possibility in 1945 Seattle. But tolerant forces in Seattle animated by the nation's ideals in its antifascist struggle counseled restraint and tolerance; they decried antiresettlement voices as affronts to the antifascist war being waged overseas. Although these voices had fallen silent amid anti-Japanese hysteria following Pearl Harbor, in 1945 the War Relocation Authority, the Army's moral authority, the ongoing claims of Japanese Americans on their rights, and grassroots moral agitation helped elected leaders to bring about a relatively peaceful resettlement, illustrating the power of the city's progressives on at least some racial questions. Thus it was the antifascist political coalition that coalesced in the 1930s that made a difference after the war.

Seattle residents mobilized on behalf of progressive causes. As the war neared its end, a Civic Unity Committee formed in support of racial tolerance and in response to reports that African American soldiers had suffered abuse. The city's Republican mayor William Devin endorsed its mission. Devin drew support from business leaders and organized labor and positioned himself as a voice of moderation in city affairs. In 1944 he urged citizens to repudiate "unthinking people and leaders who bring to us misinformation that causes prejudices . . . against all groups." Reminding his constituents of the need for wartime unity, Devin warned that "misinformation, if allowed to go unchecked by factual statements, increases disunity of our leading citizens. . . . It is our duty as citizens to face the problem together. If we do not do that, we shall not exist very long as a civilized city or as a nation."[40]

Devin ultimately sided with the Seattle Council of Churches and the Civic Unity Committee and backed the Army's resettlement order. Seattle's residents, Devin advised, must "put into effect those principles of democracy which we are all so justly proud as Americans." Stressing the trust that citizens should place in the US military, the city's leading newspapers and the

University of Washington's student newspaper also encouraged readers to heed the government's orders and live out the nation's wartime ideals in their own communities.[41]

While segregation persisted in Seattle's housing covenants and in some of its workplaces into the 1950s, it had reacted to wartime government interventions by adopting policies and rhetoric that favored civil rights and imbued with meaning the promises of human dignity that some citizens considered the goal of the war. In Phoenix, in contrast, which entered the war with more deeply entrenched racial inequality than Seattle, the warfare state helped deepen unequal treatment of racial minorities by empowering the city's business leaders who governed their enterprises and their city according to their own deep-felt racial prejudices. The federal government refused to challenge the city's racist codes and practices due to the overwhelming strength of Anglo businessmen, and Phoenix's ascendant manufacturing elites exploited their rising status to enshrine racist hiring, education, and housing policies in the city. In contrast to Seattle's steps toward greater civil rights, the federal government, especially the FEPC, deferred to local traditions rather than challenge segregation in Phoenix; racially oppressive norms, attitudes, and policies were so entrenched that the federal government's behavior failed to dent them.[42]

Phoenix experienced some postwar civil rights achievements, but racial inequality nonetheless persisted and festered. Civil rights leaders Lincoln and Eleanor Ragsdale and the NAACP and the Greater Phoenix Council for Civic Unity (GPCCU) won support from some white business owners in their postwar campaign in the state legislature to allow local school districts to desegregate on a voluntary basis. But, as Shermer points out, civil rights activists "preferred incrementalism in order to keep the peace and protect their children." The business community's openly anti–civil rights politics circumscribed the possibilities of what civil rights activists could achieve.[43]

Barry Goldwater used his Goldwater's store newsletter, "As Pedro Sees It," to inform his employees about manager-labor relations and what he deemed the proper role of racial minorities in the workplace. Depicting a poncho- and sombrero-wearing Mexican American cartoon character as lazy and inept, his newsletter reinforced the out-in-the-open prejudices that pervaded wartime Phoenix. As the federal government empowered business leaders such as Goldwater to determine the city's future, their own practices—Goldwater's refused to hire minorities in jobs where they would interact with clients—gained even more acceptance among much of Anglo Phoenix. Just prior to the start of World War II, Goldwater summed up prevailing racial biases, denouncing liberals and union bosses for tending to “minority groups who are causing the tax increases.”[44] (For a discussion of why some Hispanic World War II veterans in the West got active in conservative Republican Party politics after the war, see Geraldo L. Cadava’s essay in this edited volume.[45]) The story of desegregation in Phoenix tracked more closely with events in Birmingham, Alabama, in the 1960s than with Seattle during World War II and the early Cold War. It was the civil rights movement of the 1960s that helped end segregation in education, employment, and public accommodations in Phoenix. In 1965 the city elected its first African American City Council member, a sign that the all-white businessmen’s grip on city government was slipping.[46]

Labor Rights

Franklin Roosevelt’s 1935 National Labor Relations Act established the right of unions to bargain collectively with employers, and the World War II–era National War Labor Board conferred even stronger protections on organized labor, guaranteeing unions a chance to organize the workplace. These government interventions helped swell the ranks of Arizona’s unions from 16,600 members in 1939 to more than 50,000 by 1953, and the union organization effects were especially strong in Phoenix’s downtown business district. The federal government had helped bring good jobs to Phoenix and secured benefits for labor as part of the goal of keeping workers on the job and supportive of the war effort.

Victory for Phoenix’s anti-union forces was hardly a slam dunk. Unions had made some gains in the city during the war years. When war brought the downtown business district to life, new members flooded into unions. Local 631, the Hotel and Restaurant Employees and Bartenders Union, pressured downtown restaurants for better wages and working conditions, and its ranks expanded from nine hundred members in 1941 to thirty-five hundred members in 1946, more than tripling over five years.[47] The nation’s war aims and Franklin Roosevelt’s promise of an economic bill of rights further emboldened organized labor in Phoenix. During the war the president of the Arizona State Federation of Labor argued for greater racial equality in the union movement, and the Phoenix City Employees Unity Council came together as a joint AFL-CIO project to defend labor’s gains in local politics. Even though wartime Phoenix teemed with a host of local AFL affiliates, their high profile antagonized business leaders who resented the AFL's success at establishing baseline workplace standards and saw them infringing on their freedom to operate workplaces as they thought appropriate. Unions had made substantial strides in Phoenix and the state as a whole since the New Deal.

In 1946, Republicans gained control of Congress and soon enacted the Taft-Hartley Act despite President Harry Truman's veto. The law limited tactics unions could use and gave states the authority to ban closed shops requiring all workers in a workplace to join the union. In this climate Arizona voted in favor of Initiative 107, a "right-to-work" law, in 1946. Although it was a statewide decision, Phoenix's politicians and media led the charge. Several factors propelled the initiative victory. Phoenix politicians were reacting to labor battles during the war, disliked the NLRB's ruling in favor of striking workers in the Tovrea meat-packing operation, and worried that union strength had expanded in wartime and had to be curbed to attract new industries from elsewhere. Local politicians feared labor strife in Phoenix after the war and worried that union strength would mean little turnover and shut white combat veterans out of the industrial workforce. Defeat of two state Senate bills that would have created right-to-work inspired them to act.

As the first successful initiative curbing unions' collective bargaining power in the Southwest, the measure illustrated not only how Phoenix's leadership was fostering a pro-business economic climate but also how the federal government tapped anti-union sentiment in the early Cold War to diminish labor activism and prop up industrialists' power. The city's business and political elite passed one of their first postwar tests of their clout.[48]

Opponents mounted a vigorous campaign to block the right-to-work ballot measure. The Phoenix-based chapter of the American Veterans of World War II (AMVETS) mobilized its membership in a No-on-107 campaign in September of 1946. A Citizens Committee against the Right to Starve in Phoenix charged that if right-to-work became law, "exploiters of labor [would have power to] destroy the wage scale."[49] Some Phoenix elected officials such as Congressman Richard Harless warned that passage of 107 would roll back the wage gains that organized labor had won in recent years.

Still, Democrats often stayed silent on the ballot initiative, and some even endorsed it. One CIO activist complained that "there are two types of Democrats here. Both are controlled by the same interests."[50] Phoenix's business leaders framed right-to-work in existential terms; freedom versus slavery, postwar tranquility versus workplace and social chaos, they claimed, were on the line.

"Federal legislation, union militancy, and labor's legitimacy united area businessmen," Shermer has written. The pro–right-to-work coalition featured not simply lawyers, bankers, retailers, and other downtown business elites but also ranchers and farmers, the Chamber of Commerce, the Salt River Valley Water Users Association, and publisher Eugene Pulliam's *Arizona Republic*. Led by a cattleman, this coalition, he said, featured "redblooded American men" eager to defend capitalism and their way of life and put a halt to "'goon squads'" who dominated unions, imperiled free enterprise, and injected corruption and communism into once wholesome business concerns.

Barry Goldwater led a group of increasingly radicalized Phoenix businessmen who fought for the initiative to thwart federally driven developments that had empowered unions and constrained entrepreneurs. Goldwater urged colleagues to campaign "in the open where [the businessman's] thoughts and arguments would do some good toward correcting the evils to which he refers in private."[51] Denouncing closed shops, tying unions to "a despotic monopoly," the right-to-work forces won 56 percent of the vote statewide in November 1946. The vote could not have taken place without federal intervention; the growing national debate about Taft-Hartley encouraged Phoenix business and political leaders to roll back federal protections for organized labor.[52]

The struggle over labor rights took a different turn in Seattle in this decade. Although Seattle's unions had an uneven record between 1940 and 1952, they had enough strength to curb Boeing's economic power, maintain labor standards and some wage hikes, and protect New Deal and wartime rights to organize and bargain collectively. The IAM Local 715 established its own newspaper to educate workers about the war effort, its rights and protections under the warfare state, and to stress unions' crucial role in the defense program. "Progress in setting up the instruments of democracy can become the mainspring of a future productive achievement surpassing all that has gone before," the *Aero Mechanic* declared on June 12, 1941. The union's paper cited federal agencies that it said were helping to ensure that labor had a seat at the table during negotiations and that unionized workers got their fair share of higher government-fueled profits in defense industries. A strong labor movement, the IAM insisted, would strengthen the defense program rather than weaken it as some business leaders had claimed. The *Aero Mechanic* boasted that the IAM had negotiated the best wages of any in the aircraft industry. "We have a decided advantage over our Southern compatriots," one headline said. The war triggered fears in the IAM that business and government would curb labor rights in the name of national defense. But it also inspired the union to organize on the theory that a strong national defense required a powerful labor movement.[53]

Boeing's leadership fretted that federal defense contracts would abruptly cease. In response, the Defend Seattle Committee was formed to urge the federal government to maintain its orders for Boeing's bombers. Still, Boeing did lose some contracts, and in April 1948 workers struck to protest Boeing's plan to undermine job security by changing seniority rules and the firm's refusal to accept a ten-cent an hour wage hike. Boeing's employees looked to the federal government to defend their hard-won wartime rights in addition to the federal contracts that gave them their employment. The NLRB failed to force management back to the negotiating table, yet its fines on Boeing ($172,000 a day), along with the military's pressure on Boeing to speed production of B50 bombers, helped force Boeing to take the workers back. The results of the strike were a mixed bag, but the IAM had become sufficiently strong during the war, and with some warfare state backing in the early Cold War, to initiate a major labor action and still retain the loyalty of most of its members. The IAM's clout in Seattle strengthened its status as a check on management's power, and the IAM and Boeing set the pattern for labor relations in the area. One indication of labor's relative strength in Seattle was that in contrast to Phoenix's leading role in the passage of Arizona's right-to-work ballot initiative, Seattle's unions and progressives managed to defeat Washington's 1956 right-to-work initiative (known as 198) by a two-to-one margin.[54]

Anticommunism

The warfare state also shaped distinct outcomes in each city's anticommunist politics. Seattle retained some strong voices in defense of citizens' civil liberties, while Phoenix represented a more virulent brand of anticommunist activism. In wartime Seattle the national government turned the University of Washington into a more visible center of education. The University's scientists and engineers helped develop torpedo exploders, instruments used in atomic bomb tests, and a wind tunnel that enabled development of air power. The Far Eastern, Physics, Chemistry, and Engineering Departments worked with the federal government during the war, and UW faculty increasingly trained enlisted Army and Navy men.[55] The University also became an uneasy fusion of political activism, federally funded defense research, and publicly financed elite education. Its antiwar and antifascist student movements in the 1930s and early 1940s, which won sympathy from some faculty, turned the University into a ripe target for conservatives concerned about communist inroads in the years before and during World War II and in the early Cold War. The war had strengthened the University, and Seattle generally, into durable progressive forces within statewide politics.

During the war, UW housed soldiers in dorms, hosted a Navy unit, trained students in canning food for overseas shipment, had a chemical warfare laboratory, loaned buildings to the military, experienced antiwar, anti-ROTC protests led by the American Students' Union, and became such a hotbed of radicalism that the University's dean supplied the FBI with information about student dissenters. The 1944 passage of the GI Bill of Rights would over time help it become Washington's leading institution of higher education, and UW president Raymond Allen's inauguration in 1947 marked a new era in which faculty had more say over governance, received higher salaries and benefits, and gained access to unprecedented research grants.[56]

Although Washington experienced a Red Scare after World War I, federal actions during the 1940s helped make the state a new front in a seemingly existential battle against fascism and, later, communism. The 1942 Coulee Dam, Boeing's Seattle location, and the nuclear facility in Hanford, Washington, which produced plutonium for use in atomic bombs, turned the Pacific Northwest into what one single-minded anticommunist state legislator termed "the most important defense area in the free world." In 1946, Washington Republicans campaigned to purge the Democratic Party of communists. Spokane-area Republican freshman State Rep. Albert Canwell soon won enough support to set up the Washington State Joint Legislative Committee on Un-American Activities (known simply as the Canwell Committee) to investigate the presence of communist threats within Washington institutions, and one Republican state senator announced that communists had gained a foothold in the University of Washington. "There isn't a student who has attended this University who has not been taught subversive activities and when they come home it is very hard for parents to change their minds," he complained.[57]

The campus's profile had risen due to federal largesse and partnerships, prompting a backlash from rural legislators. Communists should be deprived of "a place [to preach] sedition" so one state representative proposed a bill to bar communist speakers from public university campuses.[58] The government's defense spending had turned Washington into a battleground, in Canwell's mind, and his probe focused on a half-dozen UW professors suspected of communist ties. Three tenured professors were ultimately fired for having refused to tell Canwell's Committee if they were communists or for allegedly misleading the University's president. (Three others stayed but only after they signed loyalty oaths and agreed to two years' probation.)[59]

The progressive response in Seattle to Olympia's anticommunist investigations was noteworthy. Canwell's committee drew some early blood, and the firings and reprimands, as Ellen Schrecker has argued, "had cleared the way… for academic institutions to turn against other types of political undesirables."[60] The University of Washington case later came to be seen on campus as a dark chapter in UW's history in particular and in the history of higher education in general.[61]

Yet Canwell's victory ultimately proved short-lived. There were undercurrents of discontent on the campus. Some six thousand students (out of sixteen thousand total) had signed a petition in favor of lifting the rule barring political speakers from campus, while Progressive Party presidential candidate Henry Wallace attracted twenty-five hundred students to his address given atop a sound truck feet from the campus.[62] Some of Seattle's politicians and activists attacked the committee's work as "despicable," in the words of one legislator from the Puget Sound area. Canwell's witch hunt represented an assault on academic freedom and free speech, eroding the values for which the war had been waged. A letter protesting the university's actions toward alleged faculty subversives was signed by 103 professors.[63] Seattle-area legislator R. R. "Bob" Grieve asserted that the government had to uphold even communists' Constitutional rights.[64] While the AFL-affiliated Seattle Central Labor Council lauded the faculty dismissals as a defense of "red-blooded Americanism," CIO workers criticized the firings, and one thousand students and professors attended a protest rally assailing the University's crackdown.[65]

Although the Red Scare was beginning to crest and although public opinion in the state sided with anticommunism, the city's voices of dissent were not rendered completely mute. The *Seattle Times* exposed the committee's false smears against professor Mel Rader, and the series won the paper a Pulitzer. Four out of six of the committee's members lost reelection as part of a Democratic surge in 1948, giving Democrats sufficient numbers in the state legislature to block the committee's reestablishment. In addition, with strong support from Seattle voters, the state approved Initiative 172 with 57 percent of the vote in 1948. Conceived by the Popular Front–led Washington Pension Union (WPU), the initiative provided a basic income of sixty dollars a month to the elderly and secured access to health care for all state recipients of public assistance—a model for a national health insurance program in the eyes of liberals nationwide.[66] Formed in 1937 and composed of peace, union, and civil rights activists, communists, timber workers, mothers receiving aid, and pensioners, the WPU also helped elected communists to office and sponsored successful initiatives expanding statewide pension benefits.[67] Amid the national climate of anticommunist hysteria, Seattle's struggle over civil liberties and anticommunism on campus underscored the city's relatively fluid political conditions in the late 1940s.

The anticommunist movement in Phoenix was even more potent than Seattle's.[68] The growing militarization of Phoenix in the 1940s—the introduction of soldiers, veterans, defense plants, and international antifascist, anticommunist alliances—sparked a debate about internal communist threats in the southwestern city. Just as federal (and state-level) support for the defense industry thrust communism into the spotlight of Seattle's politics, the national government's adoption of loyalty oaths, military buildup, and anticommunist pronouncements enabled Phoenix's Sunbelt capitalist political leaders to seize on the communist issue in their city to dramatize the capitalism versus slavery struggle and solidify the city's status as an antiradical, business-friendly mecca.

In 1946 some veterans demonstrated the way that domestic anticommunist fears had gained traction in Phoenix's politics. The city's American Legion post established a committee to investigate communist activities in the city's school district. The committee charged that the allegedly communist-run American Youth for Democracy had a foothold in the district, and the American Legion worked with the school board to ferret out and expel communists from the school system. The board had threatened to suspend one sixteen-year-old student from Phoenix Union High School, and only lifted the threat when he resigned from American Youth for Democracy. The American Legion also published names and addresses of half a dozen district teachers whom it claimed had communist ties.[69] An American Legion–backed campaign to ban textbooks from the schools that contained un-American views won plaudits from the *Arizona Republic*.[70] In the 1950s the American Legion announced that a plan by seven Russian journalists to visit Phoenix was "dangerous to the safety and security of our people and property." While there were some anti-anticommunist voices in the city, the American Legion was one example of a rising culture of anticommunism. The charge of communism was so pervasive that the city's business elites whom the World War II warfare state had empowered hurled it against union bosses, civil rights organizations, and liberal economic proposals. In fact, the warfare state had given the businessmen-politicians a cudgel that they used in defending the city's moral virtues and competitive growth policies.[71]

For the most part, Phoenix's political leaders succeeded in curbing labor power and civil rights and eradicating any hints of communism from civic institutions. Phoenix became a seat of conservative mobilization in the 1940s, while Seattle, with its coastal location, diversified economic base, and stronger labor and civil rights networks, became more firmly associated with liberal action. The political divergence that occurred in Phoenix and Seattle in response to federal wartime activities may well constitute a pattern that recurred not just in cities in the West but also in nonwestern urban parts of the country. This phenomenon may ultimately be relevant to understanding the roots of partisan divisions in modern America. More work studying the ways that cities (western and non-western) developed distinct political cultures during the 1940s should be undertaken. As Phoenix's and Seattle's trajectories indicate, the political divisions accentuated by wartime federal interventions have a deeper history than is typically appreciated. These fault lines remain important in the American polity to this day.

5

THE ROOTS OF HISPANIC CONSERVATISM IN THE WARTIME WEST

GERALDO L. CADAVA

In 1967 a few Mexican Americans attending a conference in Washington, DC, bonded over their experience during World War II. They all believed that the war had shaped their lives afterward, including the evolution of their conservative beliefs. Their names were Benjamin Fernandez, Manuel Luján, Fernando Oaxaca, Martin Castillo, and Francisco Vega.[1] They were businessmen, politicians, and lawyers. Some of them had served in the military. All had come of age during the war years. Except for Vega, a cemetery-owning businessman from Michigan, all were from the American West. Fernandez was from California, via Kansas and Indiana. Luján was from New Mexico. Oaxaca was from California, via Texas. Castillo was born and raised in California. They formed the Republican National Hispanic Council, which soon became the Republican National Hispanic Assembly (RNHA).

It didn't take long for the Republican Party to take notice of them. Luján was elected to Congress in 1968 and became the chair of the Spanish Speaking Advisory Committee to the Republican National Committee (RNC). Castillo was the chairman of Nixon's Inter-Agency Council for Mexican American Affairs, which became the Cabinet Committee on Opportunities for Spanish Speaking People (CCOSSP). Fernandez served as chair of the National Hispanic Finance Committee for the Re-election of President Nixon, and some years later would become the first Hispanic to run for president of the United States—a Republican, from California. Within a few years of their first meeting in DC,

George H. W. Bush, when he was chair of the RNC, brought their organization into the Republican Party as an official RNC auxiliary.

These Mexican Americans all pointed to World War II as a pivotal experience that offered them lessons in patriotism and service. They credited the war with their professional accomplishments. The GI Bill paid for college for some of them. They attended universities that grew as a result of federal spending and demographic growth in the West. Some of them worked in private industries that boomed as a result of the war. They moved from California, New Mexico, and Texas to Washington, DC, to represent the interests of Hispanics in the West and nationally in the federal government. They helped recruit Hispanics into the Republican Party and influenced policy decisions on issues such as counting Hispanics in the US Census, bilingual education, and undocumented immigration. Their upbringing, their educational achievements, their economic success, and their political influence were made possible because of the war and its aftermath in the West—the war and the West that it wrought.

They had risen from the West to play roles in the Republican Party nationally, and at just the same time that the West itself was playing an increasingly important role in the conservative movement and national politics more generally, as Matthew Dallek and Richard White explain in their contributions to this edited volume. Their rise in politics was hitched to the rise of western politicians such as Barry Goldwater, Richard Nixon, and Ronald Reagan, who were more at home in a western racial landscape shaped by Anglo-Mexican more than white-black relations. The evolution of their politics in the West led them to see Mexican Americans like Fernandez, Castillo, Oaxaca, and Luján as the right kind of minorities: hardworking, law-abiding, devout, and loyal, unlike the African Americans who rioted in Watts and across the United States. They were the Republican Hispanics that Goldwater, Nixon, Reagan, and other Republican leaders thought of as increasingly valuable voters, since African Americans were fleeing the Republican Party.[2]

Even more than the widely recognized Cuban exiles who arrived in Florida after the Cuban Revolution of 1959, the Republican Mexican Americans who came of age in the West during World War II built a national conservative movement among Hispanics, which rose in the 1960s and 1970s and peaked in the early 1980s. The same Mexican Americans who built the movement, then back in California after decades of government work that required them to shuttle back and forth between the East and the West, increasingly questioned whether the Republican Party was the home they thought it would be.

This story about Republican Mexican Americans who came of age during World War II, and how they shaped politics in the American West and nationally after the war, is, of course, hardly the only story to be told about race in the West during and after World War II. The influx into the region of African Americans who worked in the war industries, the internment of Japanese Americans in camps throughout the region, or Native American ambivalence about their military service are critical to understanding the racial politics of the American West and the United States during World War II.

The relatively small number of Republican Mexican Americans who came of age during the war, then built the conservative Hispanic movement nationally, isn't even representative of the war's legacy for Mexican Americans in the region. Many prominent Mexican Americans who came of age during the war were Democrats, including Congressman Edward Roybal and Lyndon Johnson's aide Vicente Ximenes. Other Mexican American veterans, not unlike the Republican Mexican Americans discussed in this chapter, described their military service as a formative experience that motivated them to fight for their civil rights—as members of the American GI Forum or the League of United Latin American Citizens, for example—and enabled their education, move to the suburbs, and middle-class lives.[3]

Others still would describe World War II not as an important turning point that made their upward mobility possible, but rather as a period of crushing nationalism and xenophobia, when they were dragged into the streets and beaten for wearing zoot suits, were refused service at restaurants, or whose loved ones were refused burial in local cemeteries after they had given their lives fighting for the United States.[4] Finally, for many Mexican and Mexican American laborers the war years represented a time when they continued to work in difficult and dangerous conditions, continued to experience workplace discrimination, and had little recourse or redress because of wartime restrictions against union activism.[5]

Nevertheless, the story of how Mexican Americans such as Castillo, Fernandez, Luján, and Oaxaca, as well as others including Manuel Ruiz of California and Robert Benitez Robles of Arizona, used their experiences during the war years to open the doors of higher education, launch their careers, and ultimately to build a national conservative Hispanic movement that had its roots in the West, remains an unexamined slice of the history of Latinos in the United States, Mexican Americans in the West, and the long legacies of World War II for the men who served and the men who came of age during the war. Even more important, it helps to explain the evolution of the relationship between Hispanics and the Republican Party. The story of how Mexican Americans in the West established this relationship got lost when Cuban exiles and Cuban Americans in Florida began to overshadow them in the 1980s and became seen as the exemplars of conservatism among Hispanics. But the rise of Cubans within the Republican Party has helped most of us forget the early efforts of Mexican Americans to build a national movement of conservative Hispanics. This is a story that in many ways began in the West, forged by Mexican Americans who came of age during World War II.

Historians have overlooked these conservative Mexican Americans not only because of the rise of Cuban Americans within the Republican Party but also because of the liberal narrative of World War II as the good war, which demonstrated the might of the United States and the powers of the federal government to provide for and transform the lives of veterans and all Americans during the postwar era. Mexican American veterans sparked the civil rights movements of the 1950s and 1960s. Conservative Mexican Americans subscribed to parts of this narrative, too, especially as they related to equality and rights. But they also drew other conclusions from the war. For them, the war was about fighting for American values and that also meant upward mobility made possible by capitalism—the "free enterprise system," they called it—and an almost existential struggle for the preservation of democracy that necessarily meant an all-out war against communism. These views demonstrate that other, lesser-known narratives about the legacy of World War II for Mexican Americans and the American West are possible. They offer insight into the more underappreciated aspects of Hispanic politics in the late twentieth century.

Wartime

Many Hispanics credited the international tumult of World War II with galvanizing their political activism. The stories that Hispanics from different backgrounds told about the war fixated on themes of patriotism, economic opportunity, and the United States as the defender of freedom in the world. The mission of the United States to defend and spread freedom, and Hispanics whose families had fled oppressive regimes—Mexico during the Mexican Revolution, Cuba during the Cuban Revolution of the 1930s—understood the meaning of freedom because they lacked it in their homelands. Their experiences during and after World War II led to educational opportunities and launched their careers. Hispanics fought for freedom abroad and expected it at home. These were some of the lessons that conservative Hispanics drew from World War II. Several historians of Mexican Americans in the United States have credited World War II with raising the expectations of Mexican Americans in the Southwest upon their return from war. The war created employment opportunities. Mexican Americans worked in the western defense industries described in several chapters in this edited volume, and 750,000 Hispanics served in the war, receiving more medals of honor than other minority groups. As a result of the efforts of Mexican American veterans, perhaps best represented by Hector García, the founder of the American GI Forum, "an organized effort to attain broad civil rights ensued."[6] Because of GI Bill benefits, World War II also led to a broad demographic shift in Mexican American communities, as many Mexican Americans moved from segregated barrios within cities to the exploding suburbs.[7]

Oral history collections such as *A Legacy Greater Than Words* have addressed how "notable" Mexican American veterans helped shape their communities after the war, establishing institutions such as clothing shops and tailors that outfitted President Lyndon Johnson, nightclubs where Elvis Presley performed as well as newspapers, social welfare agencies, and civil rights organizations like the American GI Forum.[8] But the founding of the Republican National Hispanic Assembly by a handful of Mexican Americans from the Southwest highlights an unexamined aspect of the legacy of World War II for Latinos in the United States: how it brought together a handful of Mexican Americans from the Southwest who became founders of a Hispanic-led conservative movement.

Like many other Hispanics, conservative Mexican Americans from western states who came of age during World War II cited their patriotism as the reason for their service. Many had parents who immigrated to the United States during or shortly after the Mexican Revolution, including Castillo, Fernandez, and Oaxaca. They themselves were born in the 1920s and were children during the Great Depression. Some were a little older, including Robert Benitez Robles, a Mexican American who was born in Clifton, Arizona, in 1908. Even though he was over the draft age, he "got fightin' mad" and joined the US Navy as a transport agent. Robles said of his service in World War II, "I was there because I felt it was my duty." He acknowledged discrimination, saying that Mexican Americans fought and died for a "country that at times has looked down upon them as second-class citizens."[9] But it was still his country. If conservative

Mexican Americans joined the war because of a shared sense of duty, their patriotic, antiradical, and anticommunist sensibilities after the war had a decidedly conservative bent.

Their service began in boot camp, and it took them all over the United States and around the world. Robles started in San Diego, then went to Oakland to "learn air transportation." He went on to Olathe, Kansas, to learn how to route mail, and finally to Winslow, Arizona. His last job in the military—in his home state, whose geography he knew well—was to help find the remains of pilots killed in airplane crashes in the Arizona mountains. Robles called himself a "dry land" sailor, meaning that he was in the Navy but never set sail. When he was discharged in December 1945, he learned of a plane transporting former GIs to Phoenix from the Lockheed Airport in Burbank, California—a wartime aviation center of the sort that Gavin Wright describes in his chapter in this book. The "pilot in civilian clothes" was none other than Barry Goldwater, who had been flying back and forth between Phoenix and Burbank two times a day, just to make sure that men from Phoenix got home in time for Christmas. As soon as Robles arrived in Phoenix, he caught a bus to Flagstaff and was home by 1:00 a.m. on Christmas morning.[10]

Fernando Oaxaca served in World War II after attending high school and some college in El Paso, where he was born on August 8, 1927. His parents had moved there from Chihuahua, Mexico, a couple decades earlier. He joined the military toward the end of the war, enlisting on his eighteenth birthday and serving in the Army for only a year and a half, but he called it a "very significant turning point" in his life. In an interview in the mid-1970s, Oaxaca recalled that he did basic training in Louisiana with "absolute illiterates" from West Virginia and the South more generally. He fancied himself an "intellectual giant" compared with them. His smarts included his ability to "work the system" to secure himself a desk job in Germany, where a colonel took him under his wing and promoted him to the rank of sergeant. Oaxaca came back to the United States "greatly matured and understanding so much more about the world and the way to exploit opportunities." He recalled being a "bookworm" in high school, and he continued to pursue his education after the war. He returned to college with GI Bill benefits, joined an "elite" fraternity for Hispanics, and got a degree in engineering.[11]

Even before joining the military, Oaxaca had a privileged background compared with many Mexican Americans. After settling in Texas, Oaxaca's father worked at a department store and then sold furniture and insurance. Oaxaca said that his father also had a "fantastic intellectual capacity," but he always "worked for someone else all his life" and "never owned his own business." Oaxaca's mother, meanwhile, was a "salesgirl." Oaxaca had light skin, spoke English fluently, and always had "Anglo friends." His mother taught him that the term "Chicano" was a bad word reserved for poor Mexicans, those who did domestic work for their family, or the Mexicans they encountered across the border in Ciudad Juárez. Her father had been a Mexican "baron" who owned hundreds of acres of ranchland, so she claimed an "aristocratic background." When she pointed out "los chicanitos," she meant it as an "endearing put-down."[12]

Like Oaxaca, Benjamin Fernandez was also the child of Mexican immigrant parents. For most of his life, he went by the nickname "Boxcar" Ben, because he was born in 1925 in a railroad boxcar in Kansas City, where his parents worked at the time. Beginning at the age of five, Fernandez worked alongside his parents in midwestern fields. He moved from school to school until his family settled in East Chicago, Indiana, where his dad got a job at Inland Steel. After graduating from Washington High School, Fernandez enlisted in the US Air Force, in which he served for three years during World War II. As it was for Oaxaca and other conservative Mexican Americans, the war was an important turning point for Fernandez. His service paved the way for his education.[13]

Fernandez headed west, to the University of Redlands, in Redlands, California, which grew during and after World War II. Like the University of Washington in Seattle, as Matthew Dallek describes in his chapter in this book, the University of Redlands offered classes for soldiers stationed at Camp Haan and March Field. Whole military units enrolled at the school, because of the GI Bill and special acts of Congress that created space at the university for veterans and their families. Fernandez's education jump-started his graduate studies and his first professional opportunities. From there he found opportunities in politics, becoming the national chairman of the RNHA and the first Hispanic to run for president of the United States in 1980, as a Republican in a primary race headlined by Ronald Reagan and George H. W. Bush.

Conservative Mexican Americans who didn't serve in the military during the war nevertheless saw the war years as an important period in their lives. They defended the United States at home against anyone who threatened it, even other Hispanics. The Los Angeles lawyer Manuel Ruiz, for example, served as chairman of the Citizens Committee for Latin American Youth. He had already spent several years writing and speaking about the supposed "delinquency" of Mexican American teens, who sparked demands for the increased attention to children's needs that Rebecca Jo Plant writes about in her essay in this book. In general, Ruiz argued that Mexican American youth could not be labeled uniformly as troublemakers. Individuality and equality before the law were the best aspects of a democracy, so they should be judged as individuals. Many of them had immigrated from Mexico within the past couple of decades. Solving their problems required only adjustment to life in the United States. If given a chance, they would assimilate as other immigrants had done. During the war it was especially important to give them a chance, since Mexico was an important ally that the United States shouldn't alienate by discriminating against Mexican youth.[14]

But Ruiz found himself in a tight spot in the summer of 1943, when the Zoot Suit Riots broke out in downtown Los Angeles between American sailors and alleged members of Mexican American gangs. He was torn between defending Mexican American youth against their accusers and scolding them for their participation in the unpatriotic violence. Along with other members of his committee, Ruiz demanded investigations into reports that Los Angeles police officers stood idly by as sailors tore the clothes off of Mexican American teens and beat them. But he also called for the punishment of Mexican Americans who participated in the riots.[15]

When "Johnny" from the Army Flying School in Victorville, California, wrote Ruiz to ask what was going on with those "god-damn Mexican punks" who were "raping women and knifing lone soldiers" in Los Angeles, Ruiz responded that there were "hot heads on both sides." Most Mexican American youth were law-abiding citizens. Many men served in the military, and many women worked in defense industries. A few, however, gave all Mexican Americans a bad name. The Mexican American community was "getting after the trouble makers," many of whom were already in prison. He reassured Johnny that Mexican American servicemen, in particular, "feel like you do" about the zoot-suiters. He waged a politics of respectability to distinguish himself from the more undesirable elements of the Mexican American community.[16]

Business

Between their wartime experience and political rise, several conservative Mexican Americans who came of age during World War II became successful businessmen. Their service in the military had given them some of the professional skills they relied on after the war, but they also credited their education. It has become commonplace to note that Hispanic veterans of World War II used the benefits of the GI Bill to attend college, secure home loans, and launch their professional careers. While the GI Bill didn't benefit all veterans equally, for many Hispanics it was a "golden ticket," as one historian has written.[17] This was as true for Republican Hispanics as for other Hispanics who had served in the war, even though the postwar careers of Mexican American conservatives are virtually unknown. Oaxaca used his GI Bill benefits to finish his degree at the University of Texas at El Paso. Fernandez used his GI Bill benefits to pursue degrees at the University of Redlands in California and New York University. They formed the conservative edge of a generation of Hispanics who entered skilled and semiskilled positions after World War II in greater numbers than ever before.

Their degrees paved the way for their lucrative careers. Oaxaca majored in engineering because he believed it would lead to a profession with "reasonable economic expectations." For much of the 1950s and 1960s he worked as an engineer in the "aerospace business," trying, he said, "to build the best hydrogen bombs in the world." He worked exclusively in the defense industry to develop products that "had nothing but a destructive output."[18] These, too, were the industries that Gavin Wright and Daniel Kevles demonstrate in their contributions in this book were central to the economic growth of the postwar West. They provided opportunities to Mexican American professionals in addition to other scientists, professors, and entrepreneurs.

In 1969, Oaxaca got out of government defense work and, with a few others, started a research and consulting business called Ultrasystems, where he began to earn a high salary and to live a life of "relative affluence." In the 1970s, as he became involved in politics, he founded media company in Los Angeles called Coronado Communications. The Immigration and Naturalization Service hired his company to advertise the federal amnesty program established by the Immigration Reform and Control Act of 1986. To conduct research for the marketing campaign, Oaxaca drove his Jaguar through East Los Angeles, knocking on doors to survey Mexican immigrants about what they knew of the law.[19] As Oaxaca gained wealth, he became more conservative. Like other conservatives in the West and across the country, he didn't like seeing all of the taxes he paid go to poor people whom he didn't think worked as hard as he had. "It's very hard, when you're fortunate," Oaxaca said, "to relate to those who are not," unless he saw them "out there truly, literally sweating," like he did.[20]

Fernandez, meanwhile, used his degree in economics to gain admission to New York University's business school and then to secure a job with General Electric at the same time that Reagan worked with the company. From there, Fernandez returned to California to start a management consulting company. He had come a long way from the railroad boxcar in Kansas City where he was born. When Fernandez was in college in California, he dreamed of becoming rich, and he linked his desire for wealth to his reason for becoming a Republican. In the late 1970s, Fernandez told *Washington Post* columnist George Will that a friend at Redlands said that the Republican Party was the party for rich people. He said, "Sign me up! I've had enough of poverty."[21] Fernandez claimed that his consulting company had made him a millionaire, which gave him the freedom to enter the nonprofit world. He headed up the National Economic Development Agency (NEDA), a government creation funded by the Small Business Administration and the Office of Minority Business Enterprise, to help Hispanics start businesses.

The Arizona insurance salesman Robert Robles cashed in on his military service, just as Oaxaca and Fernandez had. His World War II experience became a credential that he listed on his vita, a kind of kind of calling card that helped him secure employment in the private sector. "Better credentials led to better jobs" for Hispanics, as one historian put it.[22] Robles found work easily after the war. He recalled that he had been home for just a week when an executive at the Transcontinental Freight Bureau called him and said, "We have a job for you if you want it." He represented the company in western Mexico, from the border all the way to Guadalajara. Robles already spoke Spanish and English, but in his position with the freight company he "became well acquainted with towns, cities, customs, traditions, every-day language, technical language and mannerisms of the people."[23]

Robles's first job after the war set him up for a career with the New York Life Insurance Company. From Yuma, Arizona, Robles used his work with New York Life to establish relationships with "Mexican business men and professionals," including pharmacists, lawyers, dentists, and physicians. He ended up selling them insurance policies and joining them as a member of the Rotary Club, which had expanded into the West and the US-Mexico borderlands after World War II as a result of the region's economic growth. As Robles developed ties with Mexican businessmen, he climbed the ranks of organizations such as the Optimist Club of Yuma and the Yuma County Chamber of Commerce, of which he served as chairman of the Mexico-US Relations Committee.[24] Robles's career demonstrated how Mexican Americans shaped the postwar American West by nurturing cross-border business connections with Mexico that became an important part of the region's demographic and economic boom after World War II.[25]

Politics

Historians of Latinos in the United States have long recognized World War II as an important turning point for Latino political activism. As a historian of Hispanics in Congress has put it, the war was a "watershed moment in the development of Hispanic-American political activism."[26] Latinos said time and again that they had fought against the Axis powers to preserve democracy abroad, so when they returned to the United States they expected it at home as well. Demands for equality abroad and at home were the crux of their "double victory" campaign. They joined older social and political organizations or formed new ones to "galvanize political awareness, register votes, and generate leadership throughout the Southwest."[27]

Perhaps the most noted example of postwar Latino political activism has been the American GI Forum, founded by Hector García. The organization was founded specifically for Hispanic veterans, initially in Texas but then across the United States. During the war García commanded troops and then served in the Army medical corps so the military could take advantage of his medical training at the University of Texas at Galveston and during his residency at Creighton University in Nebraska. When García returned to Texas after the war, he opened a medical practice and helped Mexican American veterans file claims with the Veterans Administration. He broadened the scope of his efforts to fight discrimination against Mexican Americans nationally. The American GI Forum and other civil rights organizations, such as the League of United Latin American Citizens, struggled "in the courts and in their communities" for political and social inclusion.[28] Perhaps most famously, García lobbied for another Mexican American World War II veteran, Felix Longoria, a private in the US Army, to be buried in Arlington National Cemetery after Longoria had been refused interment in the segregated cemetery of Three Rivers, Texas, where he was born and raised. García and others in the community resented that a Mexican American could fight and die in the war and then be discriminated against after giving his life. The American GI Forum was also important in the establishment of the Viva Kennedy clubs that formed to help elect John F.

Kennedy, just as Viva Nixon groups of Republican Hispanics formed to help elect Nixon, in 1960.[29] Such groups signaled the rise of Hispanic political influence in the Southwest and were followed up by Viva Johnson and Latinos con Goldwater groups, and so forth. Both parties had begun to seek the votes of Mexican Americans.

Other Democrats besides García have received considerable attention from scholars, including Edward Roybal, Raymond Telles, and Vicente Ximenes. In 1949, Roybal became the first Latino elected to the Los Angeles City Council since the nineteenth century, and in 1962 he got elected to the US House of Representatives. Roybal served on the Veterans Affairs Committee for several years, and in 1976 he cofounded the Congressional Hispanic Caucus. Telles also had a distinguished political career. In 1957 he was elected as the mayor of El Paso; in 1961, President Kennedy appointed him as ambassador to Costa Rica; in 1967, President Johnson appointed him as director of the US-Mexico Border Commission; and in 1971, President Nixon appointed him as chairman of the Equal Employment Opportunity Commission.

Finally, after retiring from the military, Ximenes became a member of García's GI Forum. Kennedy chose Ximenes as the economist for the US Agency for International Development, Johnson appointed him as chairman of the Equal Employment Opportunities Commission and then as chairman of the Inter-Agency Committee on Mexican American Affairs, established in 1967 as the first cabinet-level advisory board to advocate for Hispanic affairs. The significance of their achievements is undeniable.

But in the decades after World War II, Mexican Americans who came of age during the war led the effort to bring Hispanics in the West and across the United States into the Republican Party. Their own grassroots organizing effort was of paramount importance, but they were also drawn to the personae of the first three western presidential candidates after World War II: Richard Nixon, Barry Goldwater, and Ronald Reagan. Each politician claimed to represent the region and said that they were deeply familiar with the interests of Hispanics because of the relationships they had developed with Mexican Americans. For their part, conservative Mexican Americans favored these western politicians because they shared their support for bilingual education, military interventions in countries taken over by "Communists," right-to-work laws, and free-market capitalism generally, as well as their opposition to busing programs.[30]

At the same time, Mexican Americans argued that Democrats took their votes for granted, made promises but didn't keep them, and were concerned almost exclusively with the civil rights of African Americans and Jewish Americans. Mexican Americans, they said, were always taking a back seat. The "current emphasis on Negro recognition," said one Republican Mexican American from Colorado, had "relegated" Mexican Americans to "third class status." Republican candidates encouraged such thinking and knew they would rely increasingly on Hispanics; they needed "the Latin vote" to "counteract the loss of the Negro vote."[31]

Mexican Americans were personally drawn to these western Republicans. Nixon's Mexican American supporters said that the president "was once a poor white man who worked alongside poor Mexicans in the orchards and fields" surrounding Whittier, California. That was where he "got to know us," CCOSSP chairman Henry Ramirez wrote, "while we lived our culture in accord with our values: God, family, hard work, respect for the law, and an aversion to handouts."[32] They credited Nixon with launching one of the first Hispanic outreach efforts during his campaign for a US Senate seat in 1950.

In his failed bid for the presidency in 1964, Goldwater said that he lived his "whole life on the Mexican border" and that he "spoke Spanish about the same time that I spoke English." He was a son of the borderland.[33] Reagan fashioned himself as a cowboy, like the *rancheros* of the US-Mexico borderlands. Riding alongside Mexican Americans, Reagan ceremoniously traveled on horseback from his Rancho del Cielo—the western White House near Santa Barbara—into northern Mexico.[34] Conservative Hispanics saw all of these men as candidates who were familiar with their interests as cohabitants of a region that had become increasingly relevant politically and economically in the decades after World War II.

In politics, like in business, the conservative Mexican Americans from the West who had served in World War II were committed to increasing social, economic, and political opportunities for other Hispanics. They established the RNHA, which advocated for Hispanic interests within the Republican Party. The RNHA became something of a bullpen for presidential appointments to federal government posts, such as special assistant to the president, chairman of the Small Business Administration, treasurer of the United States, or chairman of the Equal Employment Opportunity Commission. They struggled for influence with Republican presidents, lobbying for policies that would be beneficial to Hispanic Americans and Latin American immigrants throughout the United States, including "amnesty" for undocumented immigrants, jobs programs, and an extension of the Voting Rights Act to make it easier for Spanish speakers to vote. These were all positions supported by conservative Mexican Americans from the Southwest, including Luján, Fernandez, and Oaxaca, as well as western leaders of the Republican Party.

Another priority for conservative Mexican Americans after World War II was hemispheric diplomacy, or "re-establishing good relations with our neighbors to the south," as they put it, which in their opinion had been damaged by the foreign policies of successive Democratic presidential administrations.[35] Kennedy attempted to strengthen relationships throughout the hemisphere with the Alliance for Progress, which used economic development as diplomatic strategy. But buying the loyalty of Latin Americans was not how you demonstrated true friendship, conservatives said. Kennedy's bungling of the Bay of Pigs Invasion didn't help his standing among Hispanics, especially with Cuban exiles. Lyndon Johnson and Jimmy Carter, meanwhile, were soft on Communism and enabled Castro's continued influence in the Americas. By the time Reagan became president, conservative Hispanics said, he had to clean up after their mess by supporting counterrevolutions in Latin American countries that had been taken over by leftists.

Representative Manuel Luján Jr. of New Mexico was the most prominent conservative Hispanic in Congress. He was their *only* representative in Congress actually. He, too, had come of age during World War II. Born in 1928, he was only seventeen in 1945, too young to serve in the military. But the war years and New Mexico's postwar economies had shaped his worldview. Luján had helped found the RNHA and stood for the core principles of the Republican Party in the mid-1970s. He was elected in 1968 and quickly became the chairman of the RNC's Spanish Speaking Advisory Committee. Luján also shepherded through the review process the RNHA's application to become an official auxiliary of the RNC.

By the time Hispanic Democrats formed the Congressional Hispanic Caucus in 1976, Luján had served in Congress for almost a decade. Democrats said that he could join the group "if he would support its objectives."[36] He declined at first but then signed on in 1978. Throughout the 1970s Luján was a member of the House Interior and Insular Affairs Committee, which oversaw not only western lands but also Puerto Rico and other island territories. Luján served ten terms in a district that was 40 percent Hispanic, 10 percent Native American, and 50 percent white, where Democrats outnumbered Republicans by more than two to one.

In part because he had managed to win in a largely Democratic district, Luján believed that his thinking was "in tune" with that of Hispanic Democrats in Congress, but once he opened up about his views on issues from land conservation to social protest, the differences became clear. Far more than Democrats, Luján supported the economic development of western lands—mineral extraction, water use for commercial purposes, the burning of fuel without regard for pollution. The public lands that Jared Farmer writes about in his chapter in this book were always vulnerable to business interests in Luján's New Mexico, and Luján wanted it that way, or at least he said that it was important to balance environmental and business interests, which wasn't the environmentalist's view.

Even though Luján recognized how the Spanish language enriched his life and opened many opportunities to him, especially as a cultural broker between US and Latin American officials, he reduced funds for New Mexico's bilingual education programs. Discrimination was real, Luján acknowledged, since many Americans held stubborn attitudes toward Hispanics, African Americans, Native Americans, and other minorities. Yet he rationalized a preference for lighter skin by suggesting it was a matter of personal comfort. "You can identify better with that guy who's not jet black," he said. Many Hispanics called that racism.[37] Like Mexican American Democrats, Luján opposed restrictive immigration reforms proposed in the 1970s, but he did so for different reasons. Most Mexican Americans opposed their employer sanctions provisions, which would have fined employers for knowingly hiring undocumented immigrants, because the threat of penalties could lead companies to discriminate against Hispanics in the hiring process whether they were citizens or not. Luján, however, opposed sanctions because he considered them to be unfair punishment of businesses for the government's failure to prevent undocumented immigration.[38]

Lastly, Luján's views of US–Latin American relations were representative of the views of conservative Hispanics after World War II and were opposed to the views of his Democratic counterparts in Congress. He stressed that the role of the United States after the war was to defend the world, and especially the Americas, against the spread of Communism. He supported military aid to Anastasio Somoza, the right-wing dictator in Nicaragua, while Democrats did not. Luján wanted to hold on to the Panama Canal, whereas Hispanic Democrats wanted to cede control to Panama. He opposed the "leftist" Mexican president, Luis Echeverría, for his alleged support of Fidel Castro and Salvador Allende, the socialist president of Chile recently ousted by the conservative

Augusto Pinochet.[39] These views were no different than those held by Cuban exiles in Miami, but they had roots that dated back to World War II and the early years of the Cold War, instead of the Cuban Revolution.

The Mexican Americans who came of age during World War II and built the conservative Hispanic movement became increasingly involved in national politics in the 1960s and 1970s. Robles, Castillo, Oaxaca, and Fernandez are just a few examples. Slightly older than the others, Robles represented an earlier generation of conservative Hispanics, before there was a truly national movement started by Mexican Americans from the West. But he was an important bridge between the earlier generation and what he called a "new generation" of Hispanics that was no longer beholden to the Democratic Party because of how Franklin Delano Roosevelt had helped their families during the Great Depression, providing them relief and employment.[40] While their parents were irreversibly Democrats, this new generation was frustrated with the Democratic Party. Presidents Kennedy and Johnson had promised appointments and real solutions to their financial, educational, and social problems, but these went unrealized. They were willing to hear the Republican sales pitch.

In 1964, Robles worked for the Goldwater campaign as chairman of the Hispanic Division in Goldwater's home of Arizona. Robles's efforts to convince Hispanics to vote for Goldwater were a failure—fewer than 10 percent did so, even in the West. A few years after Goldwater's historic loss, Robles sent the Arizona senator a postmortem analysis of what had gone wrong among Hispanics in 1964. Namely, Republicans couldn't expect success if they only reached out to them in the weeks before the election. Robles laid out a plan for Republicans to recruit Hispanics in 1968 and beyond. The Republican Party's breakout moment came in 1972, when Nixon won a third of the Hispanic vote after capturing a paltry 5 percent to 10 percent in 1968.[41]

Between 1968 and 1972, Nixon completely revamped his approach, with the help of a crew of Mexican American advisers from the West. He changed the name of Johnson's Inter-Agency Committee for Mexican American Affairs to the Cabinet Committee on Opportunities for Spanish-Speaking People (CCOSSP), primarily because of pressure from Puerto Ricans who didn't feel included in the "Mexican American" agency. Mexican Americans still dominated the Hispanic conservative movement, and Puerto Ricans, who also were gaining a national voice in politics, didn't like it. For the first chairman of the new CCOSSP, Nixon appointed the World War II veteran Martin Castillo. Henry Ramirez, who succeeded Castillo as chairman of the CCOSSP, wrote in his memoir, *A Chicano in the White House*, that Castillo became a "feisty criminal trial lawyer" after serving in the war as a "jet fighter pilot." He was one of a "horde of young, very educated, and aggressive Mexican Americans in the hallways of Washington's bureaucracy" in the late 1960s.[42]

Castillo was a Democrat for much of his life, but he consorted with Republicans more than Democrats and served in three Republican administrations. Nixon "wanted to change Washington," Ramirez wrote, and "Chicano ex-GIs would be the change agents." For Ramirez, as the title of his memoir suggests, the term "Chicano" included conservatives like him, even though it was mostly applied to more liberal and radical Hispanics. He called himself a "civil rights warrior," demonstrating how conservatives embraced different tactics for achieving inclusion and equality but were nevertheless on board with pursuing a civil rights agenda. They didn't see themselves as the "sell outs" that many Hispanics considered them to be.[43] Fernando Oaxaca had Castillo to thank for bringing him to work for Nixon. He recalled that as a younger man, he had run with a "bohemian," liberal crowd after college. Oaxaca became a member of a "Democratic club" in Los Angeles, supported Kennedy in 1960 and Johnson in 1964, and said he thought Goldwater was "a nut" because he was going to "defoliate Vietnam and then use atom bombs and all this sort of thing."[44]

But by 1968, Oaxaca had decided that it was "time to change parties." Mainly his decision had to do with Nixon's promise to "do something positive" about Vietnam. As the owner of his own media firm whose rise was made possible by the growing influence of Mexican Americans and Hispanics in general, in both business and politics, Oaxaca began to live a life of "affluence" that made him "more politically conservative."[45] After his conversion, Oaxaca became the most loyal of Republicans; according to his obituary in the *Los Angeles Times*, his friends called him "Mr. Republican." One recalled how Oaxaca "could not be swayed from his mission of bringing the Republican philosophy to the Latino community."[46]

By the late 1960s, Oaxaca had become a leader of the conservative Hispanic movement. He himself never ran for office, but he served every Republican president from Nixon to Reagan. When Castillo was chairman of the CCOSSP, he called on Oaxaca to help him "set up" the group. Through Castillo, Oaxaca said, "a whole new world opened up for me." Oaxaca then served on Nixon's Board of Vocational Education. Benjamin Fernandez recommended him to become a "Counsellor" to President Gerald Ford. He said Oaxaca was the "kind of man who projects the finest image for all Americans." Ford appointed Oaxaca to another position instead, and he kept climbing the Republican ranks. By 1980, Oaxaca had become the chairman of the RNHA, the national cochairman of Reagan's Hispanic campaign, and a board member of the Hispanic Council on Foreign Affairs. In 1983, Reagan appointed him to the International Private Enterprise Task Force, created by executive order in 1982. Oaxaca's job was to advise the president and the heads of multiple economic development agencies on the role that "private enterprise" might play in economic assistance programs to foreign countries.[47]

By 1980, Fernandez had become the most well-known Republican Mexican American in the country, and his political career started in the West. He helped open Mexican American–owned banks in California, and it was his life's ambition to bring Republican Hispanics together nationally. The former Air Force serviceman had announced in November 1978 that he would run for president of the United States, making him the first Hispanic to do so from either party. His announcement came more than two decades before Bill Richardson (D-NM) ran in 2008, and more than three decades before Marco Rubio (R-FL) and Ted Cruz (R-TX) ran in 2016. By the time that Fernandez ran in 1980, he had decades of business and government experience as well as decades of experience recruiting Hispanics to join the Republican Party. When Fernandez returned to California after business school, he became increasingly involved in politics. He joined Castillo and Oaxaca, working for Nixon, as the chairman of Nixon's National Hispanic Finance Committee. Through his role in Nixon's reelection campaign, he became a member of Nixon's so-called Brown Mafia. Headed by an Asian American man named Bill Marumoto, and whose other members were Mexican Americans from California, the Brown Mafia tried to funnel federal government support to Hispanics who supported the president.[48]

Fernandez became the lone Hispanic called to testify before the Senate Watergate Committee. Wearing a three-piece suit and red-and-blue-striped tie, he looked like a consummate professional as he flatly denied the accusation of a Florida contractor that he offered him a quid pro quo: Fernandez would make the contractor's troubles with the US Department of Housing and Urban Development go away in exchange for a one-hundred-thousand-dollar donation to the National Hispanic Finance Committee. Although the purpose of Fernandez's testimony was to exonerate himself of any wrongdoing, which he did, he used almost every second of his prepared remarks, at the beginning and end of his testimony, to advertise and defend his efforts to build a national movement of conservative Hispanics. Fernandez had spent the past couple of decades "fostering the free-enterprise system among Spanish-speaking people throughout the United States," bringing "Spanish-speaking voters into the two-party system of government," and doing everything he could to support President Nixon, who "embraced us as first-class citizens."[49]

Fernandez recounted his success and commitment in each of these pursuits. As a businessman, he helped "lead our people"—Hispanics—"out of the economic wilderness." Before NEDA's establishment, there were 13,500 federally insured banks, and 4,500 federally insured savings and loans in the United States, but only one of each was "organized, managed, and controlled" by a Hispanic. Fernandez changed that. As a volunteer for the Nixon campaign, he traveled some 250,000 miles in 1972, all throughout the Southwest, and raised almost four hundred thousand dollars for Nixon's reelection. Even considering all of Nixon's troubles, Fernandez, speaking for all Hispanic conservatives, said, "our dedication has not wavered."[50]

By the late 1970s, Fernandez had developed a national profile that, he believed, made him the most qualified candidate in the race to become president. What's more, he believed that America needed a Hispanic president. He said so directly. Echoing national media, which predicted that the 1980s would be the "decade of the Hispanic," Fernandez argued that the United States "needs a President of Hispanic origin, bilingual in Spanish and English, fully understanding of both cultures." Hispanics represented a growing percentage of the population and an increasing share of the electorate. They were more politically active than ever before. More of them worked as employees or appointees of the federal government, and the civil rights era had prompted more Hispanics to run for, and win, elected office than at any point since the nineteenth century. Yet they didn't have a national leader to represent them. Fernandez would be their man. He would run a campaign for all Americans, and for Hispanics in particular. "Ben Fernandez is America," he said. "Fernandez para Presidente."[51]

Mobilizing the growing political power of Hispanics and bringing them together under the same umbrella—not only as individuals of Mexican, Cuban, and Puerto Rican descent but as Hispanics—had been Fernandez's mission for almost two decades, for as long as he had been involved in politics. In his testimony before the Senate Watergate Committee, he claimed that trying to "work the Spanish-speaking people into a cohesive unit" was the "toughest thing I've ever done in my life." Hispanics, he said, had a "tradition of not working together." They came from different places and had different interests. Fernandez drove home the point with a joke: Hispanics often said that "the

FIGURE 5.1 Campaign photo. *Source*: Eugene Acosta Marin Papers, 1945–2002, Chicano/a Research Collection, Arizona State University Library. Reprinted with permission.

Mexican American does not talk to the Puerto Rican, the Puerto Rican does not talk to the Cubano, the Cubano talks to no one."[52]

But Fernandez saw himself as a unifying force. All Hispanics could rally around him because of his humble origins and meteoric rise made possible by his military service, his education, and the economic growth of the West during and after World War II. By 1980 he said he was a millionaire, but he began life as many Hispanics did, in poverty. His wealth had been the result of hard work and individual initiative. Fernandez embodied the American Dream. "Fernandez is America." He would "restore faith" that "anyone born in this country who prepares himself, who works hard, and is willing to shoot for the moon, can one day become President of the United States." This, he said, was the American Dream. Before a gathering of students and faculty at the University of Texas at El Paso, Fernandez described how an acquaintance of Bush had told him, "Ben, my god, if you can rally the Mexicano, the Hispano, call him what you will, in California, Arizona, Texas, Florida, New York, and New Jersey, you'll win." His response: "The thought has occurred to me."[53]

Nevertheless, cracks in the conservative Hispanic movement that Fernandez, Oaxaca, and others had built over the past several decades began to appear in the early 1980s. Even though they had been loyal Republicans for a long time, Oaxaca and Fernandez broke with Reagan over his support for the Simpson-Mazzoli bill in the early 1980s, which became the Immigration Reform and Control Act (IRCA) that the president signed in 1986. They supported the law's amnesty provisions but not its employer sanctions. They said the bill was a disgrace and promised to encourage Reagan to veto it if and when it landed on his desk. Oaxaca said, "I am an American first, a Mexican-American second, and a Republican third," as an explanation for his willingness to go against his party if the alternative was to support policies that were harmful to Hispanics and, in his estimation, the United States.[54] On the far right of the political spectrum, anti-immigration groups like the Federation for American Immigration Reform (FAIR) opposed Simpson-Mazzoli as well. In contrast with Fernandez, Oaxaca, and many other Hispanics, FAIR strongly supported employer sanctions but opposed the bill's amnesty provisions. The fact that Republican Hispanics distanced themselves from Reagan and the Republican Party, and aligned themselves with Democrats instead, portended deeper divisions over immigration in the years to come.

The foundation of the conservative Hispanic movement became increasingly shaky as the United States became increasingly divided over immigration and border enforcement. The grounds for its shakiness were also located in the West, because of tense debates about immigration in California and throughout the US-Mexico borderlands. Tensions over immigration were themselves the product of the demographic growth of the Mexican population after World War II, especially after 1965 and the establishment of *maquiladoras* in northern Mexico, which could not have happened without the economic growth of the borderlands after the war.[55] Some of the *maquiladoras* located in the borderlands were owned and operated by American companies that had moved their manufacturing operations from the Midwest and other regions, which only fueled the anti-immigrant sentiments that got projected upon the Southwest from other areas of the United States.[56]

Oaxaca, in particular, became increasingly vocal about his opposition in the mid-1990s. Nationally, Pat Buchanan, George H. W. Bush's primary challenger in 1992, had proposed the construction of a border wall and generally maligned Latin American migration to the United States as an assault on Western civilization (as though Latin Americans weren't part of the Western world). Locally, in California the Republican governor Pete Wilson, when he was trailing his opponent by double digits, latched on to undocumented immigration as his central campaign issue. Support for the anti-immigration ballot initiative, Proposition 187, came to define him. Oaxaca didn't like this development at all. After his years of government service, he reentered the private sector as an immigrant rights activist. He owned KSNE, a radio station in Ontario, California, that broadcast twenty-four hours a day and intermixed *ranchera* music with practical advice for immigrants about what to do if they lost their passport or green card.[57]

In the short run, the Republican Party of California lost Oaxaca because of its support for Proposition 187. In the long run, the party's support for the law caused it to lose Republican Hispanics more broadly. The early 1980s was a kind of high point for Mexican American influence within the Republican Party. It is important to remember that their ascent was the product of a movement established by Mexican Americans who had come of age in the American West during World War II. They were neither the totality of the Hispanic conservative movement, nor broadly representative of the politics of Mexican Americans. By 1980, Cuban Americans gained influence within the Hispanic conservative movement and the Republican Party in general, giving Reagan some 90 percent of their votes, while Mexican American Democrats played national leadership roles in the relatively new Congressional Hispanic Caucus.

Yet conservative Mexican Americans from the West nevertheless offer important insights into the development of Latino and Republican Party politics from World War II to the late twentieth century. They also offer a different angle for viewing the rise of conservatism in the West. Mexican Americans helped build the region's conservative movement, alongside the liberal civil rights movements started by others in their communities. From their perch in the American West, and through their travels back and forth between the West and Washington, DC, to represent Hispanic interests, they built a national movement whose result was a significant share of Hispanics voting as loyal Republicans, even in elections featuring Republican candidates whose disparaging remarks about them make their support seem inexplicable.

6

"NO PRIVATE SCHOOL COULD EVER BE AS SATISFACTORY"

The Fight for Government-Funded Child Care in Postwar Los Angeles

REBECCA JO PLANT

Following World War II, the GI Bill allowed millions of veterans to pursue education and purchase homes, but proposals for a more expansive welfare state that would benefit all Americans remained unrealized. Just as legislation to establish a universal health-care system went down in defeat, wartime child-care centers were quickly shuttered. But in California, home to by far the largest number of wartime child-care centers, a coalition of mothers and "labor unions, early childhood educators, African Americans, women's groups, Communist Party members, and left feminists" lobbied for a permanent, universal, state-funded child-care program that would be incorporated into California's public schools.[1] Although this advocacy succeeded in securing the nation's only state-funded child-care program, it fell far short of proponents' original vision.[2] Instead of keeping the centers open to all working mothers, as had been the case during World War II, the assembly restricted the program in ways that set the stage for its transformation into a welfare program once federal monies again became available during the mid-1960s.

This chapter focuses on how the debates surrounding child care played out in Los Angeles, an epicenter of wartime production and home to the most extensive network of child-care centers in the state.[3] Especially in the immediate postwar years, parents who had benefited from the wartime centers insisted that child care was not just a pressing familial need, but a social good that should be supported by the state, local communities, and public schools. Rejecting the notion that they should have to turn to charitable or church-run nurseries, expensive private nursery schools, or informal arrangements with family and friends, Angelenos demanded continued access to affordable and high-quality care for preschoolers and extended-day programs for school-age youths in state-supported and licensed facilities.

In pressing their case, parents—primarily but not exclusively mothers—gave voice to a progressive vision of social citizenship that had roots in the city's prewar history. For roughly three decades before the war, Los Angeles had been home to tax-funded nurseries based in public schools in impoverished immigrant communities—an urban child-care program unparalleled in size and scope. During the Great Depression, additional nurseries opened as part of a New Deal program designed to provide jobs to unemployed teachers. These centers became the foundation upon which the wartime program was constructed. In part because of this prior history and preexisting infrastructure, Los Angeles succeeded in meeting working women's needs to a greater extent than other war-impacted cities (though still by no means sufficiently). Parents' positive experiences with the centers in turn ratcheted up expectations, which helps to explain why so many of the city's residents emerged from the war convinced that the government—whether federal, state, or local—should shoulder significant responsibility for child-care provision.[4]

The debate about child care that played out in postwar Los Angeles is notable for the extent to which it deviated from the larger national discourse about motherhood and child care. In the national press, concerns about the effects of maternal deprivation on children and the dangers of governmental incursions into family life loomed large. But such ideologically oriented critiques were surprisingly muted in Los Angeles residents' discussions of the child-care program. Because the centers almost uniformly drew praise from parents, who often singled out beloved teachers or described their positive influence in touchingly personal terms, they could not easily be delegitimized with stridently ideological arguments. In Sacramento, critics sometimes raised the specter of communism or denounced maternal employment outside the home, but even they mostly opposed the centers on other grounds, arguing that the benefits accrued almost exclusively to urban areas, or that the state should simply not be in the business of providing early childhood education.[5]

The Los Angeles experience suggests that, at least within urban areas that had a progressive history and became centers of wartime production, the heavy reliance on women workers had the potential to radically alter beliefs about the government's obligation to parents and children. In pressing to keep centers open after the war ended, many Angelenos argued that emergency conditions persisted: the acute housing shortage and high cost of living, combined with veterans' readjustment difficulties and their uncertain employment situation, made child-care services more necessary than ever in the immediate postwar period. In a city that contributed so much to the war effort—and one that by 1948 claimed more veteran residents than any other in the nation—beleaguered parents felt entitled to assistance as they struggled to raise the nation's future citizens while contending with overcrowding, high prices, and other aggravations that plagued former centers of wartime production.[6] More than anything, the unapologetic manner in which they voiced these demands illustrates the transformative power and potential of wartime social upheaval.

In the end, however, a gradual retreat from World War II's egalitarian emphasis on shared sacrifice, along with a growing emphasis on fiscal conservatism at the state level and competing priorities on the local level, prevented the development of a comprehensive, state-funded child-care program. The fact that publicly funded centers were so closely linked to military service and wartime sacrifice also undercut the claims of those who hoped to establish a more expansive and permanent program. The fate of California's wartime child-care program thus serves as both a cautionary tale for those who still believe that affordable, high-quality early childhood education should be an entitlement and a means of understanding the uneven character of public child-care provision in the United States today.

Publicly Funded Child Care in Los Angeles prior to World War II

The history of day care as we know it today dates back to the late nineteenth century, when charitable and religious organizations began to establish "day nurseries" in many large US cities to care for the children of wage-earning mothers. These women had typically been forced into the workplace because their husbands had died, deserted the family, or become incapacitated through illness or injury. Sending children to a day nursery was seen as preferable to allowing them to roam the streets, but it was still regarded as a tragic capitulation to necessity. No institution, Americans at the time firmly believed, could adequately substitute for the loving care that mothers bestowed on children in their own homes.[7]

By the turn of the century, churches and women's voluntary organizations had established numerous day nurseries in East Coast and Midwestern cities, but southern California lagged behind when it came to addressing impoverished mothers' needs for child care. A relative paucity of day nurseries run by charities and voluntary organizations helps to explain the development of an extraordinary though little known program in the Los Angeles City public school district. It originated when truant officers began enforcing compulsory school attendance in the early 1910s and discovered that many students, especially from immigrant families with two working parents, stayed home because they had to care for younger siblings. When compelled to attend school, these "little mothers" brought along their even younger charges—who were often wet, tired, and hungry—carrying them into class or depositing them in school hallways and principals' offices.

To manage this chaotic situation, school officials appealed to the National Mothers' Congress (forerunner to the PTA). The organization's mother-volunteers responded with characteristic alacrity and established onsite day nurseries. These were classic Progressive Era institutions in the sense that the badly needed assistance they provided, including not just child care but also nutritious meals, went hand-in-hand with assimilationist efforts aimed at both mothers and children.[8] Though initially run by volunteers, the nurseries soon evolved into established operations staffed by a head teacher, another teacher, and a cook. Each nursery enrolled up to forty young children, with cribs on site for the infants. Parents who could afford to paid a modest fee (ten cents) to cover the cost of food, but there was no other cost for the service and no formal means test. The program was funded through local taxes, which the state later supplemented.

In 1917 the Los Angeles Board of Education officially assumed responsibility for the "support and supervision of all needed nurseries," having concluded that they were indispensable to the schools' mission of educating older children.[9] No other large school district in the nation had attempted something on a similar scale when it came to caring for preschool-age children.[10] However, because the state's educational code did not extend to preschool children, the nurseries operated on a questionable legal basis. In 1926 the school district tried to stave off potential challenges to the program by recasting the nurseries as "home economics laboratories" designed to teach older girls how to care for young children. (As one former teacher put it, they "bootlegged" the day nurseries into the public school system.)[11] It was a rather threadbare rationale, given the nurseries' history and hours of operation (generally 7:30 a.m. to 5:00 p.m., well beyond the length of a normal school day).[12] Yet the program survived and flourished: by 1928 more than fifty employees were running twenty day nurseries in the city schools, with a monthly enrollment of more than fourteen hundred children.[13] Then, in early 1943, state legislation enacted to facilitate the establishment of centers for women war workers brought the home economics laboratories under new legal scrutiny.[14] Over the protests of teachers and others who hoped to keep them independent, they were transformed into federally funded facilities.[15]

During these same years California was emerging as an important center of a nationwide nursery school movement. Geared toward affluent and middle-class families, private nursery schools advertised themselves as educational rather than custodial institutions. Grounded in new theories of childhood development, they emphasized the importance of free play, exposure to music and art, and the development of motor skills. Nursery schools tended to be expensive and did not stay open long enough to serve the needs of working parents; most kept children for only a few hours or at most the length of a school day. Yet proponents passionately believed that all children could benefit from nursery school, and they envisioned a future in which public schools would expand to accommodate early childhood education. By 1930, California was home to nearly a third of the nation's nursery schools, even though only 5 percent of Americans lived in the state.[16] In addition, academic programs in early childhood education at the University of California (at both the Berkeley and Los Angeles campuses) and at Mills College in Oakland established laboratory nursery schools.[17] California was therefore well poised to contribute expertise and personnel during the Great Depression, when the federal government embarked on its first foray into child-care provision, the Emergency Nursery School Program (ENSP).

Typically described as a Depression-era jobs program designed to provide relief for unemployed teachers and staff, the ENSP should also be viewed as a pioneering initiative in early childhood education—one that helped to blur the distinction between day nurseries (designed to meet poor working mothers' basic needs for custodial care) and private nursery schools (designed to foster children's social and intellectual development).[18] At the program's outset child development professionals managed to convince policymakers in the Roosevelt administration that the nursery school rather than the day nursery should serve as the federal government's model. To underscore the nurseries' educational mission, they also argued that facilities should ideally be housed in public schools.[19] Thus the ENSP schools resembled private day nurseries in many respects, though they primarily served families on relief.[20]

The ENSP program operated for nearly a decade, first under the auspices of the Federal Emergency Relief Act and then, after 1935, under the Works Program Administration (WPA). On average, nearly fifteen thousand schools provided instruction to fifty thousand children between the ages of two and five years old each year.[21] California claimed an average of sixty-two nurseries during the program's operation (only five states had more), over half of which were located in Los Angeles.[22] As the unemployment rate fell in the late 1930s and fewer families could meet the eligibility requirements, enrollments diminished. By the time the Roosevelt administration ended the WPA in 1942 and the Federal Works Agency (FWA) assumed responsibility for the program's administration, a third of the program's nurseries had already closed, but those located in defense production areas continued to operate, becoming the nucleus around which the wartime child-care program was constructed.[23] In Los Angeles thirty-four former WPA nursery schools, and eight centers for older children, were converted into wartime centers aimed at serving working mothers.[24]

Despite its designation as an "emergency" program, those who ran the WPA nurseries hoped they might become an entering wedge for making early childhood education a regular part of the public school system. The WPA's final report from 1943 strikes a wistful note: "These nursery schools everywhere demonstrated their value as an efficient and beneficial mode of child care, and caused widespread hopes that nursery schools could be incorporated generally into the public school system for the benefit of all children."[25] Although the program clearly fell far short of that goal, it did serve as an important, if often overlooked, precursor to the wartime child-care program. Everything from the daily schedules the children followed to the letters that agitated parents wrote when local centers were threatened with closure anticipated Angelenos' wartime experiences with government-funded child care.[26]

Long before World War II, a significant number of the city's residents had some experience or familiarity with publicly funded nursery schools. As one commenter remarked in 1947: "Nurseries in the Los Angeles Schools are no innovation. They started many, many years ago."[27] Between the home economics laboratories and the WPA nurseries, more than two thousand children in Los Angeles were already attending publicly supported nursery schools when the United States entered World War II.[28] In fact, the national story often told about child care—that the war introduced Americans to the concept of universal child care, but only on an emergency wartime basis that allowed for the program's rapid dismantling—in some respects has things backward when it comes to the situation in Los Angeles. By subsuming the nation's only large municipal-level initiative in nursery school care, the wartime child-care program stripped the Los Angeles City School District's nurseries of their autonomy, which in turn opened them to the rigid means testing and other restrictions in the postwar period. In addition, the war's overweening focus on maximizing women's labor power during World War II took precedence over the guiding principles at the heart of the WPA nurseries, which lay in fostering children's social development and inculcating democratic principles.[29] Once the need for women's labor had ebbed, these more expansive arguments in favor of publicly funded child care would prove difficult to revive.

Federally Funded Child Care in Wartime Los Angeles

The push for federally funded child-care centers for working mothers began in earnest in 1943. The previous year, Congress enacted an amendment to the 1941 Community Facilities Act, otherwise known as the Lanham Act, that allowed localities in "war-impacted" areas to apply for federal funds to support centers for preschool and school-age children.[30] No other major American city was as "war-impacted" as Los Angeles. Unprecedented population growth, propelled by job opportunities in the mushrooming war industries, created severe housing shortages and contributed to growing racial tensions, while the influx of women into the workforce fueled fears of family breakdown and juvenile delinquency. Between 1940 and 1944 the number of women employed in California rose dramatically, from 631,000 to 1,200,000.[31] The rate of increase in Los Angeles was even more notable, reflecting the dominance of the aircraft industry, which was unusually keen on hiring women.[32] Between April 1940 and June 1943 the number of employed women in San Francisco rose from 27 to 32 per 100 workers, while in Los Angeles, women went from 28 to 37 per 100 active workers.[33]

The large number of women workers in Los Angeles meant that the city's need for child-care services was especially acute. Because of the Los Angeles public schools' long history of child-care provision, many appealed to the Board of Education for help in seeking federal funds and establishing centers. This included not only individual parents but also manufacturers, labor unions, early childhood educators, and federal officials charged with helping to meet the nation's labor needs. But with Los Angeles schools already bursting at the seams, principals and other officials resisted pressure to expand services beyond what they felt they could reasonably accommodate. At a school board meeting in late May 1943, tensions erupted when a CIO representative warned of a coming "production breakdown" if child-care facilities were not up and running by the school year's end. Representatives from the War Manpower Commission (WMC) similarly criticized the board's plan to request support for only twenty-five new centers as woefully insufficient, claiming the city needed ten times that number. Although such an estimate might seem "almost unbelievable in size," it was in fact "realistic and conservative," these officials argued: the labor shortage in Los Angeles was of such a magnitude "that nowhere else in the country is it even approached."[34]

Faced with such pressure, the school board and school administrators readjusted their thinking, though never to the extent that the WMC hoped. By September 1943, Los Angeles had 104 nursery schools and extended-day centers caring for three thousand children; within one year, those numbers more than doubled, to 224 centers with a total enrollment of around eighty-five hundred.[35] By early 1945, Frances P. Moore, executive director of the Los Angeles Committee for the Care of Children in Wartime, could report that the city's child-care program was caring for more than five thousand preschool-age children in 123 nursery schools, along with another five thousand school-age children in extended-day centers, making it "the largest [program] in the country."[36] Because of the persistent association between day nurseries and poverty, some residents initially spurned the child-care centers, preferring to leave their children with relatives or neighbors, even when such arrangements proved far from ideal.[37] But once parents tried the centers, they typically became true converts. In fact, waiting lists in Los Angeles grew so long—with more than eleven hundred children waiting for an opening—that all efforts to publicize the centers had to be discontinued.[38]

Parents who did manage to secure a spot often felt a profound—and profoundly personal—sense of gratitude toward their local centers and the individual teachers who cared for their children. Writing to the Board of Education in 1943, a father whose wife worked at a defense job believed that "no praise was too great" for the teachers at his daughter's child-care center, who managed to "keep the children happy and the school and its yard neat and clean."[39] A mother who wrote near the war's end reported that her daughter was "a better child for having been [at the centers] with other well cared for children," while another described "the care and training" that her son had received as "priceless."[40] These anecdotal accounts appear supported by an assessment of parent satisfaction conducted at two nurseries in Los Angeles County. Asked if they agreed with the statement that "on the whole" their child or children had "enjoyed nursery school," *all* of the 173 parents surveyed replied affirmatively. "The child care program for under-fives," the author concluded, "has reduced tensions, lessened friction in the home and insecurity in non-home situations, and so benefitted the children and strengthened family living."[41]

A mixture of widespread enthusiasm and profound dependence on the centers helps to account for the outcry following the federal government's announcement, just one week after V-J Day, that funding for the centers would cease in two months' time. Letters of protests poured into DC from across the country, but the clamor from California was particularly deafening. Of all the communications the Federal Works Agency (FWA) received asking for an extension of federal funding, two-thirds came from Californians.[42] At the same time, Los Angeles parents appealed to the authority closest to home, the Board of Education, regardless of the fact that it lacked decision-making power as to the program's ultimate fate.[43] "This is to inform you that the parents of Roscoe and other parents want a bill in the new State Legislature to assure a *permanent* child day care program," wrote one mother, "without a means test, and with *adequate funds* to *insure* [*sic*] lower fees so that those most in need will receive the benefits."[44]

Especially notable in this correspondence is the degree to which parents associated the government-funded centers with affordable and high-quality child care. In August 1945, Rep. Helen Gahagan Douglas entered several letters into the *Congressional Record* from her Los Angeles constituents that testify to ways in which parents differentiated between the publicly funded centers and other kinds of child care. A serviceman's wife with a four-year-old stated that she "would be unable to function" without the "Federal nurseries," noting that private nurseries were beyond their means and "any less formal arrangement" would be wholly unsatisfactory. After having her son "in a Government school," another military wife recoiled at the idea of being forced to place him "in a haphazardly run private school where there is little or no supervision."[45] Others correspondents warned that child neglect would increase if centers closed and mothers had to leave children with neighbors, friends, or even licensed but private child-care providers. As one constituent explained to Rep. Douglas,

"You cannot expect them to take the time and trouble to watch a child and give it [the] care it would receive in a Federal nursery school."[46]

Today, when right-wing activists refer to public schools as "government schools," they do so with confidence that the term will carry a negative valence.[47] But to many California parents who relied on public child care during World War II, the phrase "federal nursery school" did not evoke fears of an overweening central government bent on manipulating young minds. Instead, it conjured up images of well-trained and conscientious teachers, predictable schedules, and nutritious meals—in other words, a healthy and orderly environment that nourished young children physically, emotionally, and intellectually. In contrast, they associated alternatives to the government-funded centers—informal babysitting arrangements, foster care, and private nursery schools—with either inferior care, exorbitant expense, or both.

Parents' outpouring ultimately helped to convince a majority in the US Congress that an abrupt end to the program would further burden the wives of servicemen who remained stationed overseas. On these grounds, legislators appropriated an additional five million dollars to fund the centers, allowing them to remain open until the end of February 1946.[48] Thereafter, anxious parents pinned their hopes on the California state government, which had emerged from the war with a healthy budget surplus. Looking to Sacramento, those who had endured long working hours, cramped living spaces, separations and deaths, along with myriad lesser trials, fought to ensure that the transition to peace would not rob them of a service upon which they had come to rely.

Fighting for a Permanent State-Supported Program

Beginning while the Lanham Act was still operative, a broad grassroots coalition waged the fight for state-funded child care, as historian Natalie Fousekis has detailed. In January 1946 the legislature's only black assemblyman, Augustus Hawkins, representing South-Central Los Angeles, introduced a bill that would have funded a permanent child-care program. The proposed legislation did not include a means test; like the wartime Lanham facilities, the child-care centers would have been available to any working mother or single father with young children. In contrast, the bill that became law, cosponsored by the right-wing, anticommunist crusader Jack Tenney, allowed for only a yearlong program, approved on an emergency basis. A hotly debated amendment further restricted the program by stipulating that, beginning in July 1947, parents had to prove financial need to qualify for the program. Despite its vague language, the means test fundamentally altered the nature of the program, transforming it into "income-based rather than universal social provision." With the passage of this legislation, Tenney achieved his real—and openly avowed—goal of forestalling "efforts of the leftwing group in the Assembly from passing permanent legislation on the subject."[49]

Working parents in Los Angeles continued to press for a more expansive program. Indeed, they found it difficult to understand why "such a worthwhile activity" serving "the citizens of tomorrow" should be ended after a year rather than *expanded.* As one woman put it: "These centers answer a crying need and should never be closed, but enlarged to give all parents the opportunity to leave their children in the care of competent supervisors while they work."[50] Appealing to the school board, they lobbied to protect their own individual centers and to gain support for their campaign. "Please give the following your active support and backing when it is presented for passage by the Legislature," one father requested. "1. An undated Child Care program; 2. The abolition of the 'means test' in said program; 3. An adequate appropriation for said program, so that fees charged the parents remain below $3.25 per week."[51] Public school administrators, however, tended to be tepid in their support of the centers; they feared the program would siphon off funds for K-12 education, and they often coveted the space the centers occupied, wanting to reclaim it for their own purposes.

In appealing to the board, mothers stressed their own dire need, arguing that they could not stop working simply because hostilities had ceased. "I am appealing to you for your support to help get this bill through as this is a very vital need, as so many mothers *must work,*" urged one woman.[52] Another, who described herself as a "working mother and sole supporter of my family," pressed the board to establish "an adequate, *permanent,* and inexpensive program," while a third mother emphasized that she relied on her "own personal labor" to support herself and her son, since she had no "other relative or interested person who might be depended upon." Nor was her situation unusual, she stressed, noting: "There are many other mothers whose circumstances are similar."[53]

To drive home the critical importance of publicly funded child care, parents and other concerned citizens forecast the unhappy scenarios that would unfold should the centers be shuttered. Many claimed that unsupervised children would exacerbate the upsurge in juvenile delinquency. This fear was particularly acute in Los Angeles, where the annual arrest rate for youths under age eighteen had doubled between 1940 and 1943, and racism and xenophobia permeated discussions of juvenile delinquency.[54] By claiming that child-care centers helped to prevent juvenile delinquency, parents flipped the wartime argument advanced by alarmists like FBI director J. Edgar Hoover on its head. In early 1944, even as the War Manpower Commission sought to recruit women workers, Hoover had cautioned, "there must be no absenteeism among mothers" lest youths drift into delinquency.[55] In contrast, Los Angeles parents portrayed well-run child-care facilities as helping to *prevent* juvenile delinquency. "It is a known fact that the child who is permitted to run free and undisciplined, as it would of necessity do if the centers were closed, is a problem delinquent," wrote one mother.[56] Even more emphatically, Frank G. Pellet of the Railroad Brotherhoods' Legislative Council warned that workers would have to "quit their jobs or permit their children to run the streets with no supervision at all" should the centers close. This outcome would "materially increase the already high juvenile delinquency figures," he argued, adding pointedly, "and to that extend [*sic*] your board will be charged with the responsibility if you act to close the centers now operating in this area."[57]

Just as parents claimed that the centers helped to avert rather than cause juvenile delinquency, so they disputed the tendency to associate publicly funded child care with socialism and communism; on the contrary, they argued, child care should be viewed as an *antidote* to radical politics and social unrest. "The way to keep from objectionable forms of government, is for our present government to prevent the necessity," explained one mother, noting that "hardship and many social problems" would ensue if the centers closed.[58] Advocates similarly rebutted the Catholic Church's claims that child care weakened the family structure and eroded parental authority; on the contrary, they argued, the centers were propping up families severely damaged by the strains of war. "Face it Governor, Face it America. The American home is broken," one woman wrote to California Governor Earl Warren in late 1946. "War casualt[ies] and emotional maladjustments and economic conditions force many a mother to get out and make a living for her family. . . . The Child Care Centers are aware of their great task. Its teachers are trained to mold their impressionable young charges into sociably desirable and trustworthy citizens. . . . Governor, the 'child care centers' are our salvation!!"[59]

Veterans and their wives made especially forceful claims when demanding that the centers remain open. Some appeared to view government-funded child care almost as a military benefit, while others saw them as an essential component of the public school system. Protesting plans to shut down the extended-care program at his children's elementary school, one disabled veteran argued that it would be "like closing the schools of our nation, for these care-centers are a most necessary part of our educational system."[60] A petition protesting a proposed closure, signed by dozens of parents, took pains to note that "among us are veterans with our problems of readjustment" and others who "have the unfortunate responsibility of rearing our children single-handed to broken homes and sacrifices made to a country at war." Chastising the school board for its "selfish and limited point of view," the petitioners' appeal harkened back to the wartime ethos of shared sacrifices and mutual obligations: "We must all work together to provide the bare necessities of an American life for our children."[61] Another petition, claiming to represent the views of nineteen American Veteran (AMVET) posts in Los Angeles County, similarly demanded the benefit of continued child care based on the conviction that such services should be considered "a basic and integral part of American democratic life." As the petitioners reminded the school board, "all of the citizens of this country owe a moral and material obligation to the widows of our fighting men, as well as the wives at home whose husbands are still in the service."[62]

The problem with portraying child-care centers in this manner—as fulfilling a debt to those who fought, or as meeting a dire social need created by the war—is that the argument had an inevitable if imprecise expiration date. When advocates portrayed child-care centers as fulfilling a "moral and material" obligation to war wives and war widows, or as a stabilizing influence that would alleviate the social and economic upheaval caused by demobilization, they reinforced the notion that publicly subsidized child care was a short-term solution to an emergency situation. That in turn raised the question: For how long after a war did a society remain in crisis? As the years ticked by and the program's initial wartime justifications receded, child-care advocates would find themselves pressed to defend the centers in new ways.

California's Post–World War II Child-Care Centers

Between 1947 and 1951 parents and the educators allied with them had to fight every year to sustain the centers. Public opinion—so far as it can be gauged by letters to the governor, assemblymen, and school boards, as well as published letters-to-the-editor—ran strongly in favor of the centers. Beach Vassey, legislative secretary to Governor Warren, reported in February 1948 that two subjects dominated correspondence from constituents: child care and rent control. Whereas letters concerning rent control were "evenly divided for and against," those addressing child care skewed strongly toward support for state financing.[63] Vassey emphasized public support for the centers even more forcefully in an internal memo to the governor. "For a period of months we have been flooded with correspondence from individuals and organizations of all sorts favoring . . . child care centers. No attempt has been made even to count this correspondence which has been most numerous and prolonged."[64] Yet despite this support, the fate of the child-care program remained precarious, as parents and teachers each year had to await the legislature's verdict as to whether or not to renew funding.

In this climate of uncertainty and retrenchment, arguments in favor of the centers gradually grew more defensive. Some residents continued to portray child care as a general social good, as did a Los Angeles woman who in 1947 demanded to know, "Why isn't the child-care center placed on a permanent basis by the state? Isn't is as important as any of the State's social institutions?"[65] The ground upon which to make such broad-based claims was receding, however, as the idea that state-funded child care should be exclusively for the needy solidified. Child-care advocates had always defended the centers on fiscal and pragmatic grounds, noting that they allowed mothers who would otherwise be forced to go on relief to remain productive citizens, but this became an ever more dominant theme stressed by those defending the program.

For instance, the *Los Angeles Times* ran a letter-to-the-editor in 1947 that portrayed clients as both needy and deserving. "No career-girl-by-choice is among us, for the State nurseries and centers will not accept any child whose mother is not its main support," the writer explained, noting that all parents paid a fee (though "still much less than private care of equal quality would cost us"). She went on to argue that all parents should support the centers, not out of a sense of solidarity, nor because evidence pointed to the benefits of early childhood education, but rather on the basis on self-interest: "These State nurseries and extended day care centers are truly a service to all people who have little children, for unless you can afford enough health and accident and life insurance to keep your family in comfort in case of disaster someday could find your children among us."[66] This more crabbed framing of the issue hints at the effects of the nation's right-wing lurch in the late 1940s and early 1950s.[67]

When the California Assembly revisited the matter yet again in the June 1949, it altered the education code to signal its intent to stop funding the centers in one year's time, due to the fact that "wartime emergency" conditions were "rapidly disappearing." But just as June 1950 rolled around, the United States embarked on a new war in Korea, which helped the centers secure yet another reprieve. The following year, Governor Warren for the first time expressed support for making the program permanent. He noted that "many of our men in arms" had left behind families, and that their wives had to seek employment "to supplement their meager allotments." He pointed to the federal government's call for increased labor power, stating, "We are told by government that at least 6,000,000 more people must be brought into the work force of our country during the coming months. Many of them must be women." Child care would help the state to achieve its employment goals, he argued, while preventing the "children of working mothers from becoming community problems."[68] The California Assembly bought these arguments and enacted the Geddes-Kraft Child Care Centers Act, for the first time granting the program a two-year extension, until June 1953.

The bill breathed new life into the association between child care and wartime conditions and sacrifice. It emphasized that the child-care centers were "a means for meeting an emergency, existing in certain communities in the State, created by the employment of women with children, due to the increased drafting of men in the armed forces, and the extended operations increase in industries, as a result of the troubled and unsettled world conditions."[69] In 1953 the California Assembly used the same language when renewing the program for another two years. Thus the centers were once again rationalized as a response to the demands of war and the need to support soldiers, war wives, and essential workers. But rather than leading to an expansion of the program, as scholar Emilie Stoltzfus has noted, the Korean War "simply allowed state legislators to prolong their delay in finding a peacetime rationale for publicly subsidized Child Care Centers."[70]

In fact, by the time the child-care program acquired permanency in 1957, it had notably contracted, even as the state's population surged. In 1947–48 the state had about 293 centers, with a combined average daily enrollment of 12,038; by 1954–55 the numbers had dropped to 246 centers with a total enrollment of 10,405. During this same period the number of centers operating in Los Angeles fell from 157 to 140.[71] These declines reflected not a drop-off in demand, but rather the impact of the means test; a study conducted in 1951–52 showed that more than thirty-three hundred California families had applied for the service but were deemed ineligible because of their income. The new rules also had a major effect on the demographics of the clientele. Prior to the imposition of the means test, 40 percent of children came from single-parent families; by 1950, 56 percent of the children came from single-parent homes.[72] In subsequent years, the proportion of single-parent homes continued to rise. When the *Los Angeles Times* ran a feature on the centers in 1957, it observed that single mothers constituted a full three-fourths of the parents served, and that "the problem of deserted families" had "replaced the wartime need."[73]

According to historian Natalie Fousekis, so long as California's child-care program was administered by the Department of Education rather than the Department of Social Welfare, meaning that parents were not assigned case workers, it remained free of the stigma of welfare; the real change, she argues, occurred during the War on Poverty, when it evolved into a social program primarily aimed at transitioning welfare mothers into the workforce.[74] But the stage for this transformation was set long before. The establishment of means testing in 1947 gradually led to a different clientele: the families served became poorer, less likely to have a connection to the military or a career in public service, more likely to be headed by single parents, and almost certainly more racially diverse.[75] And with these changes came subtle shifts—changes that are difficult to pinpoint but spoke volumes to how parents experienced the program.

In 1955 one Los Angeles father fired off an indignant letter to the school board after center administrators made what he considered unreasonable demands to prove that his family qualified for care, even going so far as to contact his place of work. Complaining bitterly about their meddlesome interference, he stated that he was withdrawing his children for fear that future "harassment" of his employer might cause him to lose his low-paying, part-time job. To require him to divulge how many hours he worked and for what pay was one thing; to demand a notarized document detailing exactly which hours of which days was another thing entirely. Such treatment, he argued, seemed more fitting for "some police state or in the case of an ex-convict on probation, but is far out of line for an [*sic*] free American citizen." For this man—an immigrant from the Netherlands who arrived in the United States in 1940 and was naturalized in 1946—to be a "free American citizen" did not just mean freedom from government interference.[76] It also meant freedom to enjoy a certain standard of living, even if that meant turning to government programs or provisions in difficult times. To be constantly reminded of his dependency and treated with suspicion felt like more than a personal insult; it felt like an attack on his claim to membership in the social and civic body.

Conclusion

Today, left-leaning politicians, popular writers, and even some academics look back to World War II as a time when the United States enjoyed a "universal" child-care program.[77] They convey the impression of a comprehensive national system by noting that, at its height in mid-1944, the federal government funded more than thirty-one hundred child-care facilities, with centers located in every state save for New Mexico. In reality, this is a fiction, for state-funded child care was never truly widespread, not even in California, which claimed far more centers than any other states. By February 1946, the last month of federal funding, California retained about 390 of its child-care centers—more than the *combined total* of the 37 states with the fewest centers. The state of Washington, home to the second largest number, could claim 103 centers, whereas Los Angeles alone had more than 250 centers.[78] In other words, Los Angeles had nearly two and a half times as many child-care centers as any *state* outside of California.[79] These numbers challenge the image of a truly nationwide system that exposed the American people to the basic concept of child care outside the home as something other than a charitable service for the very poor. Instead, the wartime program is better seen as one that led working parents in select cities—industrial areas that experienced enormous population growth in a short time span, along with the myriad stresses that such growth entailed—to begin to think of government child-care centers as a stabilizing influence and a social good.

Looking back from the vantage point of 1992, Augustus F. Hawkins, the former California assemblyman who had proposed a universal child-care program in 1946, explained to an interviewer that child care and other progressive social programs "continued to exist" but on a scale that made them "more symbolic than real." California still awaited "a comprehensive child care program... that any child can qualify for and one that will provide the type of services that are needed."[80] The failure to establish such a system meant that when the US Congress revisited the question of the federal government's responsibility for caring for its youngest citizens in the 1960s and early 1970s, no state could serve as a viable model for a potential federal program.[81]

Beginning in 1989, however, the United States did establish a high-quality, federally subsidized child-care system that has remained free of the stigma of welfare. Yet like the health care provided by the Veterans Administration, it is not a universal entitlement but one derived from military service. With the passage of the bipartisan Military Child Care Act, the military dramatically reformed what had previously been an underfunded and poorly supervised program: by raising child-care workers' pay (and hence reducing turnover), instituting strict new accreditation and oversight standards and procedures, and providing ongoing training in childhood development, it built and has since maintained a child-care system that today is widely lauded. The program's success rests above all on the government's willingness to acknowledge that high-quality child care simply costs more than most families can afford. Parent fees, which are set on a sliding scale and capped to never exceed 10 percent of a family's income, cover only about a third of the cost, while the rest is paid for by the federal government. This was roughly the same funding model—one-third parent contribution, two-thirds government subsidy—that supported California's child-care program.[82]

It should not surprise us that the only Americans who today enjoy low-cost, high-quality child care—child care that is publicly funded yet carries none of the stigma of "welfare"—are the nation's servicemen and women. California managed to sustain its centers in the immediate postwar period, while other states did not, in large part because it had a much larger and more established program that people fought hard to defend. But their success, at least initially, rested in good measure on their ability to define the program as a response to an ongoing emergency. Though not officially a military benefit, child care in this period remained closely associated with wartime sacrifice—with war wives, widows, disabled veterans, and essential workers, all of whom made claims upon the state that were widely perceived as legitimate. Those associations, resuscitated during the Korean War, lingered just long enough to help advocates achieve a permanent state program in 1957, even as the social reality behind them dissipated.

By then, the number of children attending the child-care centers in Los Angeles had been dramatically reduced. The program's public image had also changed, as state-supported child care came to be portrayed as a service for poor and often abandoned single mothers compelled by necessity to join the workforce. From this vantage point, it must have been hard to recapture that heady postwar moment, just over a decade earlier, when so many Angelenos had argued for publicly funded child care as a social right and part of "the American way of life."

7

HOW THE PACIFIC WORLD BECAME WEST

MARY L. DUDZIAK

> The strategic boundaries of the United States were no longer along the western shores of North and South America; they lay along the eastern shores of the Asiatic continent.
>
> —*General Douglas MacArthur to George Kennan (1948)*

On July 22, 1944, Jose Torres paddled furiously in a handmade outrigger canoe toward an American destroyer, the USS *Wadsworth*, off the coast of Guam.[1] Torres and five other Chamorros, indigenous people of the Island of Guam, approached the ship with great hope and with a white sheet at the bow of their canoe.[2] The men and their communities had endured thirty-two months of a brutal Japanese occupation. Before World War II the Chamorro people had been, at best, ambivalent about the United States, their colonial governor since the Spanish–American War. In 1944 the US reinvasion was liberation. As Chamorro scholar Laura Torres Sauder has written, "survival became synonymous with American Armed Forces."[3] The Chamorros would "feel as if life itself is not possible" without the United States, Michael Lujan Bevacqua, also a scholar of the Chamorro people, writes.[4]

Guam, an American territory, is 9,349 miles across the Pacific Ocean from San Francisco, about two and a half times the distance between San Francisco and Hawai'i. It is much closer to Tokyo, Japan—2,520 miles away. Guam is so far to the west of the North American continent that it falls on the other side of the International Date Line. This is why Guam's motto is: "Where America's Day Begins." For historian Arrell Morgan Gibson, Guam is part of the American western frontier.[5] If directionality is an element in defining "the West," the island certainly has a claim to inclusion. Using stories from Guam in the Mariana Islands and Bikini Atoll in the Marshall Islands, this chapter explores whether the American projection of sovereign power over Guam, Bikini, and the Pacific

Ocean itself in the years after World War II made the vast ocean region part of the (or at least "an") American West. Guam's Chamorros may not have thought of themselves as westerners, but they certainly thought of themselves as Americans.

During the Japanese occupation of Guam, identification with the United States was a form of resistance. Chamorros sometimes sang a song in English, a language forbidden by the Japanese, with the refrain:

> Oh, Mr. Sam, Sam, my dear Uncle Sam,
> Won't you please come back to Guam?[6]

Affinity with the United States could motivate brutality. In two massacres of Chamorros by the Japanese military, some victims were selected because of their service, or that of their family members, in the US Navy.[7] Still, when American troops liberated two thousand Chamorros from a concentration camp in 1944, some carried with them tiny American flags they had kept hidden. Possessing a US flag was dangerous, but retaining a piece of America seemed to give them hope.[8] The historical memory of liberation highlights Chamorro gratitude for the United States, but the Chamorros were not without agency. Torres and his companions, armed at times only with bare hands, rose up against the Japanese who had murdered their family members, and freed their village before the arriving US troops set foot on the island shores.[9]

If World War II forged an emotional bond on the part of Chamorros with the United States, it was a bond that lacked reciprocity. In wartime references to Guam, the island was tied to the United States but was *not itself* the United States. The marginality of Guam for American leaders was clear when President Franklin D. Roosevelt took up his first task after the December 7, 1941, Japanese attack on Pearl Harbor: the need to convince the American people that an attack on a harbor they had never heard of was an attack on America. To do this, Roosevelt emphasized Hawai'i and the "American island of Oahu" throughout his short speech. That was the place where American lives were lost, as the president described it. Other places appeared in the speech one time each: Malaya, Hong Kong, Guam, the Philippines, Wake Island, and Midway Island. This reduced Guam, the Philippines, and Wake and Midway Islands—American territories under attack like Hawai'i—to part of "a surprise offensive extending throughout the Pacific area." Guam was a "Pacific area," rather than part of America.[10] Similarly, on a naval map prepared for the public, Guam was represented as a US operations base, not as an American flag territory.[11]

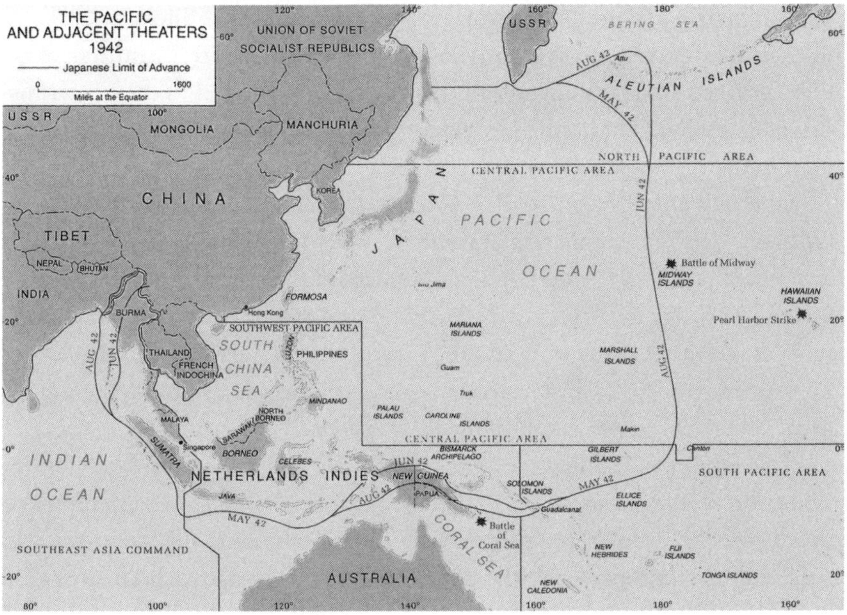

FIGURE 7.1 The Pacific Theater, World War II, 1942. *Source*: Center for Military History, US Army.

After the violent struggle to regain control of the island in 1944, the United States's relationship with the people of Guam was not much different from before. Guam was an unincorporated US territory subject to rule by the US Navy. Its residents did not have US citizenship, leaving them stateless within their own home island. The United States extended citizenship to residents of Guam in 1950, but the island remains an unincorporated territory limiting residents' political rights (they cannot vote in US presidential elections, and they have one nonvoting member in the House of Representatives).[12] In contrast, the territory of the Philippines became independent in 1946. The Hawai'ian and Aleutian Islands, along with the rest of Alaska, were fully incorporated through statehood in 1959.[13]

The greatest transformation for the United States, however, was with the great expanse of ocean itself. In the aftermath of World War II it was an American priority to project sovereign power in the Pacific.[14] The US government did in the Pacific what it had done before on the North American continent: US leaders viewed settled areas as empty spaces and occupied them. They required native peoples to migrate elsewhere or imposed military governance on their home territory. It was the oceanic analog both to the military land grabs in Jared Farmer's chapter in this edited volume, and to the longer history of displacement of indigenous peoples.[15] The effects continue to this day.

Whether or not, as Gibson argues, the Pacific was a frontier, it is certainly the case, as historian Gail M. Nomura has written, that acquisition of Pacific and Asian territories moved the western edge of the United States to Asia.[16] The United States did its best, in the aftermath of the war, to exert control over parts of the ocean itself, seeing the Pacific World as part of its national security domain. There are many works on the history of US imperialism in the Pacific, but with exceptions like historian Daniel Immerwahr's recent work, there is less attention to how power is simultaneously exercised and erased.[17]

To explore the Pacific as an American West, this chapter focuses on the projection of American power in the Pacific, forms of US sovereign presence, and the encounters of island peoples with American power. The essay examines the changing conceptions of the Pacific in law, cartography, and historiography, and takes up two examples: Bikini Atoll in the Marshall Islands, which became a nuclear testing zone, and Guam, which became the site of important US Naval and Air Force bases. The experiences of indigenous peoples on Bikini Atoll and Guam differed, with Bikini Islanders eventually turning away from formal inclusion into the United States and Guam's Chamorros seeking full US citizenship rights. In both instances, however, the United States kept these subjects of American power at arm's length. The country's ultimate interest was not in the islanders, but in the use of their Pacific homes. Especially in the Marshall Islands, this made the people themselves a liability. The absence of democratic governance in the islands has been in tension with the image the United States projected to the world.[18] The western edge of the United States appeared to require an imperial presence, and also its denial.

From "Free Sea" to Ocean Empire

Naval officer and historian Alfred Thayer Mahan called the oceans "a great highway" in his classic 1890 work *The Influence of Sea Power upon History.*[19] In 1909, Theodore Roosevelt, as naval secretary, used that highway to project an image of American power by sending a "Great White Fleet" of American naval battleships around the world.[20] During the twentieth century, and increasingly during and after World War II, the Pacific was a space where American power was exercised on sea as well as land. To the Pacific Islanders who lived there, however, the ocean was not simply a passageway. It was a site of commerce, a source of food, and was home.[21]

That the ocean is a place of power and governance is evident in the Law of the Sea. Hugo Grotius, known as the "father of international law," published what is thought of as the first book on this subject, *Mare Liberum*, or *Free Sea*, in 1609. "The sea is common to all, because it is so limitless that it cannot become a possession of any one," he wrote. The freeness of the sea derived from the idea that "it is adapted for the use of all, whether we consider it from the point of view of navigation or of fisheries."[22] As Grotius articulated it, the liberty that inhered in the oceans did not derive from a legal identity or right of the ocean itself, but rather from its utility to human users.[23] The law of the sea emerged from the idea that the oceans were empty but abundant spaces open to all. Grotius's ideas did not arise from theory alone. He wrote *Mare Liberum* to promote the interests of the Netherlands, his own nation, in its right to navigate the Indian Ocean and elsewhere for the purpose of trade with India and the East Indies at a time when they were part of the empire of Spain. His short book was part of a longer document Grotius wrote to support the legal position of the Dutch East India Company in a conflict between the Netherlands and Portugal. The law of the sea that emerged and developed from Grotius, international law scholar R. P. Anand argued, ignored preexisting maritime laws of Asian countries and was intended to serve European interests in trade.[24] In this way, legal ideas presented as transcending discreet interests instead emerged from them.

International law was not a neutral instrument when it came to the uses of the oceans. The Law of the Sea enabled the interests of the United States and other imperial powers, at the expense of island peoples. For example, Americans sought whale oil in the first half of the nineteenth century. Under international law, nations had exclusive rights and could restrict whalers in the waters up to six miles offshore. Pacific Islanders were not considered part of the community of the "civilized," so Pacific islands were not considered to be "nations." Because of this, islanders could not assert rights of a nation protected by international law. Without sovereignty, fishing and whaling in their waters was unrestricted. This created an opportunity for American whalers. They targeted the Pacific islands region, where they outnumbered the whalers of other nations from American independence through the 1860s.[25]

Without legal recognition of island sovereignty, imperial powers could absorb more than passing whales. In 1890, Mahan argued that colonies and foreign military bases mattered to the global projection of power. What he perceived as American disinclination for colonialism meant that American war ships "will be like land birds, unable to fly far from their own shores." To overcome this problem, US ships needed "resting-places" where they could refuel and make repairs. This should be "one of the first duties" of a nation seeking power at sea.[26] In the aftermath of the Spanish–American War, American bases proliferated in the Pacific and elsewhere.[27]

In the early twentieth century, Pacific islands were divided among colonial powers who assumed their right to rule indigenous peoples.[28] The United States brutally suppressed Philippine independence, intervened militarily to protect US trade interests and missionaries in China, and overthrew indigenous rule in Hawai'i.[29] In the 1930s some argued that the United States should withdraw from Guam and the Philippines to protect American security. The reason was that the islands were too close to foreign powers—not only Japan but also the German presence in the northern Mariana Islands (the rest of Guam's island chain). This could too easily draw the United States into war. The United States did not withdraw but also did not fortify the islands, leaving them vulnerable.[30] After Japan attacked Guam, the Philippines, and elsewhere hours after the assault on the Hawain'ian Island of Oahu, the Japanese occupied these territories through much of the war.[31] Hawai'i remained under US control, and its American governor imposed martial law.[32]

World War II disrupted the American, European, and Australian imperial presence in the Pacific, as Japan took control over their islands. The history of this era has traditionally been written as a military history, focusing on combatants and military leaders. The experience of Pacific Islanders was often ignored in these narratives.[33] Indigenous histories have been a focus of later work, and the islander experience is centered in the Pacific World literature. The traditional military history has retained a hold, nevertheless, in US histories of World War II.

In the Pacific islands the war was a "watershed event," anthropologists Geoffrey M. White and Lamont Lindstrom have written. It was an era of disruption, violence, and carnage. There were countless civilian casualties from American and Japanese bombing. As the Japanese and the Allies poured equipment and personnel into the islands, some islanders fought alongside foreign troops or served as laborers. The objectives of the foreign militaries were short-term, however. They "were bent on killing each other," making the occupations different than what had come before. After the war the external military presence receded on some islands, but the US military remained in the Marshall Islands and the rest of Micronesia.[34]

After World War II, American strategic interests drove the nation's presence in this region.[35] American leaders embraced empire in the Pacific as a forward line of defense.[36] Between 1945 and 1947 the United States took over the islands that Japan had occupied during the war, including the Marshall Islands and the Marianas. Concerned in part about containing the Soviet Union in Asia, American policymakers "were absolutely convinced," historian Hal M. Friedman has written, that US security required "imposing unilateral American control over these strategically placed island groups and turning the Pacific Basin into an 'American lake.'"[37] The idea that US domestic security was aided by projection and maintenance of power in faraway regions would become a central argument used politically to justify the use of force in Korea, Vietnam, and elsewhere in later years.[38] Meanwhile, the "lake" metaphor for American power in the Pacific was ubiquitous, domesticating and miniaturizing the idea of American empire in the ocean.

As if to answer Mahan's critique, the goal of pushing the borders of US power to the shores of East Asia drove the need to establish hundreds of bases throughout the Asia-Pacific region, resulting in a military network across China, Japan, Korea and other countries as well as bases scattered across islands throughout the ocean. American ships would no longer be "land birds." Bases were one form of what sociologist Walden Bello sees as the "strategic extension of the power of the U.S. state."[39] Consistent with the Truman administration's Cold War national security framework, the United States projected American power through state building in the Pacific.[40]

The United States needed more than bases to accomplish its goals. New nuclear weapons required testing sites, and where better than what Americans conceptualized as an empty space in the ocean? The result was that the Pacific became not only an "American lake" but a nuclear one. Ground zero was the Marshall Islands. Some islands were targeted, while others absorbed the nuclear detritus—the displaced people.[41] The United States depended on its Pacific sovereignty but kept the island peoples at arm's length. Although the Chamorros in Guam eventually gained US citizenship, they were beyond the nation's self-conception, excluded even from most maps of the United States.[42] Similarly, as American power moved firmly west during and after the war, American Pacific sovereignty did not disrupt the decidedly terrestrial conception of the American West. The projection of power depended, perhaps, on this erasure.

Imagining the Pacific

Cartographers have long mapped American identity in the world. The excision of American Pacific territories from conceptions of the nation supplanted a more capacious understanding of the nation's geography. As Daniel Immerwahr has shown, after US empire expanded following the Spanish–American War, cartographers mapped what was called "the Greater United States." This more capacious representation of national identity sometimes included Alaska, Hawai'i, Guam, Wake Island, American Samoa, the Philippines, Puerto Rico, and the Panama Canal Zone.[43] A broad understanding of the reach of American territory would not last, however. A legal conception of the country's relationship to its territories informed a narrower approach to mapping the United States. American legal identities were reined in in the *Insular Cases*, which addressed the legal status of goods imported from the territories. The cases took up whether goods, like a shipment of oranges from Puerto Rico to New York, was a foreign shipment subject to import taxes, or whether it was internal, since Puerto Rico was an American colony. The US Supreme Court understood that the status of imports had implications for the legal identity of people in US territories. Wishing to enable trade but not the citizenship of persons "savage not civilized," the Court defined the territories into a legal netherworld. They were unincorporated and "foreign in a domestic sense." The US Constitution was "the law of the land" within the geographic boundaries of the nation. But the territories, the Court found, were "not part of the land." This more limited conception of the nation has long appeared in US maps showing only what we call the continental United States.[44]

World War II expanded American interest in the globe as a whole and changed American cartography, shifting cultural perceptions of the Pacific Ocean. Broad engagement with a mapped image of the United States was encouraged in the early 1940s, as geography classes proliferated in American high schools.[45] After the United States formally entered the war, President Franklin D. Roosevelt prodded Americans to visualize the United States in the world, asking them to buy a world map in a February 20, 1942, radio address. A few days later, during his first "fireside chat" since the Pearl Harbor attacks, Roosevelt instructed listeners to spread out their world maps. He then reconceptualized it: "The broad oceans which have been heralded in the past as our protection from attack have become endless battlefields on which we are constantly being challenged by our enemies." Roosevelt emphasized: "The islands that lie between

Hawai'i and the Philippines—these islands, hundreds of them, appear only as small dots on most maps. But they cover a large strategic area." In the middle lay the American territory of Guam, "a lone outpost which we have never fortified."[46]

The maps that Americans spread out on their tables would have featured the dominant approach to cartography before the war. Americans knew the world through the Mercator projection—a flattened approach to mapping the world that showed the Americas floating safely in the oceans, and distorted the relationship between continents, making Europe and Asia appear farther from the United States in the north and south. Oceana appeared in textbooks "as a distant group of scattered islands, a buffer *between* civilizations," historian Susan Schulten has written. The war "forcibly disrupted conventional ideas about geography," she argues. The attack on Pearl Harbor awakened Americans to the vulnerability of the US West Coast—a region often at the edge of world maps, with an ocean buffer.[47]

Fueled by the role of aviation in the war, cartographers drew maps of an interconnected world. New approaches showed the Pacific as "a body of water joining, rather than separating, the continents on either side," and recast Pacific islands as "steppingstones to Asia." War-era cartography also changed the angle of vision. Rand McNally's "World Map for the Air Age" put the North Pole at the center to illustrate the way aviation made the distance between belligerents closer. And through the war, the ocean was mapped as more than a passageway; it was a battlespace and a strategic territory.[48]

Oceans do not fit well with conventional approaches to writing history. As historian David Igler has written, "the 'places' usually subjected to historical analysis—nations, regions, localities—have fixed borders enclosing land and thus constitute terrestrial history."[49] The "West" that was Frederick Jackson Turner's frontier, for example, was terrestrial. Yet even the terra firma of Alaska and Hawai'i fits awkwardly in the historiography. In the *Oxford History of the American West*, the "West" is mapped with Alaska and Hawai'i out of scale and floating at the edges of the page. The Aleutian Islands are cut and pasted to fit in the frame, thereby obscuring the proximity of west to east in the Bering Sea, where the International Date Line veers sharply to enable time in the North Pacific to align with sovereignty.[50] In contrast, Igler's *The Great Ocean* captures the nineteenth-century world of the eastern Pacific as a fluid space oriented toward maritime commerce. In the aftermath of the California Gold Rush, Igler argues that this ocean space gave way to "the American Far West, part of a 'bordered' and continental empire."[51]

The Pacific "has been historically reimagined many times," historian Matt K. Matsuda has written, "from an ancient Polynesian and early modern Magellanic space of transit, to an Enlightenment theater of sensual paradise, to a strategic grid of labor movements and military 'island-hopping,' to a capitalist basin, the key to a Pacific Century of emerging wealth and 'globalization' at the end of the last millennium."[52] Igler suggests that the eastern Pacific Ocean as a historical space was somewhat displaced as terrestrial California and the Pacific Coast came to be seen as the US Far West after the Gold Rush.[53] But it is also the case that the US presence in the Pacific would be solidified over time, especially in the aftermath of World War II.

As World War II reshaped the US role in the world, it also transformed the nation's relationship with the Pacific World. General Douglas MacArthur described the Pacific after the war as "an Anglo-Saxon lake" with "our line of defense" running "through the chain of islands fringing the coast of Asia."[54] The ocean was an expansive region of contested power, but it was seen by Americans as a US security zone in which the nation exerted different forms of sovereign power. In the war's aftermath, the ocean itself—not the territory of the US West Coast, or the Hawai'ian or Aleutian Islands—became the western edge of American sovereign power, and Pacific peoples acquired new relationships to the American polity. The Territories of Hawai'i and Alaska ultimately gained statehood, but other parts of the US ocean west remained on the periphery of American identity. It seemed to be that the sea spaces and the islands mattered more than their peoples. Human residents were often an annoyance, especially in the nuclear testing zone of the Marshall Islands. Great whales and other wild animals in the ocean were rarely considered at all. Over time, the importance of ocean sovereignty continued to matter to US security, even as ties to island peoples were largely erased from American memory.

Atomic Erasure

"I remember well the day the Americans first came to Bikini," said Rubon Juda, a Bikini Islander, in an oral history interview. He was out fishing and heard "planes buzzing overhead in the distance, and we heard some noise that sounded like fighting that we thought may have been taking place way out at sea." Japanese soldiers occupying the atoll had threatened to kill Christian islanders the next morning, but instead the soldiers were strafed by an American plane and went into hiding. "We were so elated when we discovered that the Americans weren't going to hurt us," Emso Leviticus recalled. Instead, "the Navy men were very kind" and gave the islanders food and medical attention. Like the Chamorros on Guam, arriving US soldiers meant liberation for Bikini—as Juda put it, "a very fortunate event for our people."[55]

Americans would eventually bring the war's most devastating weapon to Bikini Atoll. They chose it as ground zero for an American nuclear weapons testing program. US nuclear weapons research was initially motivated by the need to outpace the Nazis and end the threat of German military power. After Germany's defeat the rationale turned to the idea of defeating Japan without a massive and deadly invasion. The atomic bombing of the Japanese cities of Hiroshima or Nagasaki extended to a horrifying level the role of American air power, in which massive destruction could be achieved with less risk to American military personnel.[56]

Bikini Atoll was the site for Operation Crossroads, the first two uses of nuclear weapons after World War II. The purpose of these explosions was to test whether naval vessels could withstand nuclear weapons. US Army leaders claimed the US Navy was obsolete in an age of nuclear arms. The Navy, of course, disagreed. A nuclear blast of naval vessels would provide an answer. To plan the tests, military leaders searched for a location away from the continental United States because of concerns about radiation. Naval officers Frederick Ashworth and Horacio Rivero recalled: "We just took out dozens of maps and started looking for remote sites." Bikini emerged as the "ideal" site because its large lagoon could accommodate naval vessels, because of its climate, rarely hit by tropical storms, and because of its small population. It was also ideal because it was located in an area under US control.[57] A judgment like this had been made before. A desert area in New Mexico was selected for the first nuclear explosion—the July 15, 1945, Trinity test—in part because it appeared to be in a wasteland, although it was not seen that way by the Mescalero Apache who lived nearby.[58]

On February 10, 1946, Navy Commodore Ben H. Wyatt, military governor of the Marshall Islands, approached residents of Bikini with a bible in hand. The islanders had just finished church services, and they sat cross-legged on the ground under the shade of coconut palms. Wyatt later wrote that he "compared the Bikinians to the children of Israel whom the Lord saved from their enemy and led into the Promised Land." This was how he began his request that the islanders move so that the Americans could destroy their island. Though Wyatt's superiors requested that he ask for their consent, the decision had already been made by President Harry S. Truman, and preparatory blasting of the lagoon was under way. Wyatt reported at the time that the islanders agreed, and that their chieftain told him that they were happy to move and "very proud to be part of this wonderful undertaking" of nuclear testing.[59] Lore Kessibuki remembered it differently: "We didn't feel we had any other choice but to obey the Americans. . . . It had just been the end of the war. We were still afraid and we wanted to heed his words." Emso Leviticus, a young girl at the time, was sad to leave and felt strange "having to leave behind the bones of my ancestors while strangers would be walking around on our island." Everyone appeared to believe, however, that the move would be only temporary.[60]

How could the United States make a decision to drop an atomic bomb on the islanders' home and seek their consent afterward when plans were already in motion? This action was enabled by the way Americans thought of the Pacific islands and their peoples. Americans needed a "hole in the map" for a nuclear test site, cultural geographer Denis Cosgrove has written. "It alone created the necessary marginality for experimentation to be deemed acceptable."[61] Emptiness is not an automatic product of a physical environment, however, but a matter of perception. The idea of empty space that is then filled by social life depends on "hypothetical initial 'purity,' identified as 'nature' and as a sort of ground zero of human reality," the philosopher Henri Lefebvre explained. Empty space as a void "is actually merely a representation of space."[62]

The meaning of the Pacific islands was shaped by the intersection of humans with different ideas and social practices, and the landscape itself. Understandings of place "do work," geographer Jeffrey Sasha Davis has argued, legitimizing some uses and prohibiting others.[63] That a long-settled island was conceptualized as an empty "hole" illustrates the way representations of place are political. The imagined emptiness of indigenous land had a brutal and tragic history on the continental United States as well. These episodes were driven, in part, by the racism enabling whites to see native peoples as lacking the "civilized" personhood required for sovereignty.[64]

The war itself reinforced the idea that the islands held nothing worth valuing. When Americans captured Kwajalein in the Marshall Islands, for example, the landscape was devastated. Structures on the island were flattened, and trees and shrubs were dead. It "looked as if it had been picked up to 20,000 feet and then dropped," said a US Army observer.[65] The destruction of war produced a landscape that seemed valueless to Americans. It could be made "useful" if filled with a military base, like Kwajalein, or it could be destroyed, like Bikini.

FIGURE 7.2 The second nuclear explosion at Bikini Atoll, detonated underwater, July 25, 1946. *Source*: US Department of Defense.

Americans did not see their bulldozers as flattening a home territory to make way for an airfield, but as builders creating something where nothing had been.

As portrayed in American media, Bikini Islanders were simple and primitive people who had gotten in the way of civilization. This conceptualization was reinforced by Commodore Wyatt's story about the way grateful islanders welcomed their move. An American reporter suggested that they would not be disadvantaged because, in essence, all atolls were the same. Rongerik, the atoll islanders were initially moved to, and Bikini "look as alike as two Idaho potatoes." Two months after the move, however, with inadequate supplies of food and water, the islanders began requesting unsuccessfully to return to their home.[66] Ultimately, Bikini's purpose, as journalist James Cameron put it, "was to be remote, far away, as inaccessible as possible from anything valued by man, because it was to be destroyed."[67] The US government sought a space where the world's most devastating weapon could be tested without disturbing anyone that mattered.

On June 30, 1946, an American plane released an atomic bomb named Gilda over Bikini's lagoon. It was a plutonium bomb, identical to the one used on Nagasaki, Japan. When it exploded, a column of water half-a-mile wide rose to the sky.[68] Relocated at Rongerik Atoll, 128 miles from Bikini, the islanders heard it rumble "like a huge roar." The Americans invited their leader, the chieftain King Juda (the father of Rubon Juda, mentioned earlier in this chapter), to watch the test with them. King Juda reported back that there was much "noise, smoke and mist," but the atoll was still there. "The hermit crabs could still be seen on the beach. The trees... continued to blow in the wind." This gave the islanders hope that they would return to Bikini soon.[69]

The islanders' longing for home would continue, however. They were shunted from island to island. Poor conditions at Rongerik, leading to starvation, prompted the first move. They were moved again to make room for residents of another island affected by nuclear fallout from further testing. Without their traditional means of subsistence, the Bikini Islanders became more dependent on the United States for survival.[70] They blamed Americans for their fate. As Kessibuki put it: "The Americans moved us here, then they forgot about their responsibilities to us, and again we were starving." Islander Kilon Bauno recalled: "We were always asking ourselves, 'What are we doing here?'" Anger remained tinged with hope as they "clung desperately to the belief that the Americans would again be our saviors."[71]

Meanwhile, the 1946 tests were followed by several others in the Marshall Islands. A successful Soviet atomic test in 1949 reinforced American leaders' beliefs that bigger and better bombs were a necessary deterrent.[72] The first explosion of a hydrogen bomb was at Enewetak Atoll in 1952. It was five hundred times as powerful as the bomb dropped on Nagasaki. The largest ever US nuclear explosion was two years later at Bikini. A hydrogen bomb, Castle Bravo was one-and-a-half times the explosive power of the test at Enewetak. Because the blast was much larger than expected, and the wind shifted, fallout contaminated fifteen islands, including settled areas. Marshall Islanders and Japanese fishermen got radiation sickness. The United States continued to use Bikini as a test site, with several more hydrogen bomb blasts, and the Marshall Islands served as "the world's most H-bombed area" until President John F. Kennedy signed a treaty banning atmospheric nuclear testing in 1963.[73]

In later years, some species of fish and birds revived at Bikini, but the coconut crab passed on strontium 90 to its later generations, making this Bikini Islander delicacy forever inedible. It is a small example of the way, as Richard White puts it in his afterword in this volume, historical changes create "their own weather," with subsequent consequences. It runs counter to his suggestion that the Holocene may shoulder on, however. The continuing impact of nuclear weapons testing is considered to be an important factor in the arrival of the Anthropocene.[74] The coconut crab is an exemplar of this, showing the way human destruction can permanently alter features of the natural world.

The atoll itself remains toxic, despite government assurance to the contrary in 1968. As a result, Bikini has never been successfully resettled, leaving its islanders "nuclear nomads."[75] Bikini is now advertised to divers as "the best wreck diving site on Earth."[76] American leaders, in essence, created what they had previously imagined: a nuclear testing space empty of people.

The Ocean Edge of the American West

As Bikini Atoll functioned for the United States as a test site, Guam instead became the site of important US bases. It was departure point for American bombers headed to Asia. Chamorro self-identity is tied to the moment in 1944 when Jose Torres and his companions reached the USS *Wadsworth* in their canoe and were welcomed by the US military that then liberated their island from the Japanese. The Chamorro idea that "life itself is not possible" without the United States has fueled great patriotism, despite the fact that the islanders still lack full citizenship rights.[77]

The Chamorros had pressed for citizenship before World War II, but Secretary of the Navy Claude A. Swanson objected, saying: "These people have not yet reached a state of development" required for citizenship. After Guam's liberation from the Japanese, the US government reinstated Naval governance and appointed Rear Admiral Charles A. Pownall to serve as both governor and military commander of the island. He put the preexisting governmental structure back in place that restricted local power in the interest of US control. Over time, residents of Guam were accorded limited self-governance, and the Guam Congress—an elected body—was granted lawmaking power in 1947.[78]

In 1949, President Harry S. Truman transferred authority for Guam from the Navy to the Department of the Interior, giving Guam its first civilian governor.[79] Although still the site of an important military base, Guam as a whole became part of the "global interior"—the long-standing civil side of US imperial oversight, as historian Megan Black has written.[80] This did not bring popular governance to Guam, since the new governor was a US federal government appointee. Even this modest easing of military rule did not sit well with the US Navy, which reacted by reinstating a requirement of Navy permission to enter the territory, essentially continuing forms of martial law.[81] For Americans, this would be like having to get a visa to go from one US state to another. The Navy excluded many from Guam, especially non-US citizens. Among the reasons given for exclusion was that "their long-term presence would be detrimental to the effective use of Guam for its primary mission of defense."[82] The United Nations criticized continuing Navy rule as "colonial" and "departing from the principles of a democratic nation." Roy E. James, who served in the US Naval Government in Guam, observed: "The Guamanian is loyal to the form of government we have imposed upon him, but he finds it difficult to understand why the United States still governs his island as though it were conquered enemy territory."[83]

Seeking broader rights, residents of Guam testified in April 1950 before the US Senate Committee on Interior and Insular Affairs. Leon Guerrero told the committee: "Our loyalty has never been questioned. There has been and always shall be only one 'ism' in Guam and that is Americanism." Emphasizing the military service and sacrifice of Guam's people, Guerrero asked for US citizenship as "simple justice in memory of our loved ones who died."[84] Congress passed the Guam Organic Act of 1950, putting the people of Guam on the road to citizenship, though without full political rights. But this came after Congressman John McSweeney of Ohio during the House debate pressed the question of whether the bill "safeguarded American rights . . . so that in case of emergency we can go in, without any restrictions upon the part of the citizens, and exercise our rights for our Navy and for our Army." Congressman William Lemke of North Dakota answered: "Absolutely so!"[85]

And so, as the United States welcomed the islanders into US citizenship, it was with an understanding that rights of citizenship would be subordinate to the "rights" of the US Army and Navy. Self-governance as an American territory was conditioned on the persistent relinquishment of sovereignty. Governance in Bikini Atoll and the Marshall Islands would take a different path. The United States maintained control over the islands, first as part of a postwar security zone. The UN Security Council formalized this in 1947, creating the Trust Territory of the Pacific Islands. The US Navy controlled the region, until it was transferred to the Department of the Interior in 1951. The area was divided into six districts along earlier colonial lines. The UN dissolved the Trust Territory in 1990. Guam's neighbors, the Northern Marianas, became a US Commonwealth, with US citizenship for its residents. The Republic of the Marshall Islands rejected this path and became self-governing. Its residents are citizens of the Republic of the Marshall Islands. They maintain a formal relationship with the United States, however, under a Compact of Free Association that allows the United States to retain an American military base on Kwajalein Atoll, home to the Ronald Reagan Ballistic Missile Defense Test Site.[86]

Through a trust fund, the United States provides annual support to the Republic of the Marshall Islands, which in turn delegates its military defense to the United States. Its citizens can travel to the United States without a visa and have other US benefits. An objective of this arrangement was to settle remaining claims from the nuclear testing era. The nature of Marshallese sovereignty is perhaps the political equivalent of the impact of radiation on the coconut crab. Despite self-governance, the legacy of American power in the Marshall Islands remains contested but has become built-in and is passed on to future generations. A new threat to Marshall Islanders is now the rising ocean itself and the failure of the United States and other nations to arrest global warming.[87]

The difference in outcomes was surely driven in part by Guamanians' desires for closer ties to the United States, and Marshall Islanders' distrust. It also mattered that the importance of control of the Marshall Islands as a whole was diminished with the end of ocean-based nuclear testing once atmospheric testing was forbidden. Guam continued to play a significant role in American military conflict. The island was a strategic support base for the United States during the war in Vietnam, for example, when B-52 bombers could be heard taking off and landing all hours of the night and day. Guam was also the first stop for refugees fleeing from Vietnam as the war ended.[88] As a strategic location aiding the United States through the Cold War and after, Guam has been controlled by the United States, which imposed restrictions on the democratic rights of the island's people. The United States could claim to protect democratization and avoid charges of hypocrisy as long as Chamorro voices of protest remained muted.[89]

Like the District of Columbia, residents of Guam now have a nonvoting member of the US Congress, and no representation in the Senate. Many Chamorros remain staunchly patriotic, and residents of Guam serve in the US armed forces at a rate three times the rest of the country.[90] The self-identity of many Chamorros is tied to the moment of Guam's liberation in 1944. The island's historical memory is increasingly contested, however. Michael Lujan Bevacqua, a scholar of the Chamorro people, writes that the historical memory of the American liberation is missing an essential element, undermining the dignity of the Chamorro and reinforcing their sense of dependence on the United States. His case in point is the story of Jose Torres and the small group of Chamorros who overthrew their Japanese guards and freed their own village, showing that Chamorros played a role in their own liberation.[91] Nevertheless, as psychologist Patricia Taimanglo Piers has written:

"Chamorros live with the frustration that Guam . . . has not yet been given the right to end colonial rule."[92]

The Pacific World, islands and ocean, is important to the history of the American West because the United States has a ragged edge that extends to the shores of Asia. Its boundaries are best measured by its impact on those touched by it. In the aftermath of World War II, American efforts to use the ocean as an American lake were challenged by islanders from Bikini and elsewhere who sought to preserve remnants of sovereignty. Like the coconut crab's inherited radiation, however, the mark of American power remains. The only way to disentangle Guam, the Marshall Islands, and the Pacific Ocean from the history of the American West would be to more fully erase from American memory Pacific peoples, soil, and sea. It would be better instead to work to reveal it.

AFTERWORD

RICHARD WHITE

In the 1980s and 1990s a scholarly consensus emerged that World War II formed a watershed for the western United States; the history of the West flowed in a different direction after the war than it had before. Yet, as the chapters in this edited volume confirm, many of the trends visible after the war had their roots in the prewar years; others attributed to World War II are better seen as products of the Cold War. World War II was in this case more like a western water project than a watershed. It captured, redirected, and accelerated older flows and put them to new purposes, as, for example, Jared Farmer vividly demonstrates in his discussion of the war and public lands. The essays that compose this book both ratify and revise the reigning scholarly consensus. Mary L. Dudziak shows how the war made the Pacific basin into an American frontier. And as with Indians on the nineteenth-century frontier, wartime Americans would have preferred that their newly enlarged Pacific sphere came without occupants. Similarly, Geraldo L. Cadava highlights how responses to Mexican immigration proved more variable and less monolithic than is often claimed. Yet with all their caveats and modifications, the contributions herein substantiate the transformative impact of the war and its immediate aftermath.

I would like to expand on the volume's theme, by way of suggesting a new reading of the recent past of the West and the larger impact of World War II. The context I have in mind is the so-called Great Acceleration, a term John McNeil and Peter Engelke use as the title for their 2016 book. The Great Acceleration that began in 1945, they write, is "the most anomalous and unrepresentative period in the 200,000-year long history of relations between our species and the biosphere." A short list of global changes following the war summarizes their case. Since 1945, 75 percent of the total of human-generated carbon dioxide has entered the atmosphere; the number of motor vehicles has expanded from

40 million to 850 million. Human population has tripled, and the number of city dwellers increased from 700 million to 3.7 billion. Their longer list includes dam construction, water depletion, the destruction of fisheries, and the rise in per capita income and consumption.[1]

Apply these developments to the West, and it is check, check, double-check. The Great Acceleration describes a world that is a doppelganger of the post–World II West. The planet is certainly much larger than the American West, but changes in the American West fit very well within the Great Acceleration's conceptual frame. McNeil and Engelke are long on description and short on explanation, but given that the American West was a mighty hardscrabble place during the Great Depression, and that most of the world was even worse off, the appeal of the Great Acceleration concept to westerners and the neglect of its dangers is understandable. How could sustained prosperity, rapid growth, shrinking inequality, robust public institutions, and the relative tolerance of the period between World War II and Vietnam not seem near utopian? The urbanizing West could also seem bland, confining, and under constant threat of nuclear annihilation to those growing up within it, but as their parents never tired of telling them, it was paradise compared to their own childhoods.

The Great Acceleration describes the world as a West writ large, but the flip side of this is that it also diminishes the singularity of the postwar American West. Western historians don't have much to explain if the West has just been swept along in the draft of changes that have altered most of the planet. But analyzing the West as part of the Great Acceleration may give the region greater importance even if it costs the West some of its singularity. McNeil and Engelke offer an American-centric interpretation of the Great Acceleration, and the themes in this edited volume reinforce such an interpretation. American economic and military hegemony following the war, the tremendous growth in US technology, and the development of mass consumer society all helped precipitate the Great Acceleration.

Often for very good reasons historians have spent considerable time railing against such American-centric explanations, but the war against national histories that has raged in many history departments has created blind spots. Nationalism has obviously not retreated to its grave in the late twentieth century and early twenty-first century. Even a global story like the Great Acceleration can have deep national—and regional—roots. The stories told in this collection, explicitly and implicitly, do more than just echo McNeil and Engelke. They indicate how an understanding of the West can be analytically helpful to understanding the broader changes that followed World War II. McNeil and

Engelke's *Great Acceleration* treats the period from 1945 down to the present as a single historical moment, even as it recognizes that some of the era's earliest characteristics have faded away. The contributors in this edited volume present a more nuanced periodization. For Gavin Wright a real break in California's development takes place with the end of the Cold War, as the various knowledge economies he examines take different trajectories.

In terms of the larger history of the American West, I would emphasize a similar but slightly different chronology. I think that the West following World War II has two distinct phases, both now behind us, and a third one just emerging that is more difficult to describe. The West from roughly Pearl Harbor to the Vietnam War was not the same place as the West of the post–Vietnam era that extends into the early twenty-first century. The easiest marker is that in the immediate postwar period the West was liberal and the New Deal coalition persisted. In the post–Vietnam period the West grew more conservative and the New Deal coalition fractured. More recently the consequences flowing from those first two periods have caused the coastal states harboring the bulk of the West's population to turn various shades of blue.

The larger Great Acceleration, too, needs to be periodized. For all the sense it might make to see the Great Acceleration as a globally continuous process since 1945, it is more useful analytically to disaggregate it. In Europe and the United States the period between World War II and the early 1970s seemed to a significant segment of the population—as we have witnessed in recent elections—to be a time when all was as it should be. White people in the United States, and native-born citizens of Europe, prospered, and the demands of those who were not white and prosperous could either be met or ignored. Those who in 2016 wanted to "make America great again," for all their lip service to Ronald Reagan, were not talking about the period that began with Vietnam. Many Americans read the second phase of the Great Acceleration beginning in the 1970s as a decline, but for people in China, India, and Southeast Asia, and parts of the Arab world, things have been different. Their Great Acceleration really began only in the 1970s. This segment of the Great Acceleration marks the decline of Western hegemony.

As with the Great Acceleration itself, my periodization is easier to describe than explain, but the American West can suggest some at least tentative hypotheses. The American West is analytically useful not because it was unique—quite the contrary—but rather because so many aspects of the broader Great Acceleration took root so early beyond the hundredth meridian and flourished there so extravagantly. Rapid economic and population growth, prosperity, and declining inequality were typical of both the West and much of the world, sucked into the vortex of the Great Acceleration.

My first suggestion goes to the central paradox of the Great Acceleration. It has improved the living conditions of hundreds of millions of human beings, even as it has also generated the social, political, and environmental conditions that threaten sustaining those conditions.[2] I am not really concerned with the inability of any advanced nation with a stable or shrinking population to maintain the national rates of growth in GDP that are a central feature of the Great Acceleration. I will take that as a given. Nor am I particularly concerned, at least analytically, with the inability to sustain the population increases that contributed to high GDP growth rates. In one way or another this rate of population growth had to decline. I am more concerned with the environmental, political, and social consequences of the Great Acceleration, which I argue will manifest themselves first in those countries where rapid growth has slowed and inequality increased. That would be the Western world and the western United States.

The essays in this book confirm why the Great Acceleration took root so quickly in the American West. The war, and the Cold War that followed, triggered demographic shifts, large investments of capital, institution building, and a rapid increase in research and technological capacity. The West for better or worse—and for Japanese Americans it was for worse—had an existing administrative and technical capacity to take advantage of the changes that the war set in motion. Not everything worked. Public funding of research and education did; public funding of child care did not. Much federal activity seemed benign, but it also involved concentration camps, Indian relocation, and Operation Wetback.

I am less interested in the growth of the West during the takeoff phase of the Great Acceleration than what the West can reveal about what happens when growth slows, when inequality increases, when environmental damage becomes apparent, and when a body politic rejects many of the institutions that had been the engines of change. As the chapters in this book amply demonstrate, this is what happened in the West following Vietnam. When scholars first forged the consensus on the impact of World War II on the West in the 1980s and 1990s, they did not quite realize that the direct influences of the war, while hardly vanishing, had already created their own weather that would disrupt further progress. Consequences of consequences began to counter some of the changes that the war had brought. The high growth rates in GDP—albeit growth marred by sharp recessions—had begun their decline. Growth in the early 1970s came with high inflation, and overall the trend was relentlessly downward. The Cold War unexpectedly ended. The globalism that had welcomed both the international flow of labor and goods that Cadava notes hardly vanished, but it spawned a reaction. The cheerleading for prosperity, an open border, and mutual growth that dominated media rhetoric about the Mexican border in the immediate postwar years sounds odd today because we live amid a nationalism that began its resurgence during the period Cadava describes.

Environmentalism may be another phase of consumerism rather than a reaction against it, but it nonetheless signifies a change in thinking about how people should produce and what people should consume. Opposition to dam building, nuclear testing, nuclear power plants, and pollution ran against the trends of the immediate postwar years. Understanding what happened in the American West as the Great Acceleration entered its later phases is critical. Events in the West will not necessarily be predictive of what happens elsewhere, but they might allow us to isolate factors that we would otherwise ignore. What I would emphasize is hardly novel but it is, along with environmental issues, the great problem of our time: rising inequality.

In the West the acceptance of federal power, trust in governance, and liberal politics seem to have crucially depended on a delivery of prosperity and a basic equality. After Vietnam an inequality reminiscent of the late nineteenth century rather than the brief mid-twentieth-century window of the early Great Acceleration resurfaced. Faith in government declined on both the left and the right. With the end of the Cold War, American hegemony, already under attack on the left, seemed costly and without clear ends. The growth of a new conservatism in the West accompanied this increasing inequality, a decline in optimism, a loss of confidence in governance, and an anger—often well placed—at governing elites. Conservatism in the West, which had usually been local in orientation, embraced nationalism. A concomitant movement against globalism was reflected in a backlash against immigration and immigrants. But there were other, crosscutting developments. Mounting environmental problems yielded bitter political battles across the western region in the years after Vietnam, culminating in the Carter administration's declaration that the era of dam building on western rivers had come to an end. In the breakup of a liberal consensus amid rising inequality and environmental crises, the West anticipated events in Europe and elsewhere in North America. Asia may follow a similar path, though there is no guarantee.

I am cautious about seeing such developments as indicative of the end of the changes sparked by World War II in the West, or predictive of how things will play out globally. The Great Acceleration is usually linked to the concept of the Anthropocene. I think the idea of the Anthropocene is as analytically flawed as the Great Acceleration is descriptively revealing. To combine the Great Acceleration with the Anthropocene is to make it another installment of the "End of..." series that has run like sequels of some bad intellectual blockbuster since the 1960s. Turn the Great Acceleration into the Anthropocene, and we can subtitle it "The End of the Holocene." It is the latest installment of the series that began with Daniel Bell's *The End of Ideology*. Since then, we have had Francis Fukuyama's *The End of History*, and Bill McKibben's *The End of Nature*. Ideology, history, and nature slog on, and so, I suspect, will the Holocene.[3]

Another more optimistic way of reading the West, or at least large parts of it, is that in trying to come to terms with a more diverse, more populous, more unequal, and more environmentally threatened society, the West is coming to terms with the unanticipated consequences of the Great Acceleration produced by World War II. For the moment in its politics, its relative globalism, and its environmentalist leanings, it is either out of step with—or in advance of—much of the rest of the United States or Europe. I don't much care which one it is. It presents yet another example of what we try to teach our students. There are always alternatives.

At this point I run the danger of becoming predictive and thus almost certainly wrong. Historians are most useful when they refrain from proclaiming a future and instead inform the present moment in which decisions about the future will be made. Historians can assess the inertia of the past and gauge how and in what direction the weight of all that has gone seems to be pushing us. By recognizing what is old, they can assess what is new and perhaps influential in the ongoing present. In the 1980s and 1990s historians of the West shrewdly, and I think quite accurately, recognized that World War II had introduced new elements that had reshaped the region over the half century since 1940. But what they failed to recognize was that what was new in the 1940s and 1950s had already become part of the inertia of the past. The war had not lost its influence, but by concentrating on it—seeing it only in its creative phase—historians neglected even newer developments that rose in reaction to that phase. They failed to recognize changes taking place around them. The consequences of World War II had their own consequences that needed to be added to the mix.

We seem to be in a similar moment. The present of the West may be prologue to the eventual denouement of the Great Acceleration.

NOTES

INTRODUCTION

1. Richard White, *"It's Your Misfortune and None of My Own": A New History of the American West* (Norman: University of Oklahoma, Press, 1991), 496.

2. Gerald D. Nash, *The Federal Landscape: An Economic History of the Twentieth-Century West* (Tucson: University of Arizona Press, 1999), 42; and Bruce Cumings, *Dominion from Sea to Sea: Pacific Ascendancy and American Power* (New Haven: Yale University Press, 2009), 308–309.

3. Cumings, *Dominion from Sea to Sea*, 309.

4. Cumings, *Dominion from Sea to Sea*, 301.

5. Cumings, *Dominion from Sea to Sea*, 309.

6. Cumings, *Dominion from Sea to Sea*, 309.

7. Cumings, *Dominion from Sea to Sea*, 309; and Bernard DeVoto, "The West: A Plundered Province," *Harper's Monthly Magazine* (August 1934), 355–64.

8. Cumings, *Dominion from Sea to Sea*, 334.

9. Stalin quoted in David M. Kennedy, *Freedom from Fear: The American People in Depression and War* (New York: Oxford University Press, 1999), 190.

10. Cumings, *Dominion from Sea to Sea*, 340.

11. White, *"It's Your Misfortune and None of My Own,"* 503–504.

12. Quintard Taylor, *In Search of the Racial Frontier: African Americans in the American West, 1528–1990* (New York: Norton, 1998), 253.

13. Mark Brilliant, *The Color of America Has Changed: How Racial Diversity Shaped Civil Rights Reform in California, 1941–1978* (New York: Oxford University Press, 2010), chapter 4.

14. Cumings, *Dominion from Sea to Sea*, 334.

15. Phillip Roth, *American Pastoral* (New York: Houghton Mifflin), 40.

16. Nicholas Kristof, "An Idiot's Guide to Inequality," *New York Times*, July 23, 2014. For a more extended discussion of this point, see Michael Lind, *Land of Promise: An Economic History of the United States* (New York: Harper, 2012), chapter 13.

17. Estelle Sommeiller and Mark Price, *The Increasingly Unequal States of America: Income Inequality by State, 1917 to 2012* (Washington, DC: Economic Policy Institute, 2015). See especially the regional comparative data at the bottom of Table 6. Among regions, income was most widely distributed in the West during pre-1979 economic

expansions and then least widely distributed in the post-1979 expansions—by a considerable amount.

18. Frederick Jackson Turner, "The Significance of History," *Wisconsin Journal of Education* 21 (October 1891) in Ray A. Billington, ed., *Frontier and Section: Selected Essays of Frederick Jackson Turner* (Englewood Cliffs, NJ: Prentice-Hall, 1961), 17.

1. EXECUTIVE DOMAIN

1. See Carol Hardy Vincent et al., *Federal Land Ownership: Overview and Data*, Congressional Research Service Report 42346 (December 29, 2014); Department of Defense, *Base Structure Report Fiscal Year 2015 Baseline* (Washington, DC: Office of the Under Secretary of Defense for Acquisition, Technology and Logistics, 2014); and US Congress, Senate, *Military Land Withdrawals: Report to Accompany S. 1309*, 113th C., 2d. Sess., S. Report 113-161 (Washington, DC: Government Printing Office, 2014).

2. Brandon C. Davis, "Defending the Nation, Protecting the Land: Emergency Powers and the Militarization of American Public Lands," in *Proving Grounds: Militarized Landscapes, Weapons Testing, and the Environmental Impact of U.S. Bases*, edited by Edwin A. Martini (Seattle: University of Washington Press, 2015), 19–41, esp. 19. See also Brandon C. Davis, "Grounds for Permanent War: Land Appropriation, Exceptional Powers, and the Mid-Century Militarization of Western North American Environments," PhD diss., University of British Columbia, 2017. US historians of World War II have disregarded military land withdrawals. More surprisingly, historians of the American West and US land policy have done relatively little with the topic. In addition to Davis, my interpretation builds on the following: Alvin T. M. Lee, *Acquisition of Use of Land for Military and War Production Purposes, World War II*, War Records Monograph 5 (Washington, DC: USDA, 1947); Charles F. Wheatley, *Study of Withdrawals and Reservations of Public Domain Lands* (Washington, DC: Public Land Law Review Commission, 1969); David H. Getches, "Managing the Public Lands: The Authority of the Executive to Withdraw Lands," *Natural Resources Journal* 22 (April 1982): 279–335; John D. Leshy, "Shaping the Modern West: The Role of the Executive Branch," *University of Colorado Law Review* 72 (Spring 2001): 287–310; and Harold H. Bruff, "Executive Power and the Public Lands," *University of Colorado Law Review* 76 (Spring 2005): 503–19.

3. Mary Dudziak, *War Time: An Idea, Its History, Its Consequences* (New York: Oxford University Press, 2014).

4. Edward S. Corwin, *Total War and the Constitution* (New York: Knopf, 1947).

5. President Franklin Roosevelt, "Proclaiming a National Emergency in Connection with the Observance, Safeguarding, and Enforcement of Neutrality and the Strengthening of the National Defense Within the Limits of Peace-Time Authorizations," Proclamation 2352, *Federal Register* 4, no. 174 (September 9, 1939): 3,851.

6. President Franklin Roosevelt, "Proclaiming That an Unlimited National Emergency Confronts This Country," Proclamation 2487, *Federal Register* 6, no. 105 (May 29, 1941): 2617.

7. For historical and ethical context, see Elaine Scarry, *Thinking in an Emergency* (New York: Norton, 2011).

8. Executive Order 8578 and 8579, *Federal Register* 5, no. 213 (October 31, 1940): 4313–14. The Utah withdrawal, which became known as Wendover Bombing Range, was enlarged in 1941 by Executive Order 8652. Today it is part of the multiagency Utah Test and Training Range.

9. *An Act Making Appropriations for the Support of the Army for the Fiscal Year Ending June 30, 1919*, Public Law 65-193, *U.S. Statutes at Large* 40, pt. 1 (1918): 845–96. FDR had previously cited this authority in reserving two small tracts of land in California's Mojave Desert for a bombing range and an antiaircraft firing range; see executive orders 8450 and 8507.

10. Upon activation in 1942, the Nevada withdrawal was administered in two pieces, the Tonopah Bombing Range and the Las Vegas Bombing and Gunnery Range. Eventually the two jointly managed units became known as Nellis Air Force Range, which is now part of the multiagency Nevada Test and Training Range.

11. For context, see Vittoria Di Palma, *Wasteland: A History* (New Haven, CT: Yale University Press, 2014); Richard V. Francaviglia, *Mapping and Imagination in the Great Basin: A Cartographic History* (Reno: University of Nevada Press, 2005); and Patricia Nelson Limerick, *Desert Passages: Encounters with the American Deserts* (Albuquerque: University of New Mexico Press, 1985).

12. "'Helvidius' Number 4, [September 14] 1793," in *The Papers of James Madison*, vol. 15, edited by Thomas A. Mason, Robert A. Rutland, and Jeanne K. Sisson (Charlottesville: University Press of Virginia, 1985), 106–10.

13. Here I echo Brian DeLay, "Indian Polities, Empire, and the History of American Foreign Relations," *Diplomatic History* 39 (November 2015): 927–42; and Daniel Immerwahr, "The Greater United States: Territory and Empire in U.S. History," *Diplomatic History* 40 (June 2016): 373–91.

14. See Gregory Ablavsky, "The Rise of Federal Title," *California Law Review* 106, no. 3 (2018): 631–95.

15. *An Act to Repeal Timber-Culture Laws, and for Other Purposes*, chap. 561, *U.S. Statutes at Large* 26 (1891): 1095–1103. This law has variously been called the "Land Revision Act," the "General Land Revision Act," the "General Revision Act," and the "Forest Reserve Act."

16. *An Act for the Preservation of American Antiquities*, Public Law 59-209, *U.S. Statutes at Large* 34, pt. 1 (1907): 225.

17. See Hal Rothman, *Preserving Different Pasts: The American National Monuments* (Urbana: University of Illinois Press, 1989).

18. Theodore Roosevelt, *An Autobiography* (New York: Scribner's, 1920), 357.

19. *An Act to Authorize the President of the United States to Make Withdrawals of Public Lands in Certain Cases*, Public Law 61-303, *U.S. Statutes at Large* 36, pt. 1 (1911): 847–48.

20. *United States v. Midwest Oil Company* in *United States Reports* 236 (1915): 459–512, quotes on 472, 481.

21. Executive Order 6910, *Decisions of the Department of the Interior* 54 (1935): 539–40.

22. The General Land Office continued to manage public domain outside the jurisdiction of the Grazing Service as well as mineral claims on all federal lands. In 1946, the two agencies were combined to form the BLM. The definitive history remains Paul W. Gates, *History of Public Land Law Development* (Washington, DC: Government Printing Office, 1968), though even Gates has nothing to say about military lands. For a historiographical review, see Richard White, "Contested Terrain: The Business of Land in the American West," in *Land in the American West: Private Claims and the Common Good*, edited by William G. Robbins and James C. Foster (Seattle: University of Washington Press, 2000), 190–206.

23. "Documents Relating to the 1941 Opinion of the Attorney General," in Wheatley, *Study of Withdrawals and Reservations*, Appendix B.

24. Robert H. Jackson, "Withdrawal of Public Lands," *Opinions of the Attorney General* 40 (June 4, 1941): 73–84; and Homer Cummings, "Reservation of Public Lands for Migratory Bird Refuge," *Opinions of the Attorney General* 37 (April 30, 1934): 502–503.

25. *Youngstown Sheet & Tube Co. v. Sawyer* in *United States Reports* 343 (1952): 579–716, esp. 637. See also Martin S. Sheffer, "The Attorney General and Presidential Power: Robert H. Jackson, Franklin Roosevelt, and the Prerogative Presidency," *Presidential Studies Quarterly* 12 (Winter 1982): 54–65.

26. Executive Order 9029, *Federal Register* 7, no. 15 (January 22, 1942): 443.

27. Executive Order 9053, *Federal Register* 7, no. 23 (February 10, 1942): 840.

28. Executive Order 9146, *Federal Register* 7, no. 82 (April 28, 1942): 3067.

29. Executive Order 9337, *Federal Register* 8, no. 83 (April 28, 1943): 5516.

30. See War Relocation Authority, "Final Report, Operations Division," RG 210, Entry 16, Box 310/43.110, National Archives; and Connie Y. Chiang, *Nature Behind Barbed Wire: An Environmental History of Japanese American Incarceration* (New York: Oxford University Press, 2018), esp. 40–54.

31. See Edith C. Trunslow, *Manhattan District History: Nonscientific Aspects of Los Alamos Project Y, 1942 through 1946* (Washington, DC: Department of Energy, 1973).

32. Alvin T. M. Lee, "Land Acquisition Program of the War and Navy Departments, World War II," *Journal of Farm Economics* 29 (November 1947): 889–909. One of the largest single uses of western land occurred in summer and fall of 1943: the "Oregon Maneuver" military exercise involved some one hundred thousand soldiers across eight million acres of central Oregon, a mix of federal and private lands made available to the War Department through six-month special-use permits. Another huge temporary use zone was the Desert Training Center and associated California-Arizona Maneuver Area. See John S. Lynch, John W. Kennedy, and Robert L. Wooley, *Patton's Desert Training Center* (Fort Myer, VA: Council on America's Military Past, 1982); and George W. Howard, "The Desert Training Center/California-Arizona Maneuver Area," *Journal of Arizona History* 26 (Fall 1985): 273–94.

33. See Jeffrey Ostler, *The Lakotas and the Black Hills: The Struggle for Sacred Ground* (New York: Viking, 2010), 150, 168, 190.

34. *An Act Authorizing the Head of the Department or Agency Using the Public Domain for War Purposes to Compensate Holders of Grazing Permits and Licenses for Losses Sustained by Reason of Such Use of Public Lands for War Purposes*, Public Law 77-663, *U.S. Statutes at Large* 56, pt. 1 (1943): 654–55.

35. On ranching controversies in Utah, Nevada, and New Mexico, see, respectively, Brandon Davis, "The Desert Blossoms as a Wasteland: An Environmental History of Utah's West Desert," MA thesis, Simon Fraser University, 2007; Leisl Carr Childers, *The Size of the Risk: Histories of Multiple Use in the Great Basin* (Norman: University of Oklahoma Press, 2015); and Ryan H. Edgington, *Range Wars: The Environmental Contest for White Sands Missile Range* (Lincoln: University of Nebraska Press, 2014).

36. US Congress, Senate, *Partial Report of the Committee on Public Lands and Surveys Pursuant to S. Res. 241*, 78th Cong., 1st sess., S. Report 404 (Washington, DC: Government Printing Office, 1943), 45. For the Utah portion of the McCarran hearings, see US Congress, Senate, *Third Partial Report of the Committee on Public Lands and Surveys Pursuant to S. Res. 241: Some Public Land Withdrawals in Utah*, 79th Cong., 1st sess., S. Report 808 (Washington, DC: Government Printing Office, 1945). For context on the hearings, see Karen R. Merrill, *Public Lands and Political Meaning: Ranching, the Government, and the Property between Them* (Berkeley: University of California Press, 2002), 169–204. On the senator, see Jerome E. Edwards, *Pat McCarran, Political Boss of Nevada* (Reno: University of Nevada Press, 1982).

37. Executive Order 9526, *Federal Register* 10, no. 44 (March 2, 1945), 2423–24.

38. See Michael S. Sherry, *In the Shadow of War: The United States since the 1930s* (New Haven, CT: Yale University Press, 1995), esp. 123–87; and Michael J. Hogan, *A Cross of Iron: Harry S. Truman and the Origins of the National Security State, 1945–1954* (Cambridge: Cambridge University Press, 1998).

39. *An Act Authorizing the Head of the Department or Agency Using the Public Domain for National Defense Purposes to Compensate Holders of Grazing Permits and Licenses for Losses Sustained by Reason of Such Use of Public Lands for National Defense Purposes*, Public Law 80-561, *U.S. Statutes at Large* 62, pt. 1 (1949): 277; italics added.

40. Public Land Order 678, *Federal Register* 15, no. 211 (October 31, 1950): 7299–7300.

41. President Harry Truman, "Termination of the Wartime Emergencies," Proclamation 2974, *Federal Register* 17, no. 85 (April 30, 1952): 3813.

42. Executive Order 10355, *Federal Register* 17, no. 105 (May 28, 1952): 4831–33.

43. *An Act to Authorize the President to Provide for the Performance of Certain Functions of the President by the Other Officers of the Government, and for Other Purposes*, Public Law 81-672, *U.S. Statutes at Large* 64, pt. 1 (1952): 419.

44. Joel D. Wolfsohn to Thomas K. Finletter, October 27, 1952, reprinted in US Congress, Senate, *Military Public Land Withdrawals: Report of the Committee on Interior and Insular Affairs to Accompany H.R. 5536*, 85th Cong., 1st sess., S. Report 857 (Washington, DC: Government Printing Office, 1957), 83–84.

45. Public Land Order 833, *Federal Register* 17, no. 104 (May 27, 1952): 4822–23.

46. Atomic Energy Commission (AEC), "Location of Proving Ground for Atomic Weapons," December 13, 1950, AEC Document 141/7, copy in National Security Archive, George Washington University.

47. Public Land Order 805, *Federal Register* 17, no. 35 (February 19, 1952): 1522–23. AEC holdings in Nevada were subsequently enlarged and modified by Public Land Order 1662 (1958), Public Land Order 2568 (1961), Public Land Order 2771 (1962), Public Land Order 2834 (1962), and Public Land Order 3759 (1965). Under the Department of Energy (the successor of the AEC), the Nevada Proving Ground was renamed the Nevada Test Site. For an innovative place-based history, see Andrew G. Kirk and Kristian Purcell, *Doom Towns: The People and Landscapes of Atomic Testing* (New York: Oxford University Press, 2016).

48. Public Land Order 898, *Federal Register* 18, no. 119 (June 19, 1953): 3540.

49. Gregory W. Pedlow and Donald E. Welzenbach, *The Central Intelligence Agency and Overhead Reconnaissance: The U-2 and OXCART Programs, 1954–1974* (Washington, DC: Central Intelligence Agency, 1992), 56–57. Document available online through the National Security Archive, George Washington University.

50. Executive Order 10633, *Federal Register* 20, no. 166 (August 25, 1955): 6209–10; and *An Act to Encourage and Regulate the Use of Aircraft in Commerce, and for Other Purposes*, Public Law 69-254, *U.S. Statutes at Large* 44, pt. 2 (1926): 568–76.

51. Clair Engle, speaking on H.R. 5538, 85th Cong., 1st sess., *Congressional Record* 103, pt. 4 (April 11, 1957): 5512.

52. US Congress, House, *Military Land Withdrawals: Hearings before the Committee on Interior and Insular Affairs*, 85th Cong., 1st sess. (Washington, DC: Government Printing Office, 1957), 93–94.

53. Clair Engle, "Stopping the Military Land-Grab," *National Parks Magazine* (October–December 1956): 147–51, 186. "Land grab" entered American political vernacular in the Gilded Age, when antimonopolists characterized the railroad land grant system as the "Land Grab system."

54. *An Act to Provide That Withdrawals, Reservations, or Restrictions of More Than Five Thousand Acres of Public Lands of the United States for Certain Purposes Shall Not Become Effective Until Approved by Act of Congress*, Public Law 85-337, *U.S. Statutes at Large* 72, pt. 1 (1958): 27–30.

55. These field-defining terms are associated with the following works: Clinton L. Rossiter, *Constitutional Dictatorship: Crisis Government in the Modern Democracies* (Princeton, NJ: Princeton University Press, 1948); and Arthur M. Schlesinger Jr., *The Imperial Presidency* (Boston: Houghton Mifflin, 1973). See also Kenneth R. Mayer, *With the Stroke of a Pen: Executive Orders and Presidential Power* (Princeton, NJ: Princeton University Press, 2002); Chris Edelson, *Emergency Presidential Power: From the Drafting of the Constitution to the War on Terror* (Madison: University of Wisconsin Press, 2013); and William G. Howell, Saul P. Jackman and Jon C. Rogowski, *The Wartime President: Executive Influence and the Nationalizing Politics of Threat* (Chicago: University of Chicago Press, 2013).

56. House, *Military Land Withdrawals*, 244.

57. Senate, *Military Public Land Withdrawals*, 67. A comprehensive history of military airspace before and after the Federal Aviation Act of 1958 remains to be written. For context, see Stuart Banner, *Who Owns the Sky? The Struggle to Control Airspace from the Wright Brothers On* (Cambridge, MA: Harvard University Press, 2008).

58. See David Loomis, *Combat Zoning: Military Land-use Planning in Nevada* (Reno: University of Nevada Press, 1993), esp. 49–86; and Robert F. Durant, *The Greening of the U.S. Military: Environmental Policy, National Security, and Organizational Change* (Washington, DC: Georgetown University Press, 2007), 168–69.

59. Quoted in Loomis, *Combat Zoning*, 46.

60. See Matthew Glass, *Citizens against MX: Public Languages in the Nuclear Age* (Urbana: University of Illinois Press, 1993).

61. Chuck Yeager, *Yeager: An Autobiography* (New York: Bantam, 1985), 15.

62. See Richard Misrach and Myriam Weisang Misrach, *Bravo-20: The Bombing of the American West* (Baltimore, MD: Johns Hopkins University Press, 1990); and John P. Bieter Jr., *Showdown in the Big Quiet: Land, Myth, and Government in the American West* (Lubbock: Texas Tech University Press, 2015), 172–201.

63. *An Act to Withdraw Certain Public Lands for Military Purposes, and for Other Purposes*, Public Law 99-606, *U.S. Statutes at Large* 100, pt. 1 (1986): 3457–69. This law also clarified that military reservations do not enjoy reserved water rights.

64. *An Act to Authorize Appropriations for Fiscal Year 2000 for Military Activities of the Department of Defense, for Military Construction, and for Defense Activities of the Department of Energy, To Prescribe Military Personnel Strengths for Such Fiscal Year, and for Other Purposes,* Public Law 106-65, Title XXX, *U.S. Statutes at Large* 113, pt. 1 (1999): 885–913.

65. Barack Obama, "Statement of Administration Policy: H.R. 4909—National Defense Authorization Act for Fiscal Year 2017," May 16, 2016, American Presidency Project, http://www.presidency.ucsb.edu/ws/?pid=117501.

66. "Title XXX—Utah Test and Training Range and Related Matters" in *An Act to Authorize Appropriations for Fiscal Year 2017 for Military Activities of the Department of Defense, for Military Construction, and for Defense Activities of the Department of Energy, to Prescribe Military Personnel Strengths for Such Fiscal Year, and for Other Purposes*, Public Law 114-328, *U.S. Statutes at Large* 130 (2016): 2000–2968, esp. 2743–53.

67. The White House, Office of the Press Secretary, "Remarks by President Trump at Signing of Executive Order on the Antiquities Act," April 26, 2017. Trump, acting on the advice of Interior Secretary Ryan Zinke, subsequently reduced the two monuments to "the smallest area compatible with the proper care of the objects of scientific or historic interest to be protected"; see US President, "Modifying the Bears Ears National Monument," Proclamation 9681, *Federal Register* 82, no. 235 (December 8, 2017): 58081–87; and US President, "Modifying the Grand Staircase-Escalante National Monument," Proclamation 9682, *Federal Register* 82, no. 235 (December 8, 2017): 58089–96.

68. US President, "Declaration of National Emergency by Reason of Certain

Terrorist Attacks," Proclamation 7463, *Federal Register* 66, no. 181 (September 18, 2001): 48199.

69. For an overview, see Harold C. Relyea, *National Emergency Powers*, Congressional Research Service Report 98-508 (August 30, 2007).

70. Jack Utter et al., "Military Land Withdrawals: Some Legal History and a Case Study," University of Arizona College of Agriculture Paper 541 (Tucson, 1985).

71. President Gerald Ford, "An American Promise," Proclamation 4417, *Federal Register* 41, no. 35 (February 20, 1976): 7741.

72. *Trump v. Hawaii* (2018); "Presidential Proclamation on Declaring a National Emergency Concerning the Southern Border of the United States," February 15, 2019.

73. See Patricia Nelson Limerick, *The Legacy of Conquest: The Unbroken Past of the American West* (New York: Norton, 1987).

74. See Giorgio Agamben, *State of Exception*, trans. Kevin Atell (Chicago: University of Chicago Press, 2005).

75. See, among other titles, Rebecca Solnit, *Savage Dreams: A Journey into the Landscape Wars of the American West* (New York: Vintage, 1994); Carole Gallagher, *American Ground Zero: The Secret Nuclear War* (New York: Random House, 1994); Valerie Kuletz, *The Tainted Desert: Environmental and Social Ruin in the American West* (New York: Routledge, 1998); Mike Davis, "The Dead West: Ecocide in Marlboro Country," in *Over the Edge: Remapping the American West*, edited by Valerie J. Matsumoto and Blake Allmendinger (Berkeley: University of California Press, 1999), 339–69; Max S. Power, *America's Nuclear Wastelands: Politics, Accountability, and Cleanup* (Pullman: Washington State University Press, 2008); John Beck, *Dirty Wars: Landscape, Power, and Waste in Western American Literature* (Lincoln: University of Nebraska Press, 2010); Trevor Paglen, *Blank Spots on the Map: The Dark Geography of the Pentagon's Secret World* (New York: New American Library, 2010); and Sarah Alisabeth Fox, *Downwind: A People's History of the Nuclear West* (Lincoln: University of Nebraska Press, 2014).

76. National Research Council, *Rehabilitation Potential of Western Coal Lands* (Washington, DC: National Academy of Sciences, 1973), 86.

77. For context, see James Robert Allison III, *Sovereignty for Survival: American Energy Development and Indian Self-Determination* (New Haven, CT: Yale University Press, 2015); and Winona LaDuke with Sean Aaron Cruz, *The Militarization of Indian Country* (East Lansing, MI: Makwa Enewed, 2014). In indigenous studies "national sacrifice area" took on a life of its own, joining in the 1990s emergent vocabulary like "environmental justice," "environmental racism," "settler colonialism," and "nuclear colonialism."

78. The Sikes Act of 1960 (16 U.S. Code §670a–670o) requires the DoD to implement interagency cooperative plans for the conservation and rehabilitation of wildlife and other natural resources. For the original text, see *An Act to Promote Effectual Planning, Development, Maintenance, and Coordination of Wildlife, Fish, and Game Conservation and Rehabilitation in Military Reservations*, Public Law 86-797, *U.S. Statutes at Large* 74 (1960): 1052–53. For context, see William A. Wilcox, *The Modern*

Military and the Environment: The Laws of Peace and War (Lanham, MD: Government Institutes, 1997), 59–74; William A. Wilcox Jr. and Andrew J. Vliet III, "The Engle Act and Military Land Withdrawals: A Blueprint for Inter-agency Cooperation," *Land and Water Review* 32, no. 2 (1997): 461–78; Darrin Hostetler, "The Wrong War, with the Wrong Enemy, at the Wrong Time: The Coming Battle over the Military Land Withdrawal Act and an Experiment in Privatizing the Regulation of Public Lands," *Environmental Law* 29 (Summer 1999): 303–38; Jean A. Mansavage, *Natural Defense: U.S. Air Force Origins of the Department of Defense Natural Resources Conservation Program* (Washington, DC: Air Force History and Museums Program, 2014); and Susan Perkins Stark, "The Department of Defense Natural Resources Conservation Program: How Military Environmental Activists Conserved Thirty Million Acres for Military Use and the Protection of Endangered Species," *Western New England Law Review* 38, no. 3 (2016): 355–75.

79. See Edgington, *Range Wars*, 171–98.

80. Beth E. Lachman et al., *The Nevada Test and Training Range (NTTR) and Proposed Wilderness Areas: Issues Affecting the NTTR's Land Withdrawal Renewal* (Santa Monica: RAND Corporation, 2016), 18–19.

81. Western states have in some cases sued the federal government over inverse condemnation. For example, the taking of state lands within White Sands Missile Range was resolved through *Alex J. Armijo et al. v. the United States* (1981) in *Claims Court Reporter* 229 (1983): 34–47. See also Janice D. Paster, "School Trust Land and Federal Condemnation for Defense Purposes: Federal Laws in Conflict," *Natural Resources Journal* 24 (April 1984): 451–70.

82. For an excellent case study, see John M. Findlay and Bruce Hevly, *Atomic Frontier Days: Hanford and the American West* (Seattle: University of Washington Press, 2011).

83. See Joseph E. Taylor III et al., "Follow the Money: A Spatial History of In-Lieu Programs for Western Federal Lands," http://www.followthemoney.stanford.edu.

84. See Paul Thomas Chamberlin, *The Cold War's Killing Fields: Rethinking the Long Peace* (New York: Harper, 2018).

85. See Kate Brown, *Plutopia: Nuclear Families, Atomic Cities, and the Great Soviet and American Plutonium Disasters* (New York: Oxford University Press, 2013).

86. For an overview of the negative effects of military land use, see Howard G. Wilshire, Jane E. Nielson, and Richard W. Hazlett, *The American West at Risk: Science, Myths, and Politics of Land Abuse and Recovery* (New York: Oxford University Press 2008), 158–212. On the downwinders, see, among other titles, Howard Ball, *Justice Downwind: America's Atomic Testing Program in the 1950s* (New York: Oxford University Press, 1988); Philip L. Fradkin, *Fallout: An American Nuclear Tragedy* (Tucson: University of Arizona Press, 1989); and Stewart L. Udall, *The Myths of August: A Personal Exploration of Our Tragic Cold War Affair with the Atom* (New York: Pantheon, 1994).

87. On the U-boom, see Raye C. Ringholz, *Uranium Frenzy: Boom and Bust on the Colorado Plateau* (New York: Norton, 1989); Arthur R. Gómez, *Quest for the Golden*

Circle: The Four Corners and the Metropolitan West, 1945–1970 (Albuquerque: University of New Mexico Press, 1994); and Michael A. Amundson, *Yellowcake Towns: Uranium Mining Communities in the American West* (Niwot: University Press of Colorado, 2004). On Diné and uranium, see Peter H. Eichstaedt, *If You Poison Us: Uranium and Native Americans* (Santa Fe, NM: Red Crane Books, 1994); Doug Brugge, Timothy Benally, and Esther Yazzie-Lewis, eds., *The Navajo People and Uranium Mining* (Albuquerque: University of New Mexico Press, 2006); and Judy Pasternak, *Yellow Dirt: A Poisoned Land and the Betrayal of the Navajos* (New York: Free Press, 2011).

88. Traci Brynne Voyles, *Wastelanding: Legacies of Uranium Mining in Navajo Country* (Minneapolis: University of Minnesota Press, 2016).

89. "Treaty with the Western Shoshoni, 1863," in *Indian Affairs: Laws and Treaties*, vol. 2, edited by Charles J. Kappler (Washington, DC: Government Printing Office, 1904), 851–53.

90. For context, see Ned Blackhawk, *Violence over the Land: Indians and Empires in the Early American West* (Cambridge, MA: Harvard University Press, 2006), 267–93; and Richard O. Clemmer, "Land Rights, Claims, and Western Shoshones: The Ideology of Loss and the Bureaucracy of Enforcement," *Political and Legal Anthropology Review* 32 (November 2009): 279–311.

91. *United States v. Dann* in *United States Reports* 470 (1985): 39–50.

92. See Andrew J. Butcher, "In Search of a Remedy to the Nuclear Storage Conundrum: *Western Shoshone National Council v. United States*," *Energy Law Journal* 28, no. 1 (2007): 207–20; and Barbara McDonald, "How a Nineteenth Century Indian Treaty Stopped a Twenty-first Century Megabomb," *Nevada Law Journal* 9, no. 3 (2009): 749–74.

93. Soren C. Larsen and Timothy J. Brock, "Great Basin Imagery in Newspaper Coverage of Yucca Mountain," *Geographical Review* 95 (October 2005): 517–36.

94. See David Rich Lewis, "Skull Valley Goshutes and the Politics of Nuclear Waste: Environment, Identity, and Sovereignty," in *Native Americans and the Environment: Perspectives on the Ecological Indian,* edited by Michael E. Harkin and David Rich Lewis (Lincoln: University of Nebraska Press, 2007), 304–42; and Lincoln L. Davies, "Skull Valley Crossroads: Reconciling Native Sovereignty and the Federal Trust," *Maryland Law Review* 68, no. 2 (2009): 290–376.

95. See Jessica A. Shoemaker, "Complexity's Shadow: American Indian Property, Sovereignty, and the Future," *Michigan Law Review* 115, no. 4 (2017): 487–552; and Joseph William Singer, "Indian Title: Unraveling the Racial Contest of Property Rights, or How To Stop Engaging in Conquest," *Albany Government Law Review* 10, no. 1 (2017): 1–48.

96. Franklin D. Roosevelt, *Development of United States Foreign Policy: Addresses and Messages of Franklin D. Roosevelt* (Washington, DC: Government Printing Office, 1942), 70.

97. See Christina Duffy Burnett, "The Edges of Empire and the Limits of Sovereignty: American Guano Islands," *American Quarterly* 57 (September 2005): 779–803.

98. C. T. Sandars, *America's Overseas Garrisons: The Leasehold Empire* (Oxford: Oxford University Press, 2000); Ruth Oldenziel, "Islands: The United States as a Networked Empire," in *Entangled Geographies: Empire and Technopolitics in the Global Cold War,* edited by Gabrielle Hecht (Cambridge, MA: MIT Press, 2011); and Daniel Immerwahr, *How To Hide an Empire: A History of the Greater United States* (New York: Farrar, Straus and Giroux, 2019). See also David Vine, *Base Nation: How U.S. Military Bases Abroad Harm America and the World* (New York: Metropolitan Books, 2015); and Mary Dudziak's chapter in this edited volume.

99. See Greg Grandin, *The End of the Myth: From the Frontier to the Border Wall in the Mind of America* (New York: Metropolitan Books, 2019).

100. See J. R. McNeill and Peter Engelke, *The Great Acceleration: An Environmental History of the Anthropocene since 1945* (Cambridge, MA: Belknap Press of Harvard University Press, 2016); and Richard White's afterword to this edited volume.

101. See Jacob Darwin Hamblin, *Arming Mother Nature: The Birth of Catastrophic Environmentalism* (New York: Oxford University Press, 2013).

2. ENLISTING THE LABORATORIES

1. Judith R. Goodstein, *Millikan's School: A History of the California Institute of Technology* (New York: W. W. Norton, 1991), 153–54; and Dik Daso, *Architects of American Air Supremacy: General Hap Arnold and Dr. Theodore von Kármán* (Maxwell Air Force Base, AL: Air University Press, 1997), 99. For guidance in obtaining photos and permissions, I am grateful for Peter Collopy and Loma Karlins at the Caltech Archives, Erik Conway at the JPL Archives, and Karen Nelson and Thor Swift at the Lawrence Berkeley Archives; for research assistance, I thank Jay Weixelbaum; for consultations, I thank Peter Westwick; and for encouragement and comments, I am grateful for Mark Brilliant, Cathryn Carson, and David M. Kennedy.

2. Daso, *Architects of American Air Supremacy*, 108.

3. Michael A. Gorn, *The Universal Man: Theodore von Karman's Life in Aeronautics* (Washington, DC: Smithsonian Institution Press, 1992), 17–24.

4. Goodstein, *Millikan's School*, 156, 163; and Gorn, *Universal Man*, 26–30, 36–38.

5. Goodstein, *Millikan's School*, 164, 166; and Gorn, *Universal Man*, 44, 46, 49, 103.

6. Gorn, *Universal Man*, 63; Daso, *Architects of American Air Supremacy*, 106.

7. Daso, *Architects of American Air Supremacy*, 109–10; and Goodstein, *Millikan's School*, 175. In 1936, Clark Millikan cheered the collaborations between the Guggenheim Laboratory and the aircraft companies: "The constant contact of the academic members of the laboratory staff with the immediate problems of practical designers has a very beneficial effect upon their research and academic activities by keeping the latter up-to-date and in the current of actual aeronautical research." Goodstein, *Millikan's School*, 175.

8. Gorn, *Universal Man*, 1–2, 34, 36–38, 55, 64–65.

9. Gorn, *Universal Man*, 68–69, 71.

10. M. G. Lord, *Astro Turf: The Private Life of Rocket Science* (New York: Bloomsbury Publishing, 2009), 70–71; and Gorn, *Universal Man*, 74.

11. Lord, *Astro Turf*, 61–63, 70–73; and Gorn, *Universal Man*, 74–75.

12. Gorn, *Universal Man*, 75–76

13. Mary Terrall, "Interview with Frank J. Malina, December 14, 1978," Transcript, Archives, California Institute of Technology, Pasadena, 5.

14. Gorn, *Universal Man*, 74–76. "Sounding rockets" were named in complement of the devices used to sound the depths of the sea.

15. Gorn, *Universal Man*, 78; and Goodstein, *Millikan's School*, 262

16. Gorn, *Universal Man*, 78–79.

17. Gorn, *Universal Man*, 81.

18. Daniel J. Kevles, *The Physicists: The History of a Scientific Community in Modern America Cambridge* (Harvard University Press, 1995), 227.

19. Kevles, *Physicists*, 227–28.

20. Kevles, *Physicists*, 227–28.

21. J. L. Heilbron and Robert W. Seidel, *Lawrence and His Laboratory: A History of the Lawrence Berkeley Laboratory,* volume 1 (Berkeley: University of California Press, 1989), 75–102, 121–35, 269.

22. The 60-inch cyclotron could produce ten times as much radiation as the output of 200 milligrams of radium. K.M.G. Siegbahn, *Nobel Lectures: Physics 1922–1941*, http://www.nobelprize.org/nobel_prizes/physics/laureates/1939/press.html, accessed April 1, 2017.

23. Lawrence as quoted in Heilbron and Seidel, *Lawrence and His Laboratory*, 156–57, 34–39, 219.

24. J. L. Heilbron, Robert W. Seidel, and Bruce R. Wheaton, *Lawrence and His Laboratory: Nuclear Science at Berkeley* (Berkeley: Lawrence Berkeley Laboratory and Office for History of Science and Technology, University of California–Berkeley, 1981), 26.

25. Lawrence as quoted in Kevles, *Physicists,* 284.

26. Heilbron, Seidel, and Wheaton, *Lawrence and His Laboratory: Nuclear Science at Berkeley*, 27.

27. Daso, *Architects of American Air Supremacy*, 25, 27; and Gorn, *Universal Man*, 100.

28. Daso, *Architects of American Air Supremacy*, 27, 57, 78, n.10; and Kevles, *Physicists*, 289.

29. Goodstein, *Millikan's School*, 175–76; and Daso, *Architects of American Air Supremacy*, 59. Unhappy that so much wind-tunnel time was going to practical testing and so little to basic problems in aerodynamics and structure, von Kármán told Donald Douglas in 1940 that the company ought to support GALCIT's academic program, specifically several graduate fellowships, to encourage the new PhDs to take jobs at Douglas rather than at its competitors. Goodstein, *Millikan's School*, 177.

30. Daso, *Architects of American Air Supremacy*, 58, 64; Louis R. Johnson to Frank R. Lillie, December 15, 1938; Frank R. Lillie to the Secretary of War, December 13, 1938, September 10, 1938; Robert A. Millikan to Frank R. Lillie, June 3, 1938; [Paul Brockett] Executive Secretary [National Academy of Sciences], "Memorandum," October 4, 1938;

Louis Johnson to Secretary, National Research Council, April 2, 1938, all in "Govt Rel. & Sci. Adv. Com: Com on Army Air Corps Problems: Beginning of Program, 1938," folder in Science Advisory Board [SAB], 1934–1941, Records, Committee on Army Air Corps, 1936–1941, Jet Propulsion file, Archives, National Academy of Sciences, Washington, DC [hereafter, SAB Army Air Corps file].

31. The members are listed in Memorandum to the Secretary of War, "Preliminary Report of the Conference... December 27 and December 28, 1938," December 30, 1938, "Govt Rel & Sc Adv Com: Com on Army Air Corps Problems: Subcom on Jet Auxiliary Power," 1938–1939, folder in SAB Army Air Corps file; Kevles, *Physicists*, 122–23; Terrall, "Interview with Malina," 3; and F. J. Malina, "The U.S. Army Air Corps Jet Propulsion Research Project, GALCIT Project No. 1, 1939–1946: A Memoir," in *A History of Rocketry and Astronautics*, edited by R. Cargill Hall, *Proceedings of the Third Through the Sixth History Symposia of the International Academy of Astronautics* (AAS History Series, volume 7, part 2; IAA History Symposia, volume 2; San Diego, CA: American Astronautical Society, 1986), 154–55 [hereafter, Malina, "GALCIT"].

32. Max Mason to Members of the National Academy of Sciences Committee on Air Corps Research, n.d. [December 1938], "Govt Rel & Sc Adv Com: Com on Army Air Corps Problems: General," 1938–1939. The participants are listed in Memorandum to the Secretary of War, "Preliminary Report of the Conference... December 27 and December 28, 1938," December 30, 1938, both folders in SAB Army Air Corps file. The participant list does not include von Kármán; he had been added to the Academy committee in mid-November but appears to have been absent at the meeting. His appointment is noted in Paul Brockett to Max Mason, December 22, 1938, "Govt Rel & Sc Adv Com: Com on Army Air Corps Problems: General," 1938–1939, SAB Army Air Corps file. During the summer, in a consulting report for the Consolidated Aircraft Company (later General Dynamics/Convair) in San Diego, Malina laid out how with suitable development the GALCIT rockets might be used to assist the takeoff of their seaplanes. Malina, "GALCIT," 154–55.

33. Frank J. Malina, "Report on Jet Propulsion for the National Academy of Sciences Committee on Air Corps Research," December 21, 1938, "Govt Rel & Sc Adv Com: Com on Army Air Corps Problems: Subcom on Jet Auxiliary Power: Jet Propulsion Report," folder in SAB Army Air Corps file; Malina, "GALCIT," 155; Clayton R. Koppes, *JPL and the American Space Program: A History of the Jet Propulsion Laboratory* (New Haven, CT: Yale University Press, 1982), 9; and Goodstein, *Millikan's School*, 155.

34. Malina, "GALCIT," 155; Memorandum to the Secretary of War, "Preliminary Report of the Conference... December 27 and December 28, 1938," December 30, 1938; Max Mason to General Henry H. Arnold, January 3, 1939, "Govt Rel & Sc Adv Com: Com on Army Air Corps Problems: General," 1938–1939, folder in SAB Army Air Corps file. von Kármán recalled that at the January meeting Jerome Hunsacker from MIT, one of the nation's leading aeronautical engineers, cracked that his institution would undertake the de-icing project for the Air Corps and leave the "Buck Rogers stuff" to Caltech. Theodore von Kármán, with Lee Edson, *The Wind and Beyond:*

Theodore von Kármán, Pioneer in Aviation and Pathfinder in Space (Boston: Little, Brown, 1967), 243. Paul Brockett to Hunsacker, November 14, 1939, "Govt Rel & Sc Adv Com: Com on Army Air Corps Problems: General," 1938–1939, folder in SAB Army Air Corps file.

35. Terrall, "Interview with Malina," 4; and Gorn, *Universal Man*, 85,

36. Malina, "GALCIT,"158; and H. H. Arnold to National Academy of Sciences, June 9, 1939, and attached "Report of Conference with the National Academy of Sciences in the Office Chief of Air Corps, June 7, 1939," "Govt Rel & Sc Adv Com: Com on Army Air Corps Problems: General," 1938–1939, folder in SAB Army Air Corps file.

37. Gorn, *Universal Man*, 87; and Malina, "GALCIT," 163–64, 169–70.

38. Koppes, *JPL and the American Space Program*, 9; Lord, *Astro Turf*, 67–68; and Fraser Macdonald, *Escape from Earth: A Secret History of the Space Rocket* (New York: Public Affairs, 2019), 47–54.

39. Koppes, *JPL and the American Space Program*, 9; Gorn, *Universal Man*, 86–87; and Vannevar Bush to Frank B. Jewett, March 15, 1940, and March 19, 1940, "Govt Rel & Sc Adv Com: Com on Army Air Corps Problems: General," 1940–1941," folder in SAB Army Air Corps file.

40. Gorn, *Universal Man*, 97. Gorn dates the episode to the summer of 1940. However, Malina rightly recalled that it was in the spring; von Kármán prepared a report on the rocket project dated April 1 that did not indicate that he and Malina knew how to proceed with solid-fuel rockets; he then produced a revised report dated June 1 indicating that they now saw a way forward. Malina, "GALCIT," 163–64, 166, fig. 10; Theodore von Kármán, "Program for Jet Propulsion Research at the California Institute of Technology, 1940–1941," April 1940, "Govt Rel & Sc Adv Com: Com on Army Air Corps Problems: Subcom on Jet Auxiliary Power," 1940–1941"; and Theodore von Kármán, "Program for Jet Propulsion Research at the California Institute of Technology, 1940–1941 (revised June 1, 1940)," "Govt Rel & Sc Adv Com: Com on Army Air Corps Problems: General," 1940–1941," folders in SAB Army Air Corps file.

41. Koppes, *JPL and the American Space Program*, 10; Gorn, *Universal Man*, 85; and von Kármán, *Wind and Beyond*, 169–70.

42. Von Kármán, "Program for Jet Propulsion Research at the California Institute of Technology, 1940–1941" (Revised June 1, 1940); Frank Jewett to General H. H. Arnold, June 11, 1940; and Arnold to Jewett, June 17, 1940, "Govt Rel & Sc Adv Com: Com on Army Air Corps Problems: General," 1940–1941," folder in SAB Army Air Corps file.

43. Arnold to Jewett, July 11, 1940, and July 20, 1940, "Govt Rel & Sc Adv Com: Com on Army Air Corps Problems: General," 1940–1941," folder in SAB Army Air Corps file; and von Kármán, *Wind and Beyond*, 243.

44. Gorn, *Universal Man*, 88; and Koppes, *JPL and the American Space Program*, 11. Malina later reflected that the work was advantaged by von Kármán's "vast experience of utilizing mathematics and fundamental physical principles for the solution of difficult engineering problems, and a rare skill in negotiation and organization." Malina, "GALCIT," 158.

45. Gorn, *Universal Man*, 65; and Malina, "GALCIT," 183–87.

46. Malina, "GALCIT," 170.

47. Max Mason to F. B. Jewett, April 24, 1941; and Jewett to Mason, May 6, 1941, "Govt Rel & Sc Adv Com: Com on Army Air Corps Problems: Subcom on Jet Auxiliary Power," 1940–1941"; folder in SAB Army Air Corps file.

48. Koppes, *JPL and the American Space Program*, 14; and Lord, *Astro Turf*, 83.

49. Malina, "GALCIT," 172, 174.

50. Malina, "GALCIT," 194–95; Terrall, "Interview with Malina," 10–13l; and Macdonald, *Escape from Earth*, 97–98.

51. Koppes, *JPL and the American Space Program*, 12, 16. The GALCIT project and the company were so interleaved in time and effort that Malina later acknowledged that his group might well have been charged with conflicts of interest. They were developing JATO with federal money, advising the government on its use, and profiting from its production. But at the time no one called them to account. Rocket experts were in short supply, and there was a war on. Koppes, *JPL and the American Space Program*, 16–17.

52. Koppes, *JPL and the American Space Program*, 15.

53. Koppes, *JPL and the American Space Program*, 18–19.

54. Koppes, *JPL and the American Space Program*, 19.

55. Koppes, *JPL and the American Space Program*, 19–20.

56. Koppes, *JPL and the American Space Program*, 21–22.

57. Koppes, *JPL and the American Space Program*, 21.

58. Richard Rhodes, *The Making of the Atomic Bomb* (New York: Simon & Schuster, 1986), 303–17.

59. Siegbahn, *Nobel Lectures.*

60. Kevles, *Physicists*, 285–86.

61. Kevles, *Physicists*, 303.

62. Rhodes, *Making of the Atomic Bomb*, 380.

63. Heilbron, Seidel, and Wheaton, *Lawrence and His Laboratory: Nuclear Science at Berkeley*, 30–33.

64. Heilbron, Seidel, and Wheaton, *Lawrence and His Laboratory: Nuclear Science at Berkeley*, 32; and Rhodes, *Making of the Atomic Bomb*, 361.

65. Rhodes, *Making of the Atomic Bomb*, 369–79.

66. Rhodes, *Making of the Atomic Bomb*, 386–87.

67. Heilbron, Seidel, and Wheaton, *Lawrence and His Laboratory: Nuclear Science at Berkeley*, 32.

68. Heilbron, Seidel, and Wheaton, *Lawrence and His Laboratory: Nuclear Science at Berkeley*, 42.

69. Rhodes, *Making of the Atomic Bomb*, 409–11.

70. For Groves's family background and prewar army career, see Robert S. Norris, *Racing for the Bomb: General Leslie R. Groves, the Manhattan Project's Indispensable Man* (South Royalton, VT: Steerforth Press, 2002).

71. Norris, *Racing for the Bomb*, 249–50.

72. Heilbron, Seidel, and Wheaton, *Lawrence and His Laboratory: Nuclear Science at Berkeley*, 32, 34.

73. Heilbron, Seidel, and Wheaton, *Lawrence and His Laboratory: Nuclear Science at Berkeley*, 41.

74. Heilbron, Seidel, and Wheaton, *Lawrence and His Laboratory: Nuclear Science at Berkeley*, 34; and Norris, *Racing for the Bomb*, 205.

75. Rhodes, *Making of the Atomic Bomb*, 439–42, 497–98.

76. Stanley Goldberg, "General Groves and the Atomic West: The Making and the Meaning of Hanford," in *The Atomic West*, edited by Bruce Hevly and John M. Findlay (Seattle: University of Washington Press, 1998), 49–50.

77. Rhodes, *Making of the Atomic Bomb*, 497; and Norris, *Racing for the Bomb*, 416–21. See Farmer's chapter in this volume for an explanation of how the government acquired the 2.4 million acres that included Alamogordo, New Mexico, where the first nuclear device would be tested, on July 16, 1945.

78. Goldberg, "General Groves and the Atomic West," 48.

79. Goldberg, "General Groves and the Atomic West," 54.

80. Goldberg, "General Groves and the Atomic West," 54, 64–65.

81. Goldberg, "General Groves and the Atomic West," 54; Heilbron, Seidel, and Wheaton, *Lawrence and His Laboratory: Nuclear Science at Berkeley*, 41; and Norris, *Racing for the Bomb*, 363.

82. Heilbron, Seidel, and Wheaton, *Lawrence and His Laboratory: Nuclear Science at Berkeley*, 44–45; and Norris, *Racing for the Bomb*, 221–22.

83. Daniel J. Kevles, "Cold War and Hot Physics: Science, Security, and the American State, 1945–1956," *HSPS: Historical Studies in the Physical and Biological Sciences* 20, no. 2 (1990): 239–41.

84. Kevles, "Cold War and Hot Physics," 242–64.

85. This account of Terman and Stanford microelectronics is drawn from Stuart W. Leslie, "Playing the Education Game to Win: The Military and Interdisciplinary Research at Stanford," *HSPS: Historical Studies in the Physical and Biological Sciences* 18, no. 1 (1987): 55–88.

86. Leslie, "Playing the Education Game to Win," 59.

87. Leslie, "Playing the Education Game to Win," 69.

88. Leslie, "Playing the Education Game to Win," 70–74, 87.

89. The list of West Coast scientists who served on the advisory boards of the postwar research agencies is long. It includes Glenn Seaborg; Lee A. DuBridge, who had directed the Radiation Laboratory at MIT and succeeded Robert Millikan at the helm of Caltech in 1946; Robert F. Bacher and Charles Lauritsen of Caltech; Luis Alvarez of Berkeley; and Frederick Terman of Stanford.

90. Daso, *Architects of American Air Supremacy*, 128–30, 133–43.

91. Daso, *Architects of American Air Supremacy*, 153–74.

92. Koppes, *JPL and the American Space Program*, 24–27; and Terrall, "Interview with Malina," 14.

93. Koppes, *JPL and the American Space Program*, 27–28.

94. Koppes, *JPL and the American Space Program*, 27; and Terrall, "Interview with Malina," 13–16.

95. Terrall, "Interview with Malina," 13–16; and Macdonald, *Escape from Earth*, 219–21, 230, 234–37.

96. Koppes, *JPL and the American Space Program*, 23–24, 32–50.

97. Gregg Herken, "The University of California, the Federal Weapons Labs, and the Founding of the Atomic West," in *The Atomic West*, edited by Hevly and Findlay (Seattle: University of Washington Press, 1998), 121. For the overall transition to peacetime basic research at the laboratory, see Robert W. Seidel, "Accelerating Science: The Postwar Transformation of the Lawrence Radiation Laboratory," *HSPS: Historical Studies in the Physical Sciences* 13, no. 2 (1983): 375–400.

98. Heilbron, Seidel, and Wheaton, *Lawrence and His Laboratory: Nuclear Science at Berkeley*, 47.

99. Herken, "Founding of the Atomic West," 123; and Heilbron, Seidel, and Wheaton, *Lawrence and His Laboratory: Nuclear Science at Berkeley*, 48–49, 52, 61–62. In the East, I. I. Rabi, a Nobelist in physics at Columbia University, complained that Lawrence's enterprise amounted to an "atomic trust," a laboratory in restraint of the fundamental-particle trade. Rabi, himself a talented and effective politico of science, took the lead in persuading the AEC to establish a national laboratory at Brookhaven and fund there the powerful Cosmotron. Peter J. Westwick, *The National Labs: Science in An American System, 1947–1974* (Cambridge: Harvard University Press, 2003), 139–43.

100. Heilbron, Seidel, and Wheaton, *Lawrence and His Laboratory: Nuclear Science at Berkeley*, 76–104.

101. Heilbron, Seidel, and Wheaton, *Lawrence and His Laboratory: Nuclear Science at Berkeley*, 62.

102. Heilbron, Seidel, and Wheaton, *Lawrence and His Laboratory: Nuclear Science at Berkeley*, 65–66, 74–75.

103. Heilbron, Seidel, and Wheaton, *Lawrence and His Laboratory: Nuclear Science at Berkeley*, 75, 80, 126.

104. Herken, "Founding of the Atomic West," 127–28.

105. Daniel J. Kevles, "Hanford: The Costs of National Security," script of video unit on Hanford, accompanying Pauline Maier et al., *Inventing America: A History of the United States* (New York: W. W. Norton, 2003), in author's possession.

106. See Raye C. Ringholz, *Uranium Frenzy: Boom and Bust on the Colorado Plateau* (New York: W. W. Norton, 1989), 121.

107. Peter J. Westwick, ed., *Blue Sky Metropolis: The Aerospace Century in Southern California* (Berkeley: University of California Press, 2012), *passim*; and Koppes, *JPL and the American Space Program*, 30.

108. Macdonald, *Escape from Earth*, 237–41.

109. Lord, *Astro Turf*,, 101; and Koppes, *JPL and the American Space Program*, 30–31. On Tsien, see Iris Chang, *Thread of the Silkworm* (New York: Basic Books, 1995).

110. Patricia Nelson Limerick, "The Significance of Hanford in American History,"

in *Terra Pacifica: People and Place in the Northwest States and Western Canada*, edited by Paul W. Hirt (Pullman: Washington State University Press, 1998), 53–70, quotation on 57; and Leslie, "Playing the Education Game to Win," 68–69, 71. For an inquiry into the culture and values during the 1980s of workaday employees at the Sandia National Laboratory, in New Mexico, where the staff prepared the so-called nuclear and thermonuclear "physics packages" for detonation, see Debra Rosenthal, *At the Heart of the Bomb: The Dangerous Allure of Weapons Work* (Reading, MA: Addison-Wesley, 1990).

111. Ringholz, *Uranium Frenzy*, 148–70, 175–76, 180–88, 216–18, 260–61.

112. Limerick, "Significance of Hanford in American History," 53–70; Maier et al., *Inventing America*, 860, and accompanying Kevles, "Hanford: The Costs of National Security."

113. Heilbron and Seidel, *Lawrence and His Laboratory*, 104; and Office of Environmental Management, Department of Energy, "EM Completes Phase 1 Cleanup at Lawrence Berkeley National Laboratory," March 6, 1918, https://www.energy.gov/em/articles/em-completes-phase-1-cleanup-lawrence-berkeley-national-laboratory.

114. Koppes, *JPL and the American Space Program*, 78ff.

115. Peter J. Westwick, *Into the Black: JPL and the American Space Program, 1976–2004* (New Haven, CT: Yale University Press, 2007), 128–30, 169–71.

116. Westwick, *Into the Black*, 114–16, 119–32.

3. WORLD WAR II, THE COLD WAR, AND THE KNOWLEDGE ECONOMIES OF THE PACIFIC COAST

The author thanks the Stanford Department of Economics for support, and Jonathan Xia Zhang for outstanding research assistance. Jan De Vries, David Mowery, Paul Rhode, Steve Usselman, and Peter Westwick provided helpful comments on an earlier draft. All remaining errors are the author's responsibility.

1. Gerald D. Nash, *World War II and the West: Reshaping the Economy* (Lincoln: University of Nebraska Press, 1990), xii, 2; and Ann Markusen et al., *The Rise of the Gunbelt: The Military Remapping of Industrial America* (New York: Oxford University Press, 1991), 21. The crucial role of defense industries in California's postwar manufacturing is shown in James L. Clayton, "Defense Spending: Key to California's Growth," *Western Political Quarterly* 15 (1962): 280–93; and James L. Clayton, "The Impact of the Cold War on the Economies of California and Utah, 1946–1965," *Pacific Historical Review* 36 (1967): 449–73.

2. Stephen B. Adams, "Born on Third Base: Silicon Valley's Rich Inheritance," presented at the Business History Conference, Miami, FL, 2015.

3. Walter Isard and James Ganschow, *Awards of Prime Military Contracts by County, State and Metropolitan Area of the United States, Fiscal Year 1960* (Philadelphia: Regional Science Research Institute, 1961), Tables 2 and 3. County figures for later years are from the Defense Contract National Data System, National Archives.

4. These "agglomeration economies" are formally modeled in Paul A. David and Joshua L. Rosenbloom, "Marshallian Factor Market Externalities and the Dynamics of Industrial Localization," *Journal of Urban Economics* 28 (1990): 349–70; and W.

Brian Arthur, *Increasing Returns and Path Dependence in the Economy* (Ann Arbor: University of Michigan Press, 1994), chapters 4 and 6. The accentuated role of clustering in knowledge economies is analyzed in Enrico Moretti, *The New Geography of Jobs* (Boston: Houghton Mifflin Harcourt, 2012), 121–53.

5. This paragraph draws on Paul W. Rhode, "After the War Boom: Reconversion on the Pacific Coast, 1943–1949," in Timothy W. Guinnane, William A. Sundstrom, and Warren Whatley, eds., *History Matters: Essays on Economic Growth, Technology, and Demographic Change* (Stanford, CA: Stanford University Press, 2004), 189–94; and Marilynn S. Johnson, *The Second Gold Rush: Oakland and the East Bay in World War II* (Berkeley: University of California Press, 1993), 34–45.

6. Nash, *World War II and the West*, 42, 69. The Federal Reserve report is quoted in Rhode, "After the War Boom," 199. Robert J. Gordon has argued that the documented "learning by doing" effects in wartime production of Liberty ships and aircraft led to permanent advances in productivity for the manufacturing sector as a whole; see Robert J. Gordon, *The Rise and Fall of American Growth* (Princeton, NJ: Princeton University Press, 2016), 537–38, 548–53, 562–65. But Alexander J. Field shows that these efficiency gains were highly specialized and emerged from production conditions that for the most part were never repeated; hence, they had little relevance for the postwar civilian economy; see Alexander J. Field, "World War II and the Growth of U.S. Potential Output," Santa Clara University, Leavey School of Business working paper, May 2018.

7. Rhode, "After the War Boom," 205–13; and Arthur C. Verge, "The Impact of the Second World War on Los Angeles," *Pacific Historical Review* 63 (1994): 289–314, 312.

8. Roger W. Lotchin, *Fortress California, 1910–1961: From Warfare to Welfare* (Urbana: University of Illinois Press, 1992), 156–205, quotes on pages 159, 203. The Bay Area Council publication is quoted in Margaret Pugh O'Mara, *Cities of Knowledge: Cold War Science and the Search for the Next Silicon Valley* (Princeton, NJ: Princeton University Press, 2005), 104–105.

9. Compare the list of major aircraft manufacturers on page 93 with the list of leading missile producers 1956–61 on page 97 in Markusen et al., *Rise of the Gunbelt*. (Convair was formed in 1943 through the merger of Consolidated Aircraft and Vultee Aircraft. McDonnell and Northrop were both important wartime producers, though not in the top ten.) See also Paul A. C. Koistinen, *State of War: The Political Economy of American Warfare, 1945–2011* (Lawrence: University Press of Kansas, 2012), 91.

10. Roger L. Geiger and Creso M. Sa, *Tapping the Riches of Science: Universities and the Promise of Economic Growth* (Cambridge, MA: Harvard University Press, 2008), 10; and Judith R. Goodstein, *Millikan's School: A History of the California Institute of Technology* (New York: Norton, 1991), 255, 262. On the long-standing industrial orientation of US universities, see Nathan Rosenberg and Richard Nelson, "American Universities and Technical Advance in Industry," *Research Policy* 23 (1994): 323–48.

11. Koistinen, *State of War*, 119, 124.

12. Stuart W. Leslie, *The Cold War and American Science* (New York: Columbia University Press, 1993), 51–57; and Rebecca S. Lowen, *Creating the Cold War University: The Transformation of Stanford* (Berkeley: University of California Press, 1997) 110–11.

Terman's letter is quoted in Leslie, *Cold War and American Science*, 44. Stanford in fact offered its presidency in 1941 to Vannevar Bush, who was Terman's thesis adviser at MIT (Lowen, *Creating the Cold War University*, 52).

13. Rhode, "After the War Boom," 201. R&D estimates for years prior to 1951 are not necessarily comparable to later figures compiled by the NSF. But a series for 1930–47 was compiled in John R. Steelman, *Science and Public Policy: A Report to the President* (Washington, DC: US Government Printing Office, 1947), 10. It shows total federal R&D expenditures of $625 million in 1947, compared to a wartime average of $500 million. Of the 1947 total, $500 million were sponsored by the War and Navy Departments.

14. Lotchin, *Fortress California*, 252.

15. Roger L. Geiger, *Research and Relevant Knowledge: American Research Universities since World War II* (New York: Oxford University Press, 1993), 24–25, 44, 49.

16. Martin J. Collins, *Cold War Laboratory: RAND, the Air Force, and the American State 1945–1950* (Washington, DC: Smithsonian Institution Press, 2002), 74–85, 98–111, 119–61; and Lowen, *Creating the Cold War University*, 97–100.

17. Leslie, *Cold War and American Science*, 68.

18. US Department of Defense, Office of the Secretary of Defense, *The Changing Patterns of Defense Procurement* (Washington, DC, 1962), I, 11.

19. US Department of Defense, Office of the Secretary of Defense, *Changing Patterns of Defense Procurement*, 4.

20. Markusen et al., *Rise of the Gunbelt*, esp. 35–37, 234–37.

21. Markusen et al., *Rise of the Gunbelt*, 255–56. The warning became more explicit one year later in Ann Markusen and Joel Yudken, *Dismantling the Cold War Economy* (New York: Basic Books, 1992).

22. Peter J. Westwick, ed., *Blue Sky Metropolis: The Aerospace Century in Southern California* (Berkeley: University of California Press, 2012), 3; William Glenn Cunningham, *The Aircraft Industry: A Study in Industrial Location* (Los Angeles: Lorrin L. Morrison, 1951), 196–97; and Jacob A. Vander Meulen, *The Politics of Aircraft: Building an American Military Industry* (Lawrence: University Press of Kansas, 1991), 57.

23. Goodstein, *Millikan's School*, 168–74; and Allen J. Scott, *Technopolis: High-Technology Industry and Regional Development in Southern California* (Berkeley: University of California Press, 1993), 59–61. This paragraph also draws on Paul W. Rhode, "Technology, Markets, and the Dynamics of Business Location." Rhode argues that the isolation of the "flying-minded" regional market gave western producers an early advantage in the prewar years.

24. City of Los Angeles, Office of the Mayor, *The Economic Development of Southern California, 1920–1976*, volume 1, 29–33 (Los Angeles : Community Analysis Bureau, 1976); and Markusen et al., *Rise of the Gunbelt*, chapter 4.

25. This paragraph draws on Markusen et al., *Rise of the Gunbelt*, 93–96; Scott, *Technopolis*, 63–67, 79–82; and Reynal Guillen, "The Air Force, Missiles, and the Rise of the Los Angeles Aerospace Technopole," *Journal of the West* 36 (1997): 60–66.

26. Guillen, "Air Force," 65.

27. Scott, *Technopolis*, 96–112, 157–78.

28. Markusen et al., *Rise of the Gunbelt*, 96; Lotchin, *Fortress California*, 309–12; and Mary Lindenstein Walshok and Abraham J. Shragge, *Invention and Reinvention: The Evolution of San Diego's Innovation Economy* (Stanford, CA: Stanford Business Books, 2014), 71–94, 101–102. The role of Convair and General Atomics in the creation of UCSD is described in an oral history with physicist Marvin Stern, available at https://www.aip.org/history-programs/niels-bohr-library/oral-histories/5094. Thanks to Peter Westwick for this source.

29. Roger E. Bilstein, *The Enterprise of Flight: The American Aviation and Aerospace Industry* (Washington, DC: Smithsonian Institution Press, 2001), 25, 178–79; and Markusen et al., *Rise of the Gunbelt*, 155, 161.

30. Helke Mayer, "Entrepreneurship in a Hub-and-Spoke Industrial District: Survey Evidence from Seattle's Technology Industry," *Regional Studies* 47 (2013): 1718, 1723–24; Mia Gray et al., "Seattle: A Classic Hub-and-Spoke Region," in Ann R. Markusen, Yong-Sook Lee, and Sean DiGiovanna, eds., *Second Tier Cities: Rapid Growth Beyond the Metropolis* (Minneapolis: University of Minnesota Press, 1999), 273–79; and Richard Morrill and Paul Sommers, "Seattle as a Digital City Unexpected or Inevitable?," *Canadian Journal of Regional Science* 28 (2005): 349–68; and Jorge Nisoi and Majlinda Zhegu, "Aerospace Clusters: Local or Global Knowledge Spillovers?," *Industry and Innovation* 12 (2005): 1–25.

31. Ernest Braun and Stuart McDonald, *Revolution in Miniature*, second edition (London: Cambridge University Press, 1982), 27–30, 69; Kenneth Flamm, *Creating the Computer* (Washington, DC: Brookings Institution Press, 1988), 16–20, 29; Thomas Misa, "Military Needs, Commercial Realities, and the Development of the Transistor, 1948–1958," in Merritt Roe Smith, ed., *Military Enterprise and Technological Change* (Cambridge, MA: MIT Press, 1985), 277–84; and Thomas Misa, *Leonardo to the Internet* (Cambridge, MA: Harvard University Press, 2014), 221.

32. Flamm, *Creating the Computer*, 65–68.

33. Glenn E. Bugos, "The Aerospace Impetus to Silicon Valley," *Journal of the West* 36 (1997): 97–99; Stuart W. Leslie, "How the West Was Won: The Military and the Making of Silicon Valley," in William Aspray, ed., *Technological Competitiveness: Contemporary and Historical Perspectives on Electrical, Electronics, and Computer Industries* (Piscataway, NJ: IEEE Press, 1993), 83–84; Lotchin, *Fortress California*, 61, 125; and Walter J. Boyne, *Beyond the Horizons: The Lockheed Story* (New York: St. Martin's Press, 1998), 97.

34. This paragraph draws on Christophe Lécuyer, *Making Silicon Valley: Innovation and the Growth of High Tech, 1930–1970* (Cambridge, MA: MIT Press, 2006), 14–51.

35. The description of Silicon Valley as "social bricolage" is from Martin Kenney and Donald Patton, "The Coevolution of Technology and Institutions: Silicon Valley as the Iconic High-Technology Cluster," in Pontus Braunerhjelm and Maryann Feldman, eds., *Cluster Genesis: Technology-Based Industrial Development* (Oxford: Oxford University Press, 2006), 38. The story of Shockley and the birth of Fairchild

is recounted in many places, but good summaries are Lécuyer, *Making Silicon Valley*, 129–39; Leslie, *Cold War and American Science*, 71–72; on the planar process, see Braun and McDonald, *Revolution in Miniature*, 73–87; and AnnaLee Saxenian, *Regional Advantage: Culture and Competition in Silicon Valley and Route 128* (Cambridge, MA: Harvard University Press, 1994).

36. Flamm, *Creating the Computer*, 16; Lécuyer, *Making Silicon Valley*, 72–83, 100–16; Leslie, *Cold War and American Science*, 60–62, 212–27; and Geiger, *Research and Relevant Knowledge*, 44.

37. Braun and McDonald, *Revolution in Miniature*, 72–87; Flamm, *Creating the Computer*, 75–79; and Lécuyer, *Making Silicon Valley*, 130, 159–67.

38. On IBM, see Steven W. Usselman, "Learning the Hard Way: IBM and the Sources of Innovation in Early Computing," in Naomi R. Lamoreaux and Kenneth Lee Sokoloff, eds., *Financing Innovation in the United States, 1870 to the Present* (Cambridge, MA: MIT Press, 2007), 325–30; and David W. Kean, *IBM San Jose: A Quarter Century of Innovation* (San Jose, CA: IBM, 1977), 57.

39. Misa, "Military Needs," 267–68; Leslie, *Cold War and American Science*, 62; Lécuyer, *Making Silicon Valley*, 112–13, 165–67; John E. Tilton, *International Diffusion of Technology: The Case of Semiconductors* (Washington, DC: Brookings Institution Press, 1971), 94–95; and Martin Kenney and David C. Mowery, eds., *Public Universities and Regional Growth* (Stanford, CA: Stanford University Press, 2014), 26–27.

40. The quotation about Germany and Japan is from Markusen and Yudken, *Dismantling the Cold War Economy*, 5–6. The quotation is from Robert W. DeGrasse Jr., *Military Expansion Economic Decline* (New York: Council on Economic Priorities, 1983), 105. See also John Tirman, ed., *The Militarization of High Technology* (Cambridge, MA: Ballinger Publishing Company, 1984); and Mary Kaldor, *The Baroque Arsenal* (New York: Hill & Wang, 1981). A prominent post–Cold War statement was John A. Alic et al., *Beyond Spinoffs: Military and Commercial Technologies in a Changing World* (Boston: Harvard Business School Press, 1992).

41. Markusen and Yudken, *Dismantling the Cold War Economy*, 171, 173–81, 205; and Anthony J. Marolda, "The Commercialization of Defense Technology: The Success Factors," in R. D. Norton, ed., *Regional Resilience and Defense Conversion*, Research in Urban Economics 11 (Greenwich, CT: JAI Press, 1997), 41.

42. Lécuyer, *Making Silicon Valley*, 180–209. The Noyce quotation is from Braun and Macdonald, *Revolution in Miniature*, 142. The Moore quotations are from Gordon Moore and Kevin Davis, "Learning the Silicon Valley Way," in Timothy Bresnahan and Alfonso Gambardella, eds., *Building High-Tech Clusters: Silicon Valley and Beyond* (Cambridge: Cambridge University Press, 2004), 21–22. The continued importance of military contracting for Silicon Valley is documented in Thomas Heinrich, "Cold War Armory: Military Contracting in Silicon Valley," *Enterprise and Society* 3 (2002): 247–84. The venture capitalist is quoted by Heinrich on page 248.

43. Jeffrey T. Macher, David C. Mowery, and David A. Hodges, "Reversal of Fortune? The Recovery of the U.S. Semiconductor Industry," *California Management Review* 41 (1998): 107–36; and Shane Greenstein, *How the Internet Became Commercial:*

Innovation, Privatization, and the Birth of a New Network (Princeton, NJ: Princeton University Press, 2015), 117–18, 185, 286.

44. Robert A. Kleinhenz, Kimberly Ritter-Martinez, and Rafael De Anda, *The Aerospace Industry in Southern California* (Los Angeles: Kyser Center for Economic Research, 2012), 10–12; Maryellen Kelley and Todd A. Watkins, "In from the Cold: Prospects for Conversion of the Defense Industrial Base," *Science* 268 (1995): 525–32; Valery A. Ramey and Matthew D. Shapiro, "Displaced Capital: A Study of Aerospace Closings," *Journal of Political Economy* 109 (2001): 958–92; Luis Suarez Villa, "California's Recovery and the Restructuring of the Defense Industries," in R. D. Norton, ed., *Regional Resilience and Defense Conversion*, Research in Urban Economics 11 (Greenwich, CT: JAI Press, 1997): 99; Robert F. Schoeni et al., *Life After Cutbacks: Tracking California's Aerospace Workers* (Santa Monica, CA: RAND, 1996); Ward F. Thomas and Paul Ong, "Barriers to Rehiring of Displaced Workers: A Study of Aerospace Engineers in California," *Economic Development Quarterly* 16, no. 2 (2002): 167–78; and Michael Storper et al., *The Rise and Fall of Urban Economies: Lessons from San Francisco and Los Angeles* (Stanford, CA: Stanford University Press, 2015), 48–49.

45. Storper et al., *Rise and Fall of Urban Economics*, 40, 42,45–65, 145–62, 169–92.

46. James Hasik, *Arms and Innovation: Entrepreneurship and Alliances in the Twenty-First Century Defense Industry* (Chicago: University of Chicago Press, 2008), 183n31; Nayantara D. Hensel, *The Defense Industrial Base: Strategies for a Changing World* (Surrey, England: Ashgate Publishing Limited, 2015), 66; Mayer, "Entrepreneurship in a Hub-and-Spoke Industrial District," 1723; T. M. Sell, *Wings of Power: Boeing and the Politics of Growth in the Northwest* (Seattle: University of Washington Press, 2001), 52–53; and Nick Wingfield, "Seattle Sets a Course for Deep Space," *New York Times*, August 2, 2016.

47. James Flanigan, *Smile Southern California, You're the Center of the Universe* (Stanford, CA: Stanford University Press, 2009), 31–41; Kenney and Mowery, *Public Universities and Regional Growth*, 127–52; Stephen B. Adams, "Follow the Money: Engineering at Stanford and UC Berkeley during the Rise of Silicon Valley," *Minerva* 47 (2009): 367–90, 387; Walshok and Shragge, *Invention and Reinvention*, 90–94, 112–26; and Steven Casper, "How Do Technology Clusters Emerge and Become Sustainable? Social Network Formation and Inter-firm Mobility within the San Diego Biotechnology Cluster," *Research Policy* 36 (2007): 438–55.

4. THE POLITICS WROUGHT BY WAR

1. The author wishes to thank Bruce Cain, Jennifer Burns, Bark Brilliant, Charles Richter, Philippa Strum, Robyn Muncy, Mary-Ellen Curtin, and Marie Theresa-Connolly for their comments and insights. See, for example, Ronald Brownstein, *The Second Civil War: How Extreme Partisanship Has Paralyzed Washington and Polarized America* (New York: Penguin Books, 2008); Kevin Kruse and Julian E. Zelizer *Fault Lines: A History of the United States since 1974* (New York: Norton, 2019); Joseph Crespino, *In Search of Another Country: Mississippi and the Conservative Counterrevolution* (Princeton, NJ: Princeton University Press, 2007); Kevin M.

Kruse, *White Flight: Atlanta and the Making of Modern Conservatism* (Princeton, NJ: Princeton University Press, 2005); Pietro Divola and David Brady, eds., *Red and Blue Nation? Characteristics and Causes of America's Polarized Politics* (Washington, DC: Brookings Institution, 2006); and John A. Lawrence, *The Class of '74: Congress after Watergate and the Roots of Partisanship* (Baltimore, MD: Johns Hopkins University Press, 2018).

2. See, for example, Lisa McGirr, *Suburban Warriors: The Origins of the New American Right* (Princeton, NJ: Princeton University Press, 2001); and Elizabeth Tandy Shermer, *Sunbelt Capitalism: Phoenix and the Transformation of American Politics* (Philadelphia: University of Pennsylvania Press, 2013). The war years are covered in chapters in Shermer's *Sunbelt Capitalism* and in Philip VanderMeer's *Desert Visions and the Making of Phoenix, 1860–2009* (Albuquerque: University of New Mexico Press, 2010), but there is comparatively less recent scholarship on wartime Seattle, and the war in both cities is sometimes depicted in economic and demographic terms, rather than in terms of how a decade of war stamped the cities' politics.

3. Walter Nugent, *Color-Coded: Party Politics in the American West, 1950–2016* (Norman: University of Oklahoma Press, 2018), 4.

4. Nugent, *Color-Coded*, 241–50. Nugent argues that Washington has been a solidly blue state since the 1950s, and he reports that the Seattle-based US House District 7 has voted reliably Democratic through the decades; since 1950, only one Republican has won the seat—in 1962.

5. Nugent, *Color-Coded*, 9, 241–50.

6. James T. Sparrow, *Warfare State: World War II Americans and the Age of Big Government* (New York: Oxford University Press, 2011), 5–6.

7. See White's afterword in this volume.

8. Richard S. Kirkendall, "The Boeing Company and the Military-Metropolitan-Industrial Complex, 1945–1953," *Pacific Northwest Quarterly* 85, no. 4 (October 1994): 137–139.

9. See John C. Putnam, *Class and Gender Politics in Progressive-Era Seattle* (Reno: University of Nevada Press, 2008), introduction, chapters 2–3.

10. For brief summaries of Seattle's pioneering role in adopting municipally owned hydroelectricity, see "Public Power: A Tradition," Seattle City Light, http://www.seattle.gov/light/history/publicpower.asp, accessed April 26, 2019; and "A Brief History of City Light," Seattle City Light, http://www.seattle.gov/light/history/brief.asp, accessed April 26, 2019.

11. "The Cold War and Red Scare in Washington: Historical Context," Center for the Study of the Pacific Northwest, http://www.washington.edu/uwired/outreach/cspn/Website/Classroom%20Materials/Curriculum%20Packets/Cold%20War%20&%20Red%20Scare/II.html, accessed April 26, 2019. To learn more about both the WCF and WPU, see Jennifer Phipps, "Washington Commonwealth Federation and Washington Pension Union," as part of the project Communism in Washington State: History and Memory, University of Washington, http://depts.washington.edu/labhist/cpproject/phipps.shtml, accessed April 26, 2019.

12. Works Progress Administration, Press Release-343, December 3, 1937, Washington State Library, https://www.sos.wa.gov/legacy/images/publications/sl_wpawapressrelease_no301to400/sl_wpawapressrelease_no301to400.pdf, accessed April 26, 2019.

13. Richard Morrill, "Emerald City Emergence: Seattle and the New Deal," NewGeography.com, August 13, 2008, http://www.newgeography.com/content/00169-emerald-city-emergence-seattle-and-new-deal, accessed April 26, 2019.

14. Quintard Taylor, *The Forging of a Black Community: Seattle's Central District from 1870 through the Civil Rights Era* (Seattle: University of Washington Press, 1994), see introduction and chapter 1, especially 5–7, 52.

15. Sarah Davenport, "Battle at Boeing: African Americans and the Campaign for Jobs, 1939–1942," Seattle Civil Rights and Labor History Project, University of Washington, 2006, http://depts.washington.edu/civilr/boeing_battle.htm. Karen J. Blair, "Seattle Women's History," *Perspectives on History*, December 1, 2004, https://www.historians.org/annual-meeting/past-meetings/supplement-to-the-119th-annual-meeting/seattle-womens-history, accessed April 26. 2019. Also see Rebecca J. Mead, *How the Vote Was Won: Woman Suffrage in the Western United States, 1868–1914* (New York: New York University Press, 2004).

16. Taylor, *Forging of a Black Community*, 55, 92.

17. Morrill, "Emerald City Emergence." Also see Mead, *How the Vote Was Won;* and Blair, "Seattle Women's History." For the rich literature on Seattle's pre–World War II progressive traditions, see Dana Frank, *Purchasing Power: Consumer Organizing, Gender, and the Seattle Labor Movement, 1919–1929* (Cambridge: Cambridge University Press, 1994); Susan Starbuck, *Hazel Wolf: Fighting the Establishment* (Seattle: University of Washington Press, 2002); Doris Pieroth, *Seattle's Women Teachers of the Interwar Years: Shapers of a Livable City* (Seattle: University of Washington, 2004); and Esther Hall Mumford, *Seattle's Black Victorians, 1852–1901* (Seattle: Ananse Press, 1980). Of course, Seattle also exhibited powerful currents of anti-Japanese and other forms of racist sentiment throughout its history.

18. For more background on Seattle's pre–World War II aircraft industry, see Gavin Wright's essay on the development of the Pacific Coast's "knowledge economies" in this edited volume.

19. Shermer, *Sunbelt Capitalism*, 17, 20.

20. Heidi J. Osselaer, *Winning Their Place: Arizona Women in Politics, 1883–1950* (Tucson: University of Arizona Press, 2009), chapter 5.

21. Shermer, *Sunbelt Capitalism*, 21–23.

22. Shermer, *Sunbelt Capitalism*, 49–55, 65–70.

23. Bob Bolin, Sara Grineski, and Timothy Collins, "The Geography of Despair: Environmental Racism and the Making of South Phoenix, Arizona," *Human Ecology Review* 12, no. 2 (2005): 156–68.

24. Nugent, *Color-Coded*, 132–33.

25. VanderMeer, *Desert Visions*, chapter 4. For a discussion of how inexpensive electricity contributed to environmental degradation and economic inequality in

twentieth-century Phoenix's metropolitan area, see Andrew Needham, *Phoenix and the Making of the Modern Southwest* (Princeton, NJ: Princeton University Press, 2014).

26. VanderMeer, *Desert Visions*, chapter 4. In his chapter in this edited volume, Gavin Wright disputes the argument that "climate" was a decisive factor in the West's rise as a center of aircraft production. In Phoenix, however, its inland geographical location and its dry climate were among the varied reasons that explain why it became an important place for wartime flight training.

27. Shermer, *Sunbelt Capitalism*, 78.

28. VanderMeer, *Desert Visions*, chapter 4. This program, which Southwest Airlines eventually took over, became the second biggest in America by 1942. Brad Melton and Dean Smith, eds., *Arizona Goes to War: The Home Front and the Front Lines during World War II* (Tucson: University of Arizona Press, 2003), xix–xxi.

29. According to Shermer, "by war's end, more than 145,000 trainees had come to Arizona to earn their wings," and "by the end of 1942, Arizona's twelve vocational centers had already produced more than eleven thousand graduates"; Shermer, *Sunbelt Capitalism*, 74–77.

30. The war made "the grasstops and their investor allies [determined] to craft the policies necessary to guarantee the corporate welfare that underlay their vision for dynamic, manufacturing metropolises"; see Shermer, *Sunbelt Capitalism*, 86–90.

31. Shermer, *Sunbelt Capitalism*, 87; and see VanderMeer, *Desert Visions*, chapter 4.

32. For an example of some of the fears associated with World War II's end and demobilization, see Governor Sidney Osborn to Chester A. Smith, July 3, 1945, Arizona State Archives, http://azmemory.azlibrary.gov/digital/collection/archgov/id/347, accessed April 26, 2019. For a brief summary of Olson's tenure, see "Bio., Governor Sydney Preston Osborn," National Governor's Association, https://www.nga.org/governor/sidney-preston-osborn/, accessed April 26, 2019.

33. See Rebecca Jo Plant's essay in this edited volume in which she argues: "The fact that Los Angeles parents ultimately failed to realize their vision does not diminish its unusually progressive character."

34. Clark Kerr, *Migration to the Seattle Labor Market Area, 1940–1942* (Seattle: University of Washington Press, 1942), iii, 129.

35. James R. Warren, "World War II Home Front on Puget Sound," HistoryLink.org, September 13, 1999, http://www.historylink.org/File/1664. As Gavin Wright argues in his chapter in this edited volume, the features that gave rise to "Pacific Coast knowledge clusters" included "military demand for high-tech performance products, links between private firms and research universities, inter-firm mobility of leading inventors, and local networks of specialized suppliers and skilled labor." Some of these factors were in place in wartime Seattle.

36. Keith Murray, "Issues and Personalities of Pacific Northwest Politics, 1889–1950," *Pacific Northwest Quarterly* 41, no. 3 (1950): 213–33, 232. For Detroit and Kansas City population figures, see "Population of Detroit, MI," http://population.us/mi/detroit/, and "Population of Cities in Kansas, 1900–2010," http://www.ipsr.ku.edu/ksdata/ksah/population/2pop33.pdf, accessed April 26, 2019.

37. Jesse Kindig, "Northwest Antiwar History, Chapter 2: Cracks in the Consensus: World War II," Antiwar and Radical History Project—Pacific Northwest, University of Washington, 2008, http://depts.washington.edu/antiwar/pnwhistory_wwii.shtml, accessed April 26, 2019.

38. Davenport, "Battle at Boeing," http://depts.washington.edu/civilr/boeing_battle.htm, accessed April 26, 2019; and "N.W. Enterprise Leads Negro Labor to Victory," *Northwest Enterprise*, July 12, 1940.

39. William G. Robbins and Katrine Barber, *Nature's Northwest: the North Pacific Slope in the Twentieth Century* (Tucson: University of Arizona Press, 2011), 133–34. During the debate over internment in September 1942, however, Devin essentially withdrew from the debate, refusing to give his opinion about the round up and removal of Japanese Americans from Seattle. "I am not sufficiently well informed upon the work that is now being done to comment," he wrote one constituent. See Bill Yenne, *Panic on the Pacific: How America Prepared for a West Coast Invasion* (New York: Regnery History, 2016), epilogue. Also see Jennifer Speidel, "After Internment: Seattle's Debate over Japanese Americans' Right to Return Home," University of Washington, 2005; and "Equal Rights Promised Japs by Mayor Devin," *Seattle Times*, December 18, 1944, http://depts.washington.edu/civilr/after_internment.htm, accessed April 26, 2019.

40. Heather MacIntosh, "Mayor William F. Devin Praises Seattle's Civic Unity Committee on July 24, 1944," January 1, 2000, http://historylink.org/File/2114, accessed April 26, 2019.

41. Robbins and Barber, *Nature's Northwest*, 133–34. Also see Speidel, "After Internment"; and "Equal Rights Promised Japs by Mayor Devin," *Seattle Times*, December 18, 1944, http://depts.washington.edu/civilr/after_internment.htm, accessed April 26, 2019. Kit Oldham, "Seattle Voters Approve New City Charter and Re-elect Mayor William F. Devin on March 12, 1946," March 5, 2014, http://www.historylink.org/File/3560, accessed April 26, 2019. Speidel, "After Internment," University of Washington, 2005.

42. Bolin, Grineski, and Collins, "Geography of Despair," 156–68.

43. Shermer, *Sunbelt Capitalism*, 314–15.

44. Shermer, *Sunbelt Capitalism*, 102–103.

45. Their World War II experiences, Cadava argues in his essay in this edited volume, helped shape conservative Mexican Americans' "patriotic, antiradical, and anticommunist sensibilities after the war."

46. Hon. Elizabeth Finn, "The Struggle for Civil Rights in Arizona," July 1998, State Bar of Arizona, http://www.myazbar.org/azattorney/archives/july98/7-98a5.htm, accessed April 26, 2019.

47. Shermer, *Sunbelt Capitalism*, 93–100, 106–107

48. "Vote Petition Filing Slated," *Arizona Republic*, July 2, 1946.

49. "Fraudulent Misrepresentation," *Arizona Republic*, October 24, 1946.

50. "Harless Scores Work Bill, Water Users Urge Passage," *Arizona Republic*, October 30, 1946; and Shermer, *Sunbelt Capitalism*, 100–110.

51. Shermer, *Sunbelt Capitalism*, 100–103; and Charles A. Esser, "Amvet Feud Sparked in Fight over Labor," *Arizona Republic*, September 27, 1946

52. Shermer, *Sunbelt Capitalism*, 108–110.

53. "Labor Prepares for Major Defense Effort," *The Aero Mechanic*, June 12, 1941, http://depts.washington.edu/labhist/laborpress/images/Aero%20Mechanic/1200w/Defense%20effort--June%2012,%201941--p.1.1200w.jpg, accessed April 26, 2019. "I.A. of M. Contract with Boeing Aircraft Co. Proven To Be Best in Aircraft Industry," *The Aero Mechanic*, March 13, 1941, http://depts.washington.edu/labhist/laborpress/images/Aero%20Mechanic/1200w/Full%20page%20example3--March%2013,%201941--p.1.1200w.jpg, accessed April 26, 2019.

54. Don Brazier, *History of the Washington Legislature, 1854–1963* (Olympia: Washington State Senate, 2000), 155.

55. Jane Sanders, *Cold War on the Campus: Academic Freedom at the University of Washington, 1946–64* (Seattle: University of Washington Press, 1979), 11.

56. "University of Washington," United States History, http://www.u-s-history.com/pages/h3181.html, accessed April 26, 2019; and Sanders, *Cold War on the Campus*, 13–14.

57. Sen. Thomas Bienz quoted in Sanders, *Cold War on the Campus*, 16.

58. "Robert F. Goldsworthy: An Oral History," Washington State Oral History Program, interviewed by Sharon Boswell, 56–62. For more details about the six faculty members in question, see Sanders, *Cold War on the Campus*, 74–75.

59. "William A. Gissberg: An Oral History," Washington State Oral History Program, interviewed by Sharon Boswell, 28–29.

60. Ellen Schrecker, *No Ivory Tower: McCarthyism and the Universities* (New York: Oxford University Press, 1986), 125.

61. Nancy Wick, "The Apology: 'A Dark Day in UW History,' says President," *Columns: University of Washington Alumni Magazine*, March 13, 1998, https://www.washington.edu/alumni/columns/dec97/red6.html.

62. Sanders, *Cold War on Campus*, 32–33.

63. Nancy Wick, "Seeing Red," *Columns: University of Washington Alumni Magazine*, December 1997, https://www.washington.edu/alumni/columns/dec97/red5.html, accessed April 26, 2019.

64. "Albert F. Canwell: An Oral History," interviewed by Timothy Frederick, Introduction. "R. R. 'Bob' Grieve: An Oral History," Washington State Oral History Program, interviewed by Sharon Boswell, 34–38. "William A. Gissberg: An Oral History," 14–16, 25, 28–29.

65. Sanders, *Cold War on the Campus*, 75–77.

66. "The Cold War and Red Scare in Washington: Historical Context," Center for the Study of the Pacific Northwest, http://www.washington.edu/uwired/outreach/cspn/Website/Classroom%20Materials/Curriculum%20Packets/Cold%20War%20&%20Red%20Scare/II.html, accessed April 26, 2019. "1948 Canwell UnAmerican Activities Hearings (Seattle)," *Communism in Washington State: History and Memory*, University

of Washington, http://depts.washington.edu/labhist/cpproject/canwell_hearings.shtml, accessed April 26, 2019.

67. Phipps, "Washington Commonwealth Federation and Washington Pension Union." Phipps called the WPU "the most important Popular Front organization in the state."

68. Shermer, *Sunbelt Capitalism*, 6. Shermer argues that "racism, sexism, Christian moralism, and anticommunism were driving forces behind right-wing movements in other parts of the country during the early postwar period, but none of these traditions proved as important as the locally grown business critique of liberal governance and interventionist economic policy in Phoenix." Still, the struggle over anticommunism was fierce in early Cold War Phoenix, and its outcome revealed something of the direction of postwar politics in the city.

69. "Legion Urges Americanism Program for City Schools," *Arizona Republic*, December 19, 1946.

70. "The People Speak," *Arizona Republic*, January 30, 1947.

71. "Let Russ Feel Free, Kendall Tells Legion," *Arizona Republic*, October 21, 1955. Race relations also merged with questions of communism and American loyalty in postwar politics. As the *Arizona Republic* reported, "a few Negro youths had been induced to join the [American Youth for Democracy] organization because of the racial appeal."

5. THE ROOTS OF HISPANIC CONSERVATISM IN THE WARTIME WEST

1. Republican National Hispanic Assembly website, https://rnhanational.org/index.php/about/history/, accessed on April 26, 2019.

2. On African American flight from the Republican Party over the course of the twentieth century, especially during the 1960s, see Leah Wright Rigueur, *The Loneliness of the Black Republican: Pragmatic Politics and the Pursuit of Power* (Princeton, NJ: Princeton University Press, 2015).

3. Lorena Oropeza, ¡Raza Sí! ¡Guerra No! Chicano Protest and Patriotism during the Viet Nam War Era (Berkeley: University of California Press, 2005), especially chapter 1.

4. Luis Alvarez, *The Power of the Zoot* (Berkeley: University of California Press, 2008), chapter 5; and Maggie Rivas-Rodriguez, *Mexican Americans & World War II* (Austin: University of Texas Press, 2005).

5. Zaragosa Vargas, *Labor Rights Are Civil Rights: Mexican American Workers in Twentieth-Century America* (Princeton, NJ: Princeton University Press, 2004), chapters 4 and 5.

6. Office of the Historian and Office of the Clerk, *Hispanic Americans in Congress, 1822–2012* (Washington, DC: US Government Printing Office, 2013), 6.

7. Jerry González, *In Search of the Mexican Beverly Hills: Latino Suburbanization in Postwar Los Angeles* (New Brunswick, NJ: Rutgers University Press, 2017).

8. Maggie Rivas-Rodriguez et al., *A Legacy Greater Than Words: Stories of U.S.*

Latinos & Latinas of the WWII Generation (Austin, TX: US Latino & Latina WWII Oral History Project, 2006), 289.

9. Undated memorandum from Robert Benitez Robles to Louis Maniatis, Box 1, Folder 1, Robert Benitez Robles Papers (MS 563), Special Collections, University of Arizona; and Robert Benitez Robles, "From Barrio to Mainstream,"108, unpublished manuscript, Box 1, Folder 3, Robles Papers.

10. Robles, "From Barrio to Mainstream,"109–10.

11. Fernando Oaxaca, interview with Oscar Martinez, Interview 196, October 3, 1975, University of Texas–El Paso, Institute of Oral History.

12. Fernando Oaxaca, interview with Oscar Martinez.

13. For more on Fernandez, see Geraldo Cadava, *The Hispanic Republican: The Shaping of an American Political Identity, from Nixon to Trump* (New York: Ecco, 2020), chapter 6.

14. Minutes, Citizens Committee for Latin-American Youth, June 7, 1943, Box 4, Folder 6, Manuel Ruiz Papers (M0295), Special Collections, Stanford University.

15. Minutes, Citizens Committee for Latin-American Youth, June 21, 1943, Box 4, Folder 6, Ruiz Papers; and Minutes, Citizens Committee for Latin-American Youth, June 28, 1943, Box 4, Folder 6, Ruiz Papers.

16. Letter from "Johnny" of the Victorville Army Flying School to Manuel Ruiz, dated "mid-June," Box 1, Folder 3, Ruiz Papers; and Letter from Manuel Ruiz to "Johnny," June 20, 1943, Box 1, Folder 5, Ruiz Papers.

17. Rivas-Rodriguez et al., *Legacy Greater Than Words*, 275.

18. Fernando Oaxaca, interview with Oscar Martinez.

19. Elaine Woo, "Fernando Oaxaca, 76; Founder of Republican Latino Group," *Los Angeles Times*, June 3, 2004.

20. Fernando Oaxaca, interview with Oscar Martinez.

21. George Will, "Benjamin Fernandez: A Natural Republican," *Washington Post*, August 23, 1979, A21.

22. Office of the Historian and Office of the Clerk, *Hispanic Americans in Congress, 1822–2012* (Washington, DC: US Government Printing Office, 2013), 338.

23. Robles, "From Barrio to Mainstream," 110.

24. Robles, "From Barrio to Mainstream," 110–13.

25. See Geraldo Cadava, *Standing on Common Ground: The Making of a Sunbelt Borderland* (Cambridge, MA: Harvard University Press, 2013), especially chapters 2–3.

26. Office of the Historian and Office of the Clerk, *Hispanic Americans in Congress, 1822–2012* (Washington, DC: US Government Printing Office, 2013), 338.

27. Office of the Historian and Office of the Clerk, *Hispanic Americans in Congress*, 338; and Oropeza, ¡Raza Sí! ¡Guerra No!, chapter 1.

28. Office of the Historian and Office of the Clerk, *Hispanic Americans in Congress*, 324.

29. Ignacio García, *Viva Kennedy: Mexican Americans in Search of Camelot* (College Station: Texas A & M University Press, 2000).

30. On busing and bilingual education, see Mark Brilliant, *The Color of America*

Has Changed: How Racial Diversity Shaped Civil Rights Reform in California, 1941–1978 (New York: Oxford University Press, 2010), chapters 7 and 8; and John Skrentny, *The Minority Rights Revolution* (Cambridge, MA: Belknap Press of Harvard University Press, 2002), chapter 7.

31. Tom Gavin, "Latin-American Leaders Urge Switch from Kennedy," *Denver Post*, September 19, 1963, 46; and Manuel Ruiz to Louis P. Maniatis, October 4, 1964, Box 1, Folder 10, Ruiz Papers.

32. Henry M. Ramirez, *A Chicano in the White House: The Nixon No One Knew* (Los Angeles: Henry M. Ramirez, 2014), 21.

33. "Barry's Latin Policy Strong," *Orlando Evening Star*, July 22, 1964, 10.

34. Author interview with Albert Zapanta, August 7, 2015.

35. Fernando Oaxaca, "A Fortuitous Tool," *Los Angeles Times*, April 20, 1980, H16.

36. Manuel Luján Jr., interview with Oscar Martinez, Interview 210, March 10, 1976, University of Texas–El Paso, Institute of Oral History.

37. Manuel Luján Jr., interview with Martinez.

38. Manuel Luján Jr., interview with Martinez.

39. Manuel Luján Jr., interview with Martinez.

40. Richard Santillan and Federico Subervi-Vélez, "Latino Participation in Republican Party Politics in California," *Racial and Ethnic Politics in California* (1991): 285–319, 288.

41. Robert Benitez Robles to Barry Goldwater, October 23, 1969, Box 1, Folder 2, Robles Papers.

42. Henry M. Ramirez, *A Chicano in the White House: The Nixon No One Knew* (Los Angeles, CA: Henry M. Ramirez, 2014), 83.

43. Ramirez, *Chicano in the White House*, 83, 366.

44. Fernando Oaxaca, interview with Oscar Martinez.

45. Fernando Oaxaca, interview with Oscar Martinez.

46. Woo, "Fernando Oaxaca, 76; Founder of Republican Latino Group."

47. Appointment of Oaxaca by Reagan, *Weekly Compilation of Presidential Documents* 19, no. 18 (May 9, 1983): 639.

48. G. Cristina Mora, *Making Hispanics: How Activists, Bureaucrats, and Media Constructed a New American* (Chicago: University of Chicago Press, 2014), chapter 1.

49. Benjamin Fernandez, testimony before the US Senate Watergate Committee, November 8, 1973.

50. Fernandez, testimony, November 8, 1973.

51. "Soon: The Biggest Minority," *Time*, October 16, 1978; and Benjamin Fernandez, lecture at University of Texas–El Paso, November 10, 1978.

52. Fernandez, testimony, November 8, 1973.

53. Fernandez, lecture at University of Texas–El Paso, November 10, 1978.

54. Laurie Becklund, "2 GOP Latinos Support Foes of Measure on Immigration," *Los Angeles Times*, July 16, 1984, B3.

55. On the economic growth of the US-Mexico borderlands, see Cadava, *Standing on Common Ground.*

56. Ana Minian, *Undocumented Lives: The Untold Story of Mexican Migration* (Cambridge, MA: Harvard University Press, 2018), chapter 1.

57. Lou Cannon, "Southern California's Boom Is Latino-Led," *Washington Post*, July 12, 1997, A3.

6. "NO PRIVATE SCHOOL COULD EVER BE AS SATISFACTORY"

The author would like to thank Jennifer Ryder and Kate Flach for their research assistance as well as Mark Brilliant, Frances M. Clarke, Sandra Eder, Rachel Klein, David M. Kennedy, and the anonymous reviewers at Stanford University Press for their helpful advice.

1. Natalie Fousekis, *Demanding Child Care: Women's Activism and the Politics of Welfare, 1940–1971* (Champaign-Urbana: University of Illinois Press, 2011), 39–40.

2. Scholars seeking to explain this development have emphasized a number factors. Ellen Reese points to "favorable political conditions," including the lack of an organized opposition movement, a flush treasury, and influential allies. She also credits activist mothers who used maternalist rhetoric in politically savvy ways, arguing that child-care centers helped them to *fulfill* their maternal duties, not escape them. Ellen Reese, "Maternalism and Mobilization: How California's Postwar Childcare Campaign Was Won," *Gender and Society* 10, no. 5 (October 1996): 566–89. Emilie Stoltzfus claims that California's neoprogressive political culture, characterized by an emphasis on fact-finding and pragmatic policy making, along with a robust spirit of bipartisanship, proved more conducive for proponents of child-care legislation than elsewhere. She also argues that, because military industries remained so central to the state's economy after World War II, women could defend the legitimacy of their workforce participation more effectively in California than elsewhere. In contrast to Reese, Stoltzfus believes that California's working mothers challenged gender norms by claiming that access to child care allowed them to be "productive citizens." Emilie Stoltzfus, *Citizen, Mother, Worker: Debating Public Responsibility for Child Care after the Second World War* (Chapel Hill: University of North Carolina Press, 2004). Finally, in *Demanding Child Care*, Fousekis foregrounds the determination and sustained activism of mothers in alliance with "the remarkable number" of early childhood educators based in California who supported parent activists in their fight to maintain an education-based child-care program for the working poor. Fousekis suggests that Californians' greater openness to state-funded child care reflected their particularly acute need for such services, since so many of the residents were recent arrivals with few friends and family nearby who might otherwise help them.

3. According to Arthur Verge, "The Impact of the Second World War on Los Angeles," *Pacific Historical Review* 63, no. 3 (1994): 289–314 (quotation 290): "While the impact of the Second World War was felt throughout the American homefront, no other American urban center was so transformed by the war as was Los Angeles." See also Verge, *Paradise Transformed: Los Angeles during the Second World War* (Dubuque, IA: Kendall/Hunt Publishing, 1993); and Kevin Allen Leonard, *The Battle for Los*

Angeles: Racial Ideology and World War II (Albuquerque: University of New Mexico Press, 2006).

4. As Matthew Dallek argues in his chapter in this edited volume, divergent politics in postwar Phoenix and Seattle reflected distinctive prewar traditions that "anticipated the sharpening of divisions" during the war. This chapter tells a similar story about Los Angeles.

5. Fousekis, *Demanding Child Care*, 109–14.

6. My findings are in keeping with the arguments that Laura McEnaney advances in *Postwar: Waging Peace in Chicago* (Philadelphia: University of Pennsylvania, 2018), a finely grained study of the ways in which working-class Chicagoans negotiated the transition from war to peace. McEnaney identifies a "resilient and expectant war liberalism among the urban working class that lasted well into the next war in Korea." She holds that this "hybrid liberalism," which amounted to a set of convictions about the state's obligations to ordinary citizens who sacrificed during the war, has too often been overlooked or downplayed by historians who interpret the 1946 elections as evidence of a thoroughgoing repudiation of wartime statism (McEnaney, *Postwar*, 8). See also James T. Sparrow, *Warfare State: World War II Americans and the Age of Big Government* (New York: Oxford University Press, 2011), who explores how Americans legitimized their claims upon the state by emphasizing their connection to heroic soldiers and veterans.

7. On the history of day nurseries, see Barbara Beatty, *Preschool Education in America: The Culture of Young Children from the Colonial Era to the Present* (New Haven, CT: Yale University Press, 1995); Sonya Michel, *Children's Interests/Mothers' Rights: The Shaping of America's Child Care Policy* (New Haven, CT: Yale University Press, 1999); Elizabeth Rose, *A Mother's Job: The History of Day Care, 1890–1960* (New York: Oxford University Press, 1999); and Anne Durst, "'Of Women, by Women, and for Women': The Day Nursery Movement in the Progressive-Era United States," *Journal of Social History* 39, no. 1 (Fall 2005): 141–59.

8. Betty Lois Halper, "Recollections of Los Angeles Children's Centers' Early Days," MA thesis, California State University–Northridge, 1977, 6–11. Progressive women in Los Angeles had an expansive understanding of public schools' mission, as Judith Raftery shows in *Land of Fair Promise: Politics and Reform in Los Angeles Schools, 1885–1941* (Stanford, CA: Stanford University Press, 1992).

9. Emeline S. Whitcomb, *Progress in Home Economics Education*, Bulletin No. 4, Department of the Interior, Bureau of Education (Washington, DC: US Government Printing Office, 1926), 9, 11; and "Legal Development of Nursery Schools in California," Appendix C-3, California Legislature, *Technical Staff Report on the Joint Committee on Preschool Primary Training* (Sacramento, January 17, 1947): 31, 235–36.

10. The singular character of the Los Angeles school district's commitment to early childhood education is evident in a 1929 compendium on preschool education in the United States that identified four different types of day nurseries—independent commercial nurseries, philanthropic nurseries, those organized by industry to retain women workers, and "day nurseries in a public school system." The last group "is

limited to one city, Los Angeles," the authors noted, stressing, "no other city has undertaken this service as a part of its school work." Whipple, *Twenty-Eighth Yearbook of the National Society for the Study of Education, Preschool and Parental Education*, 90–91. Likewise, all of the nation's day nurseries listed in Department of Commerce, *Children under Institutional Care: 1923* (Washington, DC: US Government Printing Office, 1927), 209–10, were run by religious and other private, voluntary organizations, save for the Los Angeles facilities.

11. Halper, "Recollections of Los Angeles Children's Centers Early Days," 6, 8.

12. In the late 1920s the assistant superintendent still described the main goals of the program without reference to the home economics component, explaining that the nurseries "offer the first step in the Americanization of foreign children and their mothers; they afford proper education for the small children in courtesy, table manners, patriotism, etc.; they prevent the absence of larger children from school." Guy Montrose Whipple, ed., *The Twenty-Eighth Yearbook of the National Society for the Study of Education, Preschool and Parental Education* (Bloomington, IN: Public School Publishing Co., 1929), 90.

13. The number of nurseries had risen to twenty-five by the time of the 1933 earthquake, but six were destroyed and did not reopen. "Child Care Centers," January 22, 1947, Folder 2, Box 1039, Los Angeles Unified School District Board of Education Records, 1875–2012, University of California, Los Angeles, Special Collections (hereafter LAUSD Board of Education Records).

14. The Child Care Center Act (Assembly Bill No. 307) prohibited the use of state, local, or county tax money to finance centers to care for preschool-age children. The attorney general did not definitively judge the home economics laboratories to be operating without legal authority; rather, he stated that further investigation was be required to determine whether the "School District is in fact operating a nursery school and not using the so-called home economics course of study as a cloak to disguise its true purpose." But his evidently skeptical view helped to sway the Board and sealed the laboratories' fate. Attorney General Robert W. Kenny to Hon. Lee T. Bashore, July 27, 1944, Folder 2, Box 1039, LAUSD Board of Education Records.

15. Enrollments in the home economics laboratories had already declined by the time the United States entered World War II, but nineteen facilities, with a combined staff of 54 individuals, continued to provide care for over 820 preschool-age children. Untitled document, Folder 1, Box 1173, LAUSD Board of Education Records.

16. Fousekis, *Demanding Child Care*, 176.

17. Catherine Landreth, "The Nursery School of the Institute of Child Welfare of the University of California, Berkeley," typescript of an oral history conducted in 1981 by Daniel Burke, Regional Oral History Office, Bancroft Library, University of California–Berkeley, 1983.

18. A full 95 percent of federal funding for the ENSP went toward salaries for teachers, cooks, custodians, and other personnel. Rose, *A Mother's Job*, 144–45. For a thorough and illuminating account of the program, see Molly Quest Arboleda,

Educating Young Children in WPA Nursery Schools: Federally Funded Early Childhood Education from 1933–1944 (New York: Routledge, 2019).

19. According to Fousekis, *Demanding Child Care*, 31–32, Lois Meek Stolz, director of the Institute of Child Development at Columbia University, was widely credited with selling the Roosevelt administration on the idea of government nursery schools in 1933. Stolz moved to the University of California–Berkeley in 1939 and later headed the committee that designed California's wartime child-care program.

20. Unlike private nurseries, however, ENSP schools placed great emphasis on the importance of nutrition, providing children with what was often their most nourishing meal of the day. Children also received free immunizations and dental care upon enrolling. Arboleda, *Educating Young Children in WPA Nursery Schools*, Kindle location 1567–1602.

21. Arboleda, *Educating Young Children in WPA Nursery Schools*, Kindle location 199.

22. Arboleda, *Educating Young Children in WPA Nursery Schools*, Kindle location 2238.

23. Woman's Bureau, *Planning Services for Children of Employed Mothers: A Report Prepared by a Subcommittee of the Interdepartmental Committee on Children and Youth* (Washington, DC: US Labor Department, 1953), 15.

24. Frances P. Moore, "Los Angeles Child Care Program," *Vassar Alumnae Magazine* 30 (June 15, 1945), 8–10 (quotation 10).

25. *Final Report on the WPA Program, 1935–1943* (Washington, DC: US Government Printing Office, 1943), 76.

26. Arboleda argues that we suffer from "willful amnesia concerning the first federally funded early childhood education program in American history." She also claims the number of wartime Lanham-funded nursery schools never exceeded the number of WPA nursery schools, noting that the frequently cited figure of thirty-one hundred Lanham centers includes both nursery schools and extended school day facilities for older children. Arboleda, *Educating Young Children in WPA Nursery Schools*, Kindle location 3317.

27. "Child Care Centers," January 22, 1947, Folder 2, Box 1037, LAUSD Board of Education Records.

28. Moore, "Los Angeles Child Care Program," 8.

29. Frances P. Moore, executive secretary of the Los Angeles Committee for the Care of Children in Wartime, subtly acknowledged the manner in which wartime demands required a lowering of child-care standards. "Too many people have been misled into thinking of [the child-care program] as an educational or protective measure for children with no intimate relation to the war effort. This type of thinking has, in the past, resulted in a good deal of misunderstanding and has tended to slow developments." Moore, "Los Angeles Child Care Program," 8.

30. Howard Dratch, "The Politics of Child Care in the 1940s," *Science & Society* 38, no. 2 (Summer 1974): 167–204.

31. "Calif. Women Workers Double 1940 Total," *Long Beach Independent*, December 5, 1944, 16.

32. In Los Angeles, 37 percent of female aircraft workers had children under age fourteen. The Los Angeles Area Committee of the Aircraft War Production Council built sixty-four nurseries and sixty-nine extended-day centers, according to Chitose Sato, "Gender and Work in the American Aircraft Industry during World War II," *Japanese Journal of American Studies* 11 (2000): 147–71.

33. State of California, Department of Industrial Relations, Division of Labor Statistics and Research, *Handbook of California Labor Statistics, 1943–1944* (San Francisco, May 1945), 17–19.

34. H. R. Harnish to Mr. Vierling Kersey, June 1, 1943, Folder 5, Box 1035, LAUSD Board of Education Records.

35. Dorothy W. Baruch, "When the Need for War-Time Services for Children Is Past—What of the Future," *Journal of Consulting Psychology* 9 (January–February 1945): 45–57.

36. By way of comparison, six thousand children attended child-care centers in all of Michigan, a state that was also home to many war industries. Alan Clive, *State of War: Michigan in World War II* (Ann Arbor: University of Michigan Press, 1979), 195.

37. For instance, a San Diego mother testified to the California Assembly that she "wouldn't listen" when her friend first told her about the program, because she assumed "that was just like something wholesale," meaning cheap and low quality. Once she finally tried a local center, however, she was delighted with the effects on her daughter, who went from being "backward" and "quiet" to positively chatty. "Testimony of Mrs. Grace Sweet, Parent," in California Assembly, *Technical Staff Report to the Joint Committee on the Preschool and Primary Training*, Table 44b, 162.

38. The housing shortage and a lack of funds prevented further expansion of the program. Moore, "Los Angeles Child Care Program," 8.

39. Henry Zabel to the Los Angeles City Board of Education, June 30, 1943, Folder 4, Box 1035, LAUSD Board of Education Records.

40. Mrs. Joyce Well to J. Paul Elliott, August 1945, Folder 1, Box 1038; and Mrs. L. H. Hasseupflug to the Los Angeles City Board of Education, September 19, 1945, Folder 1, Box 1038, LAUSD Board of Education Records.

41. The study drew on surveys and records that parents and teachers completed over the course of three years, from December 1943 to December 1946, a period that spanned the transition from federal to state funding. An overwhelming majority of parents reported improvements in their children's eating and dressing habits, while solid majorities believed that they had grown "more cooperative" with their peers and more "obedient" and "cooperative" with adults. When asked whether the improvements they noted in their children could be attributed directly to the time they spent in nursery school, 61 percent of parents said yes, while 21 percent said they were uncertain. Ruth Pearson Koshuk, "Developmental Records of 500 Nursery School Children," *Journal of Experimental Education* 16, no. 2 (December 1947): 134–48. Given that this study's author served as the director of two child-care centers in Los Angeles County,

this glowing assessment could easily be dismissed as self-serving were it not in accord with the archival record, which includes much praise and scant criticism of the centers.

42. By the end of October 1945 the FWA received a total of 1,485 separate appeals from Californians—833 letters (of 1,155 received), 103 wires (of 318), and 549 postcards (of 794), in addition to numerous petitions with multiple signatures. Residents of Georgia sent 208 letters, wires, and cards—the second largest batch of all the states. In other words, Californians sent more than seven times as many communications concerning the child-care centers as any other state. These numbers were compiled by FWA officials at the request of Rep. Helen Gahagan Douglas, a strong proponent of publically funded child care. *Congressional Record, Appendix*, 79th Congress, 1st session, vol. 91, part 12, 3998–99.

43. As Laura McEnaney has noted of Chicago residents during this same period, they did not "distinguish between federal, state, municipal, or charitable funding streams when they leaned on local resources"; see McEnaney, *Postwar*, 9.

44. Lenore A. Aubry to Los Angeles City Board of Education, December 10, 1945, Folder 1, Box 1038, LAUSD Board of Education Records.

45. Mrs. Beatrice Kinman to Rep. Helen Gahagan Douglas, August 25, 1945, in *Appendix to the Congressional Record*, A3999. Mrs. Marvin G. Ronk to Rep. Helen Gahagan Douglas, August 27, 1945, in *Appendix to the Congressional Record*, A3999.

46. Mrs. John A. Howard to Rep. Helen Gahagan Douglas, August 27, 1945, in *Appendix to the Congressional Record*, A3999.

47. Katherine Stewart, "What the 'Government Schools' Critics Really Mean," *New York Times*, July 31, 2017, https://www.nytimes.com/2017/07/31/opinion/donald-trump-school-choice-criticism.html.

48. On October 4, 1945, President Harry S. Truman urged Congress to approve funding to extend the program through February 1946, on the grounds that working mothers needed "more time to make other arrangements for the care of their children," as did state and local governments that hoped to continue the programs in the absence of federal funding. Fousekis, *Demanding Child Care*, 50.

49. Fousekis, *Demanding Child Care*, 54–57.

50. Mrs. Jane A. Davisson to Marie M. Adams, August 15, 1946, Folder 1, Box 1038, LAUSD Board of Education Records.

51. C. Curtin Mitchell to the Los Angeles City Board of Education, December 10, 1946, Folder 1, Box 1038, LAUSD Board of Education Records.

52. Helen Makinson to the Los Angeles City Board of Education, December 10, 1946, Folder 1, Box 1038, LAUSD Board of Education Records.

53. Eleanor Phipps to the Los Angeles City Board of Education, December 10, 1946, Folder 1, Box 1038, LAUSD Board of Education Records.

54. Sensationalized press coverage of the so-called Sleepy Lagoon Murder in 1942, followed by the Zoot Suit Riots in 1943, led many white Los Angeles residents to view juvenile delinquency as a serious threat to social order. On the racialization of juvenile delinquency, see Luis Alvarez, *The Power of the Zoot: Youth Culture and Resistance during World War II* (Berkeley: University of California Press, 2008). Officials deemed

the situation so dire that some parents of repeat offenders actually faced prosecution. Verge, "Impact of the Second World War on Los Angeles," 306.

55. J. Edgar Hoover and James Madison Wood, "Mothers... Our Only Hope," *Woman's Home Companion* 71, no. 1 (January 1944): 20.

56. Mrs. H.W. Keefe to the Los Angeles City Board of Education, December 10, 1946, Folder 1, Box 1038, LAUSD Board of Education Records.

57. Frank G. Pellet to the Los Angeles City Board of Education, August 22, 1946, Folder 1, Box 1038, LAUSD Board of Education Records.

58. Margaret Briggs to the Los Angeles City Board of Education, [December 1946], Folder 1, Box 1038, LAUSD Board of Education Records.

59. Quoted in Stoltzfus, *Citizen, Mother, Worker*, 161.

60. Robert E. Schelen to the Los Angeles City Board of Education, [October 1945], Folder 1, Box 1038, LAUSD Board of Education Records.

61. [N.A.] to the Los Angeles City Board of Education, postmarked October 11, 1946, Folder 1, Box 1038, LAUSD Board of Education Records.

62. Harvey Humphrey to the Los Angeles City Board of Education, September 19, 1946, Folder 1, Box 1038, LAUSD Board of Education Records.

63. "Rent Control, Child Care Top State's Problems," *Healdsburg Tribune*, February 13, 1948.

64. Stoltzfus, *Citizen, Mother, Worker*, 287. As Fousekis shows, mothers, teachers, and other child-care advocates organized letter-writing campaigns. Fousekis, *Demanding Child Care*, 67–92.

65. "Saving Our Child-Care Centers," *Los Angeles Times*, February 3, 1947, A4.

66. Mrs. W. H. Hoff, "Saving Our Child-Care Centers," *Los Angeles Times*, February 3, 1947, A4.

67. By 1951, Washington and Massachusetts were the only other states that still funded child-care centers, and they did so on a much more modest scale; according to the Children's Bureau, Massachusetts was supporting only four centers in 1951. "Background Information on Day Care and Extended School Services for Children of Working Mothers," *Bulletin of the National Association of Nursery Education* 6, no. 4 (1951): 3–6.

68. "Child Center Plea Omits Talk of Permanency," *Los Angeles Times*, January 5, 1951, 8.

69. Assembly of the State of California, *Statutes of California* 2 (1951), chapter 1263, 3154.

70. Stoltzfus, *Citizen, Mother, Worker*, 185.

71. Senate Interim Committee on Social Welfare, "Report of the Senate Interim Committee on Social Welfare, Part 6: The Child Care Program," *Journals of the Legislature of the State of California*, 1955 Regular Session (Sacramento: California Legislature, 1955), 25.

72. Fousekis, *Demanding Child Care*, 88.

73. Anne Norman, "Child Care Centers Heed Cry of Wayward Men's Families," *Los Angeles Times*, September 7, 1957, part IV, 8–9.

74. Fousekis, *Demanding Child Care*, 140–41.

75. In 1947, 83.5 percent of the children who attended the centers were white; 8.5 percent were African American; 4.2 Mexican; 1 percent Japanese; fewer than 1 percent Chinese; and 2.1 percent identified as other. Information on the racial breakdown for later periods, or for Los Angeles in particular, appears to be lacking. However, both Oakland and Los Angeles had integrated centers that served racially diverse populations. Fousekis, *Demanding Child Care*, 74, 184. The *Los Angeles Sentinel*, an African American newspaper, frequently voiced support for the centers.

76. Daniel de Jonghe to Los Angeles City Board of Education, November 12, 1955, Folder 2, Box 1038, LAUSD Board of Education Records; de Jonghe's naturalization records are available on Ancestry.com.

77. For instance, when President Obama in 2015 made a pitch for expanded child-care subsidies for the poor and child-care tax credits for the middle class, he asserted that the federal government had provided "universal child care" during World War II. Barack Obama, State of the Union Address, delivered January 20, 2015, http://www.cnn.com/2015/01/20/politics/state-of-the-union-2015-transcript-full-text/. A spate of articles followed in the press, such as "Free Child Care in the U.S.: A Forgotten Dream?" BBC News, February 3, 2015, http://www.bbc.com/news/magazine-31051633; "U.S. Once Had Universal Child Care, But Rebuilding It Won't Be Easy," National Public Radio, January 24, 2015, http://www.npr.org/2015/01/24/379530251/u-s-once-had-universal-child-care-but-rebuilding-it-wouldnt-be-easy; and Stephanie Condon, "Obama: We Had Universal Childcare in the 1940's; Let's Do It in 2015," NBC News, January 22, 2015, http://www.cbsnews.com/news/obama-we-had-universal-childcare-in-the-1940s-so-lets-do-it-in-2015/. See also Chris T. Herbst, "Universal Child Care, Maternal Employment, and Children's Long-Run Outcomes: Evidence from the U.S. Lanham Act of 1940," *Journal of Labor Economics* 35, no. 2 (2017): 519–64, an academic paper that received significant attention in the popular press. Herbst refers to the World War II program as "broadly accessible." In a response to journalist Emily Badger, "That One Time America Almost Got Universal Child Care," *Washington Post*, June 23, 2014, he claims that the nation had a "universal child care program" but "dismantled it" after World War II. Subsidized child care was inexpensive rather than free during World War II; parents typically paid fifty cents per child each day until July 1945, when the fee was raised to seventy-five cents. In today's terms this translates to roughly $7.00 and $10.50 a day. Emilie Stoltzfus, "Child Care: The Federal Role during World War II," Congressional Research Service Report for Congress, June 29, 2000, http://congressionalresearch.com/RS20615/document.php.

78. California Legislature, *Technical Staff Report to the Joint Committee on the Preschool and Primary Training*, Table 44b, 285n9.

79. "Legislature Sent Child Care Data," *Los Angeles Times*, January 14, 1947, 14.

80. Hawkins also detected a regrettable trend toward "looking at such programs as custodial in nature rather than educational," a notable erosion of the ideals that had previously informed the centers. Augustus F. Hawkins, "Black leadership in Los Angeles oral history transcript," interviewed by Clyde Woods, 1992, Department of

Special Collections, Charles E. Young Research Library, University of California–Los Angeles.

81. In 1971, Congress enacted legislation that would have provided for a truly universal child-care system—a fact one can only marvel at today. At the urging of Pat Buchanan and others on the emergent far right, President Nixon vetoed the legislation, claiming that for "the Federal Government to plunge headlong financially into supporting child development would commit the vast moral authority of the National Government to the side of communal approaches to child rearing over against the family-centered approach." Since then, the enactment of comprehensive child-care legislation that would encompass all the nation's parents has remained elusive. On the failure of the 1971 Comprehensive Child Care Act, see Deborah Dinner, "The Universal Childcare Debate: Rights Mobilization, Social Policy, and the Dynamics of Feminist Activism, 1966–1974," *Law and History Review* 28, no. 3 (August 2010): 577–628; and Kimberley Morgan, "A Child of the Sixties: The Great Society, the New Right, and the Politics of Federal Care," *Journal of Policy History* 13, no. 2 (2001): 215–50.

82. Bryce Covert, "The U.S. Already Has a High Quality, Universal Child-Care System—in the Military," *Think Progress*, June 16, 2017, https://thinkprogress.org/universal-military-childcare-9bb2b54bd154/.

7. HOW THE PACIFIC WORLD BECAME WEST

I am grateful to Mark Brilliant, Jared Farmer, Rebecca Herman, and Tehila Sasson for very helpful comments on an earlier draft of this chapter. Thank you to Kristin Oberiano and Jana Lipman for advice about sources. For assistance with research, I thank Gabriel Gorre, my intern at the Library of Congress in the fall of 2015; former Emory students Jason Ehrenzeller and P. J. Kachmar; and Elizabeth Christian, Kelly Cobb, Amy Flick, Chrystal Lee, Thomas Sneed, and others on the staff (or previously on staff) of the Emory University Law Library.

Epigraph: Top Secret Conversation between General Douglas MacArthur and George F. Kennan, March 5, 1948, *Foreign Relations of the United States, 1948, The Far East and Australasia*, vol. 6, p. 700, https://history.state.gov/historicaldocuments/frus1948v06/d519, accessed on April 26, 2019.

1. Jose M. Torres, *The Massacre at Atate* (Mangilao, Guam: University of Guam Press and Micronesian Area Research Center, 2014, 61–62); Log of the USS *Wadsworth*, DD-516, July 22, 1944, Appendix 4, Torres, *The Massacre at Atate*, 84; and Paul Carano and Pedro Sanchez, *A Complete History of Guam* (Rutland, VT: Charles E. Tuttle, Co., 1964), 292–93.

2. The spelling of Chamorro (or Chamoru) has been a contested issue in Guam. The spelling used in this chapter is consistent with Torres's memoir and other sources relied on. See Gina E. Taitano, "Chamorro vs. Chamoru," *Guampedia*, https://www.guampedia.com/chamorro-vs-chamoru/, accessed on April 26, 2019.

3. Laura Torres Sauder, "Psyche Under Siege: Uncle Sam, Look What You've Done to Us," Sustainable Development or Malignant Growth? (Suva, Fiji: Marama

Publications, 1994), 193–94, as quoted in Michael Lujan Bevacqua, "Afterword: 'The Uprising at Atåte,'" in Torres, *Massacre at Atate*, 113.

4. Bevacqua, "Afterword," 115.

5. Arrell Morgan Gibson, *Yankees in Paradise: The Pacific Basin Frontier* (Albuquerque: University of New Mexico Press, 1993).

6. Torres, *Massacre at Atate*, 122; and Carano and Sanchez, *History of Guam*, 289.

7. Torres, *Massacre at Atate*, 112, 124.

8. Carano and Sanchez, *History of Guam*, 306. For more on resistance to the Japanese occupation, and the possession of US flags as protest, see Alvita Akiboh, "National Symbols and Constructions of Identity in the U.S. Colonial Empire, 1898–1959," PhD dissertation, Northwestern University, 2019, chapter 4.

9. Torres, *Massacre at Atate*, 50–53. Bevacqua, in "Afterword," 97–135, recaptures Chamorro agency and seeks to revise the historiography and popular understanding of Chamorro history.

10. "FDR's 'Day of Infamy' Speech: Crafting a Call to Arms," *Prologue* 33, no. 4 (Winter 2001), https://www.archives.gov/publications/prologue/2001/winter/crafting-day-of-infamy-speech.html; and Emily Rosenberg, *A Date Which Will Live: Pearl Harbor in American Memory* (Durham, NC: Duke University Press, 2003), 9–33.

11. Pacific Naval War Map of the Pacific Operations, 1942, Library of Congress Map Collection.

12. Carano and Sanchez, *History of Guam*, 319; and Doloris Coulter Cogan, *We Fought the Navy and Won: Guam's Quest for Democracy* (Honolulu: University of Hawai'i Press, 2008).

13. Patricio N. Abinales and Donna J. Amoroso, *State and Society in the Philippines* (Lanham, MD: Rowman & Littlefield Publishers, 2005), 146, 168; and Victoria Wyatt, "Alaska and Hawai'i," *Oxford History of the American West*, edited by Clyde A. Milner II, Carol A. O'Connor, and Martha A. Sandweiss (New York: Oxford University Press, 1994), 565–99.

14. "Sovereignty" often refers to formal governance: "a territory under the rule of a sovereign, or existing as an independent state." While formal sovereignty figures in this chapter, the idea of US governance in the Pacific as a whole relies on a broader conception of sovereignty: "supremacy in respect of power . . .; supreme dominion, authority, or rule." "Sovereignty, n.," OED Online, September 2019, https://www-oed.com.proxy.library.emory.edu/view/Entry/185343?redirectedFrom=sovereignty&, accessed October 12, 2019.

15. See, e.g., Ned Blackhawk, *Violence over the Land: Indians and Empires in the Early American West* (Cambridge, MA: Harvard University Press, 2006); and Heather Cox Richardson, *Wounded Knee: Party Politics and the Road to an American Massacre* (New York: Basic Books, 2011).

16. Gail M. Nomura, "Significant Lives: Asia and Asian Americans in the U.S. West," in *A New Significance: Re-Envisioning the History of the American West*, edited by Clyde A. Milner II (New York: Oxford University Press, 1996), 138.

Gibson, *Yankees in Paradise*, argues that the Pacific was an American frontier.

Posthumously published in 1993, but initially written between 1976 and 1987, the book is understandably grounded in an earlier historiography. The author was pioneering, however, in that he treated the ocean itself, rather than only land masses, as the frontier. In that way he anticipated Pacific World scholarship, including creative work like David Igler's *The Great Ocean*, which treats contiguous land and ocean on the US West Coast as a distinct region. David Igler, *The Great Ocean: Pacific Worlds from Captain Cook to the Gold Rush* (New York: Oxford University Press, 2013). See also Matt K. Matsuda, *Pacific Worlds: A History of Seas, Peoples, and Cultures* (Cambridge: Cambridge University Press, 2012); Gary Y. Okihiro, *American History Unbound: Asians and Pacific Islanders* (Oakland: University of California Press, 2015); and David Armitage and Alison Bashford, eds., *Pacific Histories: Ocean, Land, People* (New York: Palgrave Macmillan, 2014).

17. Daniel Immerwahr, *How to Hide an Empire: A History of the Greater United States* (New York: Farrar, Straus and Giroux, 2019). Leading works on US empire in the Pacific include Paul A. Kramer, *The Blood of Government: Race, Empire, the United States, and the Philippines* (Chapel Hill: University of North Carolina Press, 2006); and Sally Engle Merry, *Colonizing Hawai'i: The Cultural Power of Law* (Princeton, NJ: Princeton University Press, 2000).

18. Mary L. Dudziak, *Cold War Civil Right: Race and the Image of American Democracy*, 2nd edition (Princeton, NJ: Princeton University Press, 2011).

19. Alfred Thayer Mahan, *The Influence of Sea Power upon History, 1660–1783*, 14th edition (Boston: Little, Brown and Co., 1898), 25.

20. Kenneth Wimmel, *Theodore Roosevelt and the Great White Fleet: American Sea Power Comes of Age* (Lincoln, NE: Potomac Books Inc., 1998).

21. Igler, *Great Ocean*; Matsuda, *Pacific Worlds*; and Okihiro, *American History Unbound*.

22. Hugo Grotius, *Mare Liberum* (1609), 28.

23. For an argument that legal identity inheres in the environment itself, see Christopher D. Stone's classic work *Should Trees Have Standing? Law, Morality, and the Environment*, 3rd edition (New York: Oxford University Press, 2010).

24. R. P. Anand, *Origin and Development of the Law of the Sea* (The Hague: Martinus Nijhoff Publishers, 1982), 1–6, 159–61.

25. Ron Crocombe, *The Pacific Islands and the USA* (Suva, Fiji: Institute of Pacific Studies, University of the South Pacific, 1995), 19. On whaling and international relations, see Kirkpatrick Dorsey, *Whales and Nations: Environmental Diplomacy on the High Seas* (Seattle: University of Washington Press, 2013).

26. Mahan, *Influence of Sea Power*, 83.

27. Brian McAllister Linn, *Guardians of Empire: The U.S. Army and the Pacific, 1902–1940* (Chapel Hill: University of North Carolina Press, 1997); Walter Nugent, *Habits of Empire: A History of American Expansion* (New York: Alfred A. Knopf, 2008), 221–317; Geoffrey M. White and Lamont Lindstrom, eds., *The Pacific Theater: Island Representations of World War II* (Honolulu: University of Hawai'i Press 1989); David Vine, *Base Nations: How U.S. Military Bases Abroad Harm America and the World*

(New York: Metropolitan Books, 2015); and Catherine Lutz, ed., *The Bases of Empire: The Global Struggle against U.S. Military Posts* (New York: New York University Press, 2009).

28. Robert C. Kiste, editor's note, in Lindstrom and White, eds., *Pacific Theater*, v–vi.

29. Kramer, *Blood of Government*; Eileen P. Scully, *Bargaining with the State from Afar: American Citizenship in Treaty Port China, 1844–1942* (New York: Columbia University Press, 2001); and Merry, *Colonizing Hawai'i.*

30. Earl S. Pomeroy, *Pacific Outpost: American Strategy in Guam and Micronesia* (Stanford, CA: Stanford University Press, 1951).

31. Wakako Higuchi, *The Japanese Administration of Guam, 1941–1944* (Jefferson, NC: McFarland & Company, 2013); John Dower, *War without Mercy: Race and Power in the Pacific War* (New York: Pantheon Books, 1986); and Frances B. Cogan, *Captured: The Japanese Internment of American Civilians in the Philippines, 1941–1945* (Athens: University of Georgia Press, 2000).

32. Harry N. Scheiber and Jane L. Scheiber, *Bayonets in Paradise: Martial Law in Hawai'i during World War II* (Honolulu: University of Hawai'i Press, 2016).

33. Lamont Lindstrom and Geoffrey M. White, "War Stories," in *Pacific Theater*, edited by White and Lindstrom, 3.

34. Lindstrom and White, "War Stories," 4–34.

35. Akira Iriye, "A Pacific Century?" in *Pacific Histories*, edited by Armitage and Bashford, 97–118.

36. Walden Bello, "U.S. Imperialism in the Asia-Pacific," *Peace Review* 10, no. 3 (1998): 367–73.

37. Hal M. Friedman, "The 'Bear' in the Pacific? US Intelligence Perceptions of Soviet Strategic Power Projection in the Pacific Basin and East Asia, 1945–1947," *Intelligence and National Security*,12, no. 4 (1997): 75–101. See also Hal M. Friedman, *Governing the American Lake: The U.S. Defense and Administration of the Pacific Basin, 1945–1947* (East Lansing: Michigan State University Press, 2007).

38. Susan A. Brewer, *Why America Fights: Patriotism and War Propaganda from the Philippines to Iraq* (New York: Oxford University Press, 2009, 102–38), 141–45.

39. Bello, "U.S. Imperialism in the Asia-Pacific," 369.

40. Campbell Craig and Fredrik Logevall, *America's Cold War: The Politics of Insecurity* (Cambridge, MA: Belknap Press of Harvard University Press, 2009) 102–38.

41. Jonathan M. Weisgall, *Operation Crossroads: The Atomic Tests at Bikini Atoll* (Annapolis, MD: Naval Institute Press, 1994).

42. Daniel Immerwahr, "The Greater United States: Territory and Empire in U.S. History," *Diplomatic History* 40, no. 3 (2016): 373–91.

43. Immerwahr, "Greater United States," 377–81.

44. Daniel Immerwahr, "Greater United States," 381–82; *Downes v. Bidwell*, 182 U.S. 244 (1901); and Christina Duffy Burnett and Burke Marshall, eds., *Foreign in a Domestic Sense: Puerto Rico, American Expansion, and the Constitution* (Durham, NC: Duke University Press, 2001). See also Immerwahr, *How to Hide an Empire.*

45. Susan Schulten, *The Geographical Imagination in America, 1880–1950* (Chicago: University of Chicago Press, 2001), 133–34.

46. Franklin D. Roosevelt: "Fireside Chat," February 23, 1942, *The American Presidency Project*, edited by Gerhard Peters and John T. Woolley, http://www.presi dency.ucsb.edu/ws/?pid=16224; and Schulten, *Geographical Imagination,* 204.

47. Schulten, *Geographical Imagination*, 6.

48. Schulten, *Geographical Imagination*, 139, 141–43, 233; Ian W. Toll, *Pacific Crucible: War at Sea in the Pacific, 1941–1942* (New York: W.W. Norton & Company, 2011); and White and Lindstrom, *Pacific Theater* .

49. Igler, *Great Ocean*, 8. An exception, focusing on the foreign relations and regulation related to ocean life, is Dorsey, *Whales and Nations*.

50. *Oxford History of the American West*, inside front and back covers; "Map of world time zones," *Encyclopædia Britannica*, https://www.britannica.com/topic/International-Date-Line/media/290873/167508, accessed on April 26, 2019.

51. Igler, *Great Ocean*, 183.

52. Matt K. Matsuda, "The Pacific," *American Historical Review* 111, no. 3 (2006): 758–80.

53. Igler, *Great Ocean*, 183.

54. Daniel Scott, "An Old Soldier's View of the Early Cold War, 1949–1953," MA thesis, Illinois State University, 2015, 20; and D. Clayton James, *The Years of MacArthur*, volume 3 (Boston: Houghton Mifflin, 1970), 401.

55. Rubon Juda, as quoted in Jack Niedenthal, *For the Good of Mankind: A History of the People of Bikini and Their Islands,* 2nd edition (Majuro, Marshall Islands: Bravo Publishers, 2001), 37–40; Emso Leviticus, as quoted in Niedenthal, *For the Good of Mankind*, 40–41. On the broader impact of nuclear tests on Marshall Islanders, see Martha Smith-Norris, *Domination and Resistance: The United States and the Marshall Islands during the Cold War* (Honolulu: University of Hawaiʻi Press, 2016).

56. Michael S. Sherry, *The Rise of American Air Power: The Creation of Armageddon* (New Haven, CT: Yale University Press, 1987), 341–56; and Richard Rhodes, *The Making of the Atomic Bomb* (New York: Simon & Schuster, 1987).

57. As quoted in Weisgall, *Operation Crossroads*, 32. See also Jeffrey Sasha Davis, "Representing Place: 'Deserted Isles' and the Reproduction of Bikini Atoll," *Annals of the Association of American Geographers* 95, no. 3 (September 2005): 613–14; and Sasha Davis, *The Empires' Edge: Militarization, Resistance, and Transcending Hegemony in the Pacific* (Athens: University of Georgia Press, 2015).

58. Rhodes, *Making of the Atomic Bomb*, 652–53; and Andrew G. Kirk, *Doom Towns: The People and Landscapes of Atomic Testing* (New York: Oxford University Press, 2016), 13, 275–77.

59. As quoted in Weisgall, *Operation Crossroads*, 106–108. Weisgall discusses variations in Wyatt's account over time.

60. As quoted in Niedenthal, *For the Good of Mankind*, 41.

61. Davis, "Representing Place," 607–25 (quoting Denis Cosgrove, "Introduction: Project Plowshare," *Ecumene* 5 [1998]: 264).

62. Henri Lefebvre, *The Production of Space* (Oxford: Blackwell Publishers 1991), 190; and Davis, *Empires' Edge,* 62–63.

63. Davis, "Representing Place," 607–25.

64. Helen M. Kinsella, *The Image before the Weapon: A Critical History of the Distinction between Combatant and Civilian* (Ithaca, NY: Cornell University Press, 2011), 94–101 (discussing "civilization" as it relates to the failure to afford Native Americans the protection of the law of armed conflict).

65. As quoted in Jane Dibblin, *Day of Two Suns: U.S. Nuclear Testing and the Pacific Islanders* (New York: New Amsterdam Books, 1998), 17.

66. Davis, *Empires' Edge,* 63–64.

67. James Cameron, "23 Nuclear Explosions Later," *New York Times,* March 1, 1970, 219.

68. Cameron, "23 Nuclear Explosions Later."

69. King Juda, as quoted in Niedenthal, *For the Good of Mankind,* 46–47.

70. J. Weisgall, "The Nuclear Nomads of Bikini," *Foreign Policy* 39 (1980): 74–98.

71. Quotations from Niedenthal, *For the Good of Mankind,* 54–55, 59–60.

72. Paul Boyer, *By the Bomb's Early Light: American Thought and Culture at the Dawn of the Atomic Age,* 2nd edition (Chapel Hill: University of North Carolina Press, 1994), 336–41.

73. J. Frank Diggs, "Reclaiming the World's Most H-Bombed Area," *U.S. News and World Report* 67 (October 13, 1969): 98–101; and Richard Rhodes, *Arsenals of Folly: The Making of the Nuclear Arms Race* (New York: Alfred A. Knopf, 2007), 71–74.

74. J. R. McNeill and Peter Engelke, *The Great Acceleration: An Environmental History of the Anthropocene since 1945* (Cambridge, MA: Belknap Press of Harvard University Press, 2014), 160–68.

75. Weisgall, "Nuclear Nomads of Bikini"; and Teresia K. Teaiwa, "bikinis and others/pacific n/oceans," *Contemporary Pacific* 6, no. 1 (Spring 1994): 87–109.

76. *Indies Trader,* http://www.indiestrader.com/bikini-atoll/bikini-dive-trip/, accessed on April 26, 2019.

77. Torres, *Massacre at Atate,* 115.

78. Carano and Sanchez, *History of Guam,* 320, 346–55. The Congress's laws could be vetoed by the governor, subject to override by the Congress through a two-thirds' vote.

79. Carano and Sanchez, *History of Guam,* 320, 346–55; and Cogan, *We Fought the Navy and Won,* 151–56.

80. Megan Black, *The Global Interior: Mineral Frontiers and American Power* (Cambridge, MA: Harvard University Press, 2018).

81. W. Scott Barrett and Walter S. Ferenz, "Peacetime Martial Law in Guam," *California Law Review* 48, no. 1 (March 1960): 1–30.

82. Patricia Taimanglo Pier, "An Exploratory Study of Community Trauma and Culturally Responsive Counseling with Chamorro Clients," PhD dissertation, University of Massachusetts–Amherst, 1998, 6–7.

83. Roy E. James, "Military Government: Guam," *Far Eastern Survey* 15, no. 18

(September 11, 1946): 277; and R.D.K. Herman, "Inscribing Empire: Guam and the War in the Pacific National Historical Park," *Political Geography* 27 (2008): 630–51.

84. Carano and Sanchez, *History of Guam*, 357–58.

85. As quoted in Carano and Sanchez, *History of Guam*, 359–62.

86. "Decolonization: Issue on the Trust Territory of the Pacific Islands," United Nations Department of Political Affairs, Trusteeship and Decolonization, April 1980; "Trust Territory of the Pacific Islands," University of Hawai'i Digital Archives, http://libweb.hawaii.edu/digicoll/ttp/ttpi.html, accessed on April 26, 2019.

87. "Decolonization: Issue on the Trust Territory of the Pacific Islands"; "Trust Territory of the Pacific Islands"; Smith-Norris, *Domination and Resistance*; Davis, *Empire's Edge*; and Coral Davenport, "The Marshall Islands Are Disappearing," *New York Times*, December 1, 2015, https://www.nytimes.com/interactive/2015/12/02/world/The-Marshall-Islands-Are-Disappearing.html.

88. Pier, "Exploratory Study of Community Trauma," 70; and Jana K. Lipman, "'Give Us a Ship': The Vietnamese Repatriate Movement on Guam, 1975," *American Quarterly* 64, no. 1 (March 2012): 1–31.

89. David Vine, *Base Nation: How U.S. Military Bases Abroad Harm America and the World* (New York: Henry Holt and Co., 2015), 80–95.

90. "Island of Warriors," *America by the Numbers with Maria Hinojosa*, Futuro Media Group, 2014, http://www.americabythenumbers.org/episode/guam/.

91. Michael Lujan Bevacqua, "The Uprising at Atate," in Torres, *Massacre at Atate*, 97–135. See also Herman, "Inscribing Empire."

92. Pier, "Exploratory Study of Community Trauma," 49.

AFTERWORD

1. John McNeil and Peter Engelke, *The Great Acceleration: An Environmental History of the Anthropocene since 1945* (Cambridge, MA: Harvard University Press, 2016), 4, 5.

2. For the connections between these things, see Amitav Ghosh, *The Great Derangement: Climate Change and the Unthinkable* (Chicago: University of Chicago Press, 2016), 87–115.

3. Daniel Bell, *The End of Ideology: On the Exhaustion of Political Ideas in the Fifties* (1962; reprint, New York: Free Press, 1965); Francis Fukuyama, *The End of History and the Last Man* (New York: Free Press, 1992); and Bill McKibben, *The End of Nature* (New York: Random House, 1989). Although I disagree with large parts of it, Dipesh Chakrabarty has written a brilliant article on the Anthropocene and history; see Dipesh Chakrabarty, "The Climate of History: Four Theses," *Critical Inquiry* (Winter 2009): 197–222, 207.

CONTRIBUTORS

MARK BRILLIANT is associate professor of history and American Studies at the University of California–Berkeley. He is author of *The Color of America Has Changed: How Racial Diversity Shaped Civil Rights Reform in California, 1941–1978*, which won the Cromwell Book Prize from the American Society for Legal History and received honorable mention from the Organization of American Historians for the Frederick Jackson Turner Award.

GERALDO L. CADAVA is associate professor of history and Latinx Studies at Northwestern University. His first book, *Standing on Common Ground: The Making of a Sunbelt Borderland*, won the Frederick Jackson Turner Award from the Organization of American Historians. His second book, *The Hispanic Republican: The Shaping of an American Political Identity, from Nixon to Trump*, will be published in 2020.

MATTHEW DALLEK is professor at George Washington University's Graduate School of Political Management and a political historian specializing in American conservatism and liberalism since 1940. His most recent book is *Defenseless under the Night: The Roosevelt Years and the Origins of Homeland Security* (2016), winner of the Henry Adams prize for the best book on the history of the federal government. Dallek's first book, *The Right Moment* (2004), traced the shifting character of California's conservative and liberal politics in the mid-1960s and appeared on the annual best-of lists of the *Washington Post* and the *Chicago Tribune*. His scholarly and popular articles and reviews have appeared in the *Journal of Policy History*, the *Journal of American History*, *Politico*, the *Washington Post*, and numerous other publications.

MARY L. DUDZIAK is Asa Griggs Candler Professor of Law at Emory University and a leading legal historian and US and the world scholar. She is past president of the Society for Historians of American Foreign Relations and an Honorary Fellow of the American Society for Legal History. She is the author of *War Time: An Idea, Its History, Its Consequences* (2012); *Exporting American Dreams: Thurgood Marshall's African Journey* (2008); *Cold War Civil Rights: Race and the Image of American Democracy* (2000, 2011); and other works. Her research has been supported by the John Simon Guggenheim Foundation; the School of Social Science, Institute for Advanced Studies, Princeton; the Center for Advanced Study in the Behavioral Sciences, Stanford; the American Council of Learned Societies; and other institutions.

JARED FARMER is professor of history at the University of Pennsylvania and a former Andrew Carnegie Fellow. He holds degrees from Utah State University, the University of Montana, and Stanford University. His book *On Zion's Mount: Mormons, Indians, and the American Landscape* (2008) received the Francis Parkman Prize.

DAVID M. KENNEDY is the Donald J. McLachlan Professor of History Emeritus at Stanford University, where he has taught for more than fifty years. His publications include *Over Here: The First World War and American Society* (1980, 2004), which was a Pulitzer Prize finalist, and *Freedom from Fear: The American People in Depression and War, 1929–1945* (1999), a volume in the *Oxford History of the United States*, which was awarded the Pulitzer Prize for History in 2000.

DANIEL J. KEVLES is professor emeritus of history at Yale University. He writes about science, technology, medicine, and society past and present. His works include *The Physicists*, *The Baltimore Case*, and *In the Name of Eugenics* as well as articles, essays, and reviews in scholarly and popular journals, among them the *New York Times*, the *New York Review of Books*, *The New Yorker*, and the *Times Literary Supplement*. A past fellow of the Guggenheim Foundation, the National Endowment for the Humanities, and the Cullman Center for Scholars and Writers at the New York Public Library, Kevles has received a Page One Award, the National Historical Society Prize, the Watson Davis Prize, and the Sarton Medal for career achievement from the History of Science Society.

REBECCA JO PLANT is associate professor of history at the University of California–San Diego and coeditor of the electronic journal and database *Women and Social Movement in the United States*. The author of *Mom: The Transformation of Motherhood in Modern America*, and coeditor of *Maternalism Reconsidered: Motherhood, Welfare, and Social Policies in the Twentieth Century*, she has held major fellowships from the American Association of University Women, the Radcliffe Institute for Advanced Study, the American Council of Learned Societies, and the Australian Research Council. Together with Frances M. Clarke, Plant is currently completing a study on the problem of underage enlistment during the American Civil War.

RICHARD WHITE is the Margaret Byrne Emeritus Professor of American History at Stanford University, specializing in the American West, the history of capitalism, environmental history, history and memory, and Native American history. He is a MacArthur Fellow and a recipient of the Mellon Distinguished Professor Award. His work has won numerous academic prizes, and he has twice been a finalist for the Pulitzer Prize.

GAVIN WRIGHT is the William Robertson Coe Professor of American Economic History Emeritus at Stanford University, where he has taught since 1982. He received his BA from Swarthmore College and his PhD from Yale University. He was elected to the American Academy of Arts and Sciences in 1993 and is a past president of the Economic History Association and the Agricultural History Society. Wright's research centers on the historical record of the American economy, with a long-standing special interest in the South. His most recent book is *Sharing the Prize: The Economics of the Civil Rights Revolution in the American South*, which won the Alice Hanson Jones Prize as the best book in North American economic history during 2013–14. The paperback edition was released in 2018.

INDEX